RUGBY · A WAY OF LIFE   RUGBY · A WAY OF LIFE   RUGBY · A WAY OF LIFE   RUGBY · A WAY OF LIFE
RUGBY · A WAY OF LIFE   RUGBY · A WAY OF LIFE   RUGBY · A WAY OF LIFE   RUGBY · A WAY OF LIFE
RUGBY · A WAY OF LIFE   RUGBY · A WAY OF LIFE   RUGBY · A WAY OF LIFE   RUGBY · A WAY OF LIFE
RUGBY · A WAY OF LIFE   RUGBY · A WAY OF LIFE   RUGBY · A WAY OF LIFE   RUGBY · A WAY OF LIFE
RUGBY · A WAY OF LIFE   RUGBY · A WAY OF LIFE   RUGBY · A WAY OF LIFE   RUGBY · A WAY OF LIFE
RUGBY · A WAY OF LIFE   RUGBY · A WAY OF LIFE   RUGBY · A WAY OF LIFE   RUGBY · A WAY OF LIFE
RUGBY · A WAY OF LIFE   RUGBY · A WAY OF LIFE   RUGBY · A WAY OF LIFE   RUGBY · A WAY OF LIFE
RUGBY · A WAY OF LIFE   RUGBY · A WAY OF LIFE   RUGBY · A WAY OF LIFE   RUGBY · A WAY OF LIFE
RUGBY · A WAY OF LIFE   RUGBY · A WAY OF LIFE   RUGBY · A WAY OF LIFE   RUGBY · A WAY OF LIFE
RUGBY · A WAY OF LIFE   RUGBY · A WAY OF LIFE   RUGBY · A WAY OF LIFE   RUGBY · A WAY OF LIFE
RUGBY · A WAY OF LIFE   RUGBY · A WAY OF LIFE   RUGBY · A WAY OF LIFE   RUGBY · A WAY OF LIFE
RUGBY · A WAY OF LIFE   RUGBY · A WAY OF LIFE   RUGBY · A WAY OF LIFE   RUGBY · A WAY OF LIFE
RUGBY · A WAY OF LIFE   RUGBY · A WAY OF LIFE   RUGBY · A WAY OF LIFE   RUGBY · A WAY OF LIFE
RUGBY · A WAY OF LIFE   RUGBY · A WAY OF LIFE   RUGBY · A WAY OF LIFE   RUGBY · A WAY OF LIFE
RUGBY · A WAY OF LIFE   RUGBY · A WAY OF LIFE   RUGBY · A WAY OF LIFE   RUGBY · A WAY OF LIFE
RUGBY · A WAY OF LIFE   RUGBY · A WAY OF LIFE   RUGBY · A WAY OF LIFE   RUGBY · A WAY OF LIFE
RUGBY · A WAY OF LIFE   RUGBY · A WAY OF LIFE   RUGBY · A WAY OF LIFE   RUGBY · A WAY OF LIFE
RUGBY · A WAY OF LIFE   RUGBY · A WAY OF LIFE   RUGBY · A WAY OF LIFE   RUGBY · A WAY OF LIFE
RUGBY · A WAY OF LIFE   RUGBY · A WAY OF LIFE   RUGBY · A WAY OF LIFE   RUGBY · A WAY OF LIFE
RUGBY · A WAY OF LIFE   RUGBY · A WAY OF LIFE   RUGBY · A WAY OF LIFE   RUGBY · A WAY OF LIFE
RUGBY · A WAY OF LIFE   RUGBY · A WAY OF LIFE   RUGBY · A WAY OF LIFE   RUGBY · A WAY OF LIFE
RUGBY · A WAY OF LIFE   RUGBY · A WAY OF LIFE   RUGBY · A WAY OF LIFE   RUGBY · A WAY OF LIFE
RUGBY · A WAY OF LIFE   RUGBY · A WAY OF LIFE   RUGBY · A WAY OF LIFE   RUGBY · A WAY OF LIFE
RUGBY · A WAY OF LIFE   RUGBY · A WAY OF LIFE   RUGBY · A WAY OF LIFE   RUGBY · A WAY OF LIFE
RUGBY · A WAY OF LIFE   RUGBY · A WAY OF LIFE   RUGBY · A WAY OF LIFE   RUGBY · A WAY OF LIFE
RUGBY · A WAY OF LIFE   RUGBY · A WAY OF LIFE   RUGBY · A WAY OF LIFE   RUGBY · A WAY OF LIFE
RUGBY · A WAY OF LIFE   RUGBY · A WAY OF LIFE   RUGBY · A WAY OF LIFE   RUGBY · A WAY OF LIFE
RUGBY · A WAY OF LIFE   RUGBY · A WAY OF LIFE   RUGBY · A WAY OF LIFE   RUGBY · A WAY OF LIFE
RUGBY · A WAY OF LIFE   RUGBY · A WAY OF LIFE   RUGBY · A WAY OF LIFE   RUGBY · A WAY OF LIFE
RUGBY · A WAY OF LIFE   RUGBY · A WAY OF LIFE   RUGBY · A WAY OF LIFE   RUGBY · A WAY OF LIFE
RUGBY · A WAY OF LIFE   RUGBY · A WAY OF LIFE   RUGBY · A WAY OF LIFE   RUGBY · A WAY OF LIFE
RUGBY · A WAY OF LIFE   RUGBY · A WAY OF LIFE   RUGBY · A WAY OF LIFE   RUGBY · A WAY OF LIFE
RUGBY · A WAY OF LIFE   RUGBY · A WAY OF LIFE   RUGBY · A WAY OF LIFE   RUGBY · A WAY OF LIFE
RUGBY · A WAY OF LIFE   RUGBY · A WAY OF LIFE   RUGBY · A WAY OF LIFE   RUGBY · A WAY OF LIFE

RUGBY - A WAY OF LIFE

STANLEY
PAUL

Also available in the same series
CRICKET – A WAY OF LIFE Christopher Martin-Jenkins

RUGBY-A WAY OF LIFE

An Illustrated History of Rugby

Edited by Nigel Starmer-Smith

Foreword by Bill Beaumont

STANLEY PAUL

London Melbourne Auckland Johannesburg

Stanley Paul & Co. Ltd

An imprint of Century Hutchinson Ltd
62-65 Chandos Place, London WC2N 4NW
Century Hutchinson (Australia) Pty Ltd
16-22 Church Street, Hawthorn, Melbourne, Victoria 3122
Century Hutchinson (NZ) Ltd
32-34 View Road, Glenfield, Auckland 10
Century Hutchinson (SA) Pty Ltd
PO Box 337 Bergvlei 2012, South Africa

First published 1986
Copyright © Lennard Books 1986

Made by Lennard Books Ltd
Mackerye End, Harpenden, Herts AL5 5DR

Editor Michael Leitch
Designed by David Pocknell's Company Ltd
Production Reynolds Clark Associates Ltd

British Library Cataloguing in Publication Data
Rugby: a way of life; an illustrated history of rugby
1. Rugby football – History
I. Title
796.33'3'09 GV944.85

ISBN 0 09 165710 5

Printed and bound in Spain by TONSA, San Sebastian

Jacket Photographs

Front
Top left R.H. Sparks, hooker for Plymouth Albion, Devon and England,
    first capped in 1928.
Top centre J.P.R. Williams playing for the Barbarians v British Lions at
    Twickenham, 1977.
Top right Japanese Golden Oldie at Twickenham, 1985.

Back
Left Ciaran Fitzgerald, captain of the 1983 Lions.
Centre Willie John McBride, Lions captain in South Africa, 1974.
Right Bill Beaumont during the Lions tour of New Zealand, 1977.

CONTENTS

Much as I had enjoyed every moment of my playing career it was not until injury forced me to retire that I realized that Rugby had become much more than just a sport and a hobby – for over two decades it had been a way of life.

I have always acknowledged that the fates have been kind to me. Not many players who begin their senior careers at full-back for the 6th XV of a well-known club like Fylde can expect to play lock forward for England in a full international within four years. In fact, it only took four weeks for the guys in the Fylde 6ths to work out I had wasted the previous ten years of my life trying to master the art of full-back play. These lads explained that I had all the basic attributes of a forward, not a back – I was born to be a donkey. I was switched first to flank forward and then prop before finally settling down at lock.

Funnily enough, I was quite popular with the rest of the 6th XV because, although I lacked the vast experience of those hoary veterans, I had three rare and precious assets which invariably tended to elude the disciples of the art of coarse, Extra B Rugby – boundless energy and enthusiasm, bottomless fitness and burning ambition. For the chain-smoking, pot-bellied fading stars of the 6ths, it was manna from the wilderness to discover a keen young workaholic who was prepared to undertake all the really taboo tasks like tackling, falling on the ball, pushing in the scrums and even jumping at the lineout.

Having found just such a raw, irrepressible fanatic in their midst, they had no wish to provide an easy escape route for me. I played my heart out every week for several months only to be rewarded each week with selection for the 6ths once again. Just how brilliant, I wondered, were the 5ths? Of course, I learned afterwards that the team captain would announce at selection each Monday that young Beaumont was showing a bit of promise and, given about five years learning the ropes and gathering experience with the 6ths, he would just about be ready for better things. As no club selectors were sentenced to actually have to watch the 6ths, they happily accepted the captain's words. Had it not been for a spate of injuries happening to coincide with the outbreak of a flu epidemic, I dare say I would have spent my whole career in the Fylde 6ths.

Mind you, I had a great time in those early days and learned that Rugby catered not only for people of every conceivable shape and size but also for players with the most widely diverse aims and ambitions. Rugby has always had a place for both the dedicated athlete and also for the most unashamed hedonist. In their own quite different ways the international stars

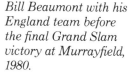

Bill Beaumont with his England team before the final Grand Slam victory at Murrayfield, 1980.

Beaumont on the charge against France, 1977.

on the one hand and the Extra B lads on the other can each derive enormous fun and pleasure from their weekly game of Rugby.

If the machiavellian junta of the 6th XV had threatened to retard my progress, my first sortie with the 3rds almost ended my career. The occasion was an away match against Percy Park 3rds in Newcastle. I told my mother that I thought I would be back from my first big away match about 11pm. Armed with a token pound (not for the beer kitty) I joined the team bus at Preston and set off on the most exciting expedition of my life up to that time. We won the match. Rather than return at once in triumph to Preston the team felt a certain moral obligation to celebrate in fitting style by drinking the North-East of England dry or at the very least to be violently sick in the attempt.

As far as I can remember we drank for six solid rather fluid hours before the natives poured us on the coach for the journey home. A rough effort at a sing-song ensued until we arrived at Scotch Corner at half past two in the morning. This was a good opportunity, I thought, to phone home and explain to my mother that I might be a trifle late. All I recall of that conversation was hearing my mother firmly tell my father that I had just played my last game of Rugby ever. With that she rang off but fortunately she mellowed a few days later

and I was given a reprieve.

The marvellous tradition of Rugby, the genuine camaraderie, the warmth, the compassion and the humour have meant as much to me as they have to the millions of other players at every level of the game in every corner of the world who have derived the fun, the enjoyment and the satisfaction from participating in such a great team game. I like to think the approach and attitude of players in the past 100-odd years has not changed all that much. The ideals, the motivation and the inspiration of Rugby have remained pretty constant. The roots of Rugby have been planted so deeply and have developed in such a firm fashion that I have every faith in the future.

In a rapidly changing society the face of Rugby is currently changing and will inevitably continue to change but I strongly believe that the individual players of the future will remain loyal to all the outstanding values which have always characterized the game of Rugby and the men who play it. So many of my friends now are people I met through Rugby and I will always look back with pride and satisfaction on the great matches I was privileged to play and the great, lasting friendships I made.

When I retired from Rugby after suffering a series of bad concussions, England scrum-half Steve Smith read in the papers that I had had a brain scan at the hospital. In the midst of my

W.B. Beaumont OBE.

depression that week, he phoned me to say he felt really that no sooner had the neurological surgeon found I actually had a brain than I had smashed it to smithereens. He was the guy who interrupted my half-time team talk during the England-Australia match at Twickenham in 1982 when the lovely Erika Roe did her famous streak behind my back. Noticing her voluptuous figure and acknowledging my rather large rear end, he suddenly exclaimed as I realized I did not have the rapt attention of my audience: 'I'd look round if I were you, Bill, there's a bloke just run on to the pitch with your backside stuck on to his chest.'

I turned round to get quite a shock, but I quickly pointed out to the lads that if they wanted to get a closer look we would have to spend the whole second-half camped near the Australian line. We did, and we won 15-11. It's nice to win but the fun and the enjoyment must always be of paramount importance. This book traces the history of the game from its origins right through to the present day. It is a fascinating story which, in describing the game's evolution, gives a deep insight into the whole ethos of Rugby. It reflects on the glories of the past and gives us every cause to look forward with real optimism and confidence to the future. Everyone who has ever had any pleasure from playing or watching Rugby will be gratified by the course of events described in this book.

Bill Beaumont

PART ONE

*T*HE EARLY YEARS TO 1914

Let's get one thing straight at the start. William Webb Ellis did not invent Rugby football. Neither did Rugby School. The game of football had been evolving for at least two thousand years, and probably more, and the boys at Rugby School in the early part of the nineteenth century played their own version of that game.

No doubt they had been doing so ever since the school was founded in 1567. Football was such a popular pastime throughout the Middle Ages that various monarchs of the realm inveighed against it because it got in the way of much more useful exercises such as archery. Certainly the boys at Rugby would have been playing football since the school moved to its present site in 1750, and just as certainly they would have been playing it since the school was rebuilt between 1809 and 1815.

By then, the game of football had long been a part of the English and Irish tradition. In 1527, the statutes of Galway forbade every sport except archery and 'the great footballe'. In 1583, the Puritan pamphleteer Philip Stubbes referred to football as 'a devilish pastime, and hereof groweth envy, rancour and malice, and sometimes brawling, murther' (remember the Irish traditions), 'homicide and great effusion of blood, as experience daily teacheth'. Football was even a part of Shakespeare's life. One of his characters, obviously a bit of a sceptic, commented: 'I shall not believe thee dead until I can play football with thy head.'

In those days, football was played either as a mad helter-skelter in the narrow streets of the towns and cities on certain feast days, or it was played in the country between entire villages. All the able-bodied males, and even some of those who were old enough to know better, formed a scrimmage on each side of a line at noon, and a ball was tossed up in the air between them. They then knocked seven bells out of each other until sunset. All the players sought to gain possession of the ball and either carry it or run with it or manoeuvre it or smuggle it towards a specific goal. That goal may have been the end of a field, or the centre of the rival village.

The historian Sir Frederick Morton Eden wrote: 'The game was this. He who at any time got the ball in his hands, ran with it till he was overtaken by a player of the opposite party, and then, if he could shake himself loose from those who were holding him, he ran on; if not, he threw the ball from him, unless it was wrested from him by one of the other party, but no person was allowed to kick it. If neither side won, the ball was cut into equal parts at sunset.'

Shrove Tuesday was the traditional day for some of the country's oldest established football matches. One was played at Derby, and from it the modern sporting expression 'local Derby' is derived.

These matches were bloody and uncompromising affairs. Street traders in London used to shutter their windows against them, and a history of the county of Derbyshire, written in 1829, observes:

'The struggle to obtain the ball, which is carried in the arms of those who have possessed themselves of it, is then violent, and the motion of the human tide heaving to and fro without the least regard to consequences is tremendous.

'Broken shins, broken heads, torn coats and lost hats are among the minor accidents of this fearful contest, and it frequently happens that persons fall, owing to the intensity of the pressure, fainting and bleeding beneath the feet of the surrounding mob. It would be difficult to give an adequate idea of this ruthless sport. A Frenchman passing through Derby remarked

The origins of Rugby football.

Right *An artist's impression of football in the streets of London during the reign of Edward II.*

Centre *An early game at Rugby School, 1845.*

Far right *The traditional game of football was still being played on Shrove Tuesday in Kingston-upon-Thames in 1846.*

that if Englishmen called this playing, it would be impossible to say what they called fighting.

'Still, the crowd is encouraged by respectable persons attached to each party, who take a surprising interest in the day's sport, urging on the players with shouts and even handing oranges and other refreshment to those who are exhausted.'

Now this was written in 1829, and it was clearly as descriptive of a typical English scene as a painting by Constable. Football had been played for centuries, and it consisted of a struggle for possession of a ball, which was then mauled, or scrimmaged, or driven, or passed, or run towards the opposing goal.

All the elements of what we now know as Rugby football were contained in that contest, the only difference being that there were a few more players on the field than there are now, and they were not allowed to kick the ball. Is it not therefore incredible that anyone should believe for one moment that the message imprinted on the famous plaque at Rugby School has any significance in the development of the game of football?

That plaque reads:

This stone
commemorates the exploit of William Webb Ellis
who with a fine disregard for the rules of football
as played in his time
first took the ball in his arms and ran with it
thus originating the distinctive feature of
the Rugby game

AD 1823

Rugby School themselves acknowledge that there is very little evidence that William Webb Ellis created a new form of football. For one thing, the only evidence to support this belief was contained in a letter written to a magazine more than fifty years after the event, and the letter was no more than hearsay. What is more, it was immediately refuted by a schoolboy contemporary of Ellis, who wrote: 'I remember William Webb Ellis perfectly. He was an admirable cricketer, but was generally inclined to take unfair advantage at football.' (Like picking up the ball and running with it?) 'I should not quote him in any way as an authority.'

One possible explanation is that the game of football at Rugby at that time was largely a kicking game, as it was at so many other schools which had only a paved quadrangle for their playing surface, and therefore could not contemplate the tackling to the ground and the scrimmaging that were part of the true football game played on the yielding surface of a soft field.

Perhaps the original buildings of Rugby School did not have a Big Side, which was the field upon which the boys played after they moved to the present site in 1750. That would explain why it took sixty or seventy years for the game at the school to revert to the true football game which had been played in the British Isles throughout the ages. And make no mistake: the game that is now known as Rugby, and which is played in one of our former colonies as American football, is the *true* football game. The game which is now called football (soccer) is an offshoot of the real game, and it was evolved in the second half of the nineteenth century to accommodate the tastes of players who were, to put it frankly, pansies. But more of that anon.

RESOLUTIONS

THAT only in cases of extreme emergency, and only by the permission of the heads of the sides, shall any one be permitted to leave the Close, after calling over, till the game be finished, and consequently, that all dressing take place before that time.
That the punishment for absenting oneself from a match, without any real and well-grounded reason, be left to the discretion of any Praeposter.
That whenever a match is going to be played, the School shall be informed of it by the Head of the School in such manner as he shall think fit, some time before dinner on the day in question.
That no unecessary delay take place in the commencement of the matches, but as soon as calling over be finished, the game be commenced.
That the old custom, that no more than two matches take place in the same week be strictly adhered to, of which, one must always take place on Saturday, without some strong cause to the contrary.

That all fellows not following up strictly prohibited from playing any game in goal, or otherwise conducting themselves in any way which shall be deemed prejudicial to the interests of their side.
That in consequence of the great abuse in the system of giving notes to excuse fagging, & c. and otherwise exempt fellows from attendance at the matches, no notes shall be received which are not signed by one of the Medical Officers of the School, and countersigned by the Head of the House, or by a Master when the case specified is not illness.
That all fellows at Tutor during calling over, or otherwise absent, shall be obliged to attend as soon as possible.
That the Head of the School take care that these resolutions be generally known among the School, and as far as the case may be they shall apply equally to the big sides.
That Old Rugbaeans shall be allowed to play at the matches of Football, not without the consent, however, of the two heads of the sides.

Resolutions passed at the meeting which established the first Laws of the game.

All the leading schools in England, schools which are now known as public schools, played their own version of football in the early part of the nineteenth century. The boys made up their own rules to suit the facilities available. What is more, they continually changed those rules, and they did so at Rugby School. Naturally, it was a slow process, but at Rugby the evolution of these rules was recorded, and the school still has the books in which the boys themselves wrote down the rules to which they played.

These were among the school's institutions when Thomas Hughes went to Rugby in the early 1830s, and he used his experiences there as the source material for his classic book, *Tom Brown's Schooldays.* Tom Hughes was never as good a football player as his fictional schoolboy hero, Tom Brown, but the book gives a most explicit account of the game and its setting.

'Tom . . . followed East across the level ground till they came to a sort of gigantic gallows of two poles eighteen feet high, fixed upright in the ground some fourteen feet apart, with a cross bar running from one to the other at the height of ten feet or thereabouts.

'"This is one of the goals," said East, "and you see the other, across there, right opposite, under the Doctor's wall. Well, the match is for the best of three goals; whichever side kicks two goals wins; and it won't do, you see, just to kick the ball through these posts; it must go over the crossbar; any height'll do, so long as it's between the posts.

'"You'll have to stay in goal to touch the ball when it rolls behind the posts, because if the other side touch it, they have a try at goal. Then we fellows in quarters, we play just about in front of goal here, and have to turn the ball and kick it back, before the big fellows on the other side can follow it up. And in front of us, all the big fellows play, and that is where the scrummages are mostly."'

East explains the bounds of the field to Tom, and tells him that when the ball goes beyond those bounds, it is in touch, and it then has to be knocked back in between two lines of opposing players. While he is explaining this, some boys bring out some balls to practise kicking, and by the time the match is due to start, 150 boys are practising hard.

The boys then split up into two sides, of by no means equal numbers, and step forward to start the game with the 'new ball you may see lie there, quite by itself in the middle, pointing towards the school or island goal'.

What could be more specific than that? The posts and the crossbar are much the same as they are now. The ball is not round, but oval, because it *points* towards the school goal. A goal has to be kicked over the crossbar and between the posts. Any defender who is beaten to the touch-down behind the posts by an opponent concedes a try at goal. The quarters play just in front of the goal, and have to kick the ball back to the big fellows in front, and that is where most of the scrummages are. If the ball goes off the field, into touch, it has to be knocked back in between two lines . . .

The field is there. The posts are there. The crossbar is there. The ball is there. The try at goal is there. The goal is there. The touch-down is there. The lineout is there. The big fellows at the front are there, where most of the scrumages occur. The little fellows are at the back. They are the quarters. Three quarters? Four quarters? Twenty quarters? It does not matter.

The ball was a sophisticated production, too. It consisted of panelled leather, stitched in much the same way as we know it today, with an inflated bladder inside. Saddlers made those balls, and obviously had done so many years before Master Ellis was born.

It is also clear from drawings made at the time that the clothing worn by the players had long been established by custom. The boys at Rugby School looked rather like modern cricketers, with long white trousers and small peaked caps. The shirts they wore were either white or striped, and the School has drawings of the formidable Headmaster, Dr Arnold, watching the proceedings of his boys at play.

The game and its equipment and customs were a part of the fabric of Rugby School less than ten years after William Webb Ellis was supposed to have 'originated the distinctive feature of the Rugby game'. If that assertion had even a shred of truth in it, we would have to assume that Rugby football had been an example of sporting evolution as instant as the invention of lawn tennis and badminton. But football was not like that, and never had been. It was a tradition, more than two thousand years old.

So who *was* William Webb Ellis? Why should he have been dredged up, more than fifty years later, as a significant figure in the history of football?

It has been suggested, somewhat mischievously, that he was both a coward and a cheat! He went on to become a man of the church, and is buried on a lovely hillside in the South of France, so we must hope that at least he was not a cheat. The chances are that he was no more than a fly on Doctor Arnold's wall, advanced in an attempt to promote the influence of Rugby School in the development of the game. This ensured at least that the fly became elevated to a plaque on the Doctor's wall, but there is no doubt that William Webb Ellis did *not* invent Rugby football.

The truly distinctive feature of what Rugby School did for the game of football was to draw up, and above all, write down, its first set of rules. Posterity is fortunate in that regard, because when the school moved to its new site in 1750, it was probably the only school in England which owned a wide open grass playground. As Sir Montague Shearman, the first major historian of the game, wrote a hundred years ago: '... hence it happens, as we should have expected, that at Rugby School alone do we find the original game survived almost in its primitive form.

'As far as we can discover, no school but Rugby played the old style of game where every player was allowed to pick up the ball and run with it, and every adversary could stop him by collaring, hacking over, and charging, or by any other means he pleased.'

Rugby School and its pupils not only provided the game of football with a set of rules, they also gave it a system of scoring. The object of the game was to kick goals, and there is not much doubt that Rugby originated the idea of touching the ball down over the opposing line to give the attacking side 'a try at goal'. They also originated the idea of giving a cap to those players good enough to take part in the play, a practice which spread to all sports.

This cap distinguished the good players from those who were only allowed to stand beyond the posts in goal. The cap entitled the wearer to follow up after the ball, rather than stand as one of a battalion of goalkeepers. It was awarded, therefore, to 'follow up', and not to play for Rugby School. It still is.

Rupert Brooke, the poet, played football for Rugby, and won his School cap. The school still has it.

Above and above left Football at Rugby School. Two illustrations from an early edition of Tom Brown's Schooldays. *Left An extract from the match records of Rugby School. The Hughes referred to at the foot of the page was Thomas Hughes's elder brother, George.*

Members of the Cotton House team who had been awarded the caps which entitled them to follow up.

The arguments about the rules of football persisted for about twenty-five years in the middle of the nineteenth century. In the end, those arguments produced two quite separate codes of football, one of which involved handling an oval ball, and the other kicking a round ball. It is easy, with the benefit of hindsight, to see that the division was both natural and inevitable, but the protagonists in the argument did not see it that way at all.

It did not occur to them to agree to go their separate ways from the beginning. Neither did it occur to them to retreat from their determination to convince the opposition of the error of their ways. Perhaps that was understandable, because what was at stake was the definition of an Englishman's belief in one of the sporting traditions of his country.

The traditionalists poured scorn on the notion that football should not be an unequivocally physical contest for possession of the ball, in which the ball was both handled and mauled. They also derided the idea that the practice known as hacking should be abolished. Hacking did not consist only of kicking at the ball. Players were allowed to hack at the legs of their opponents as well in order to get at the ball.

Men who had gone, as boys, to schools like Eton and Winchester, abhorred the traditional football game, because they had not played it. They thought that hacking was barbarous and said so as vehemently as they could. The passions aroused by this argument are documented in the correspondence columns of *The Field* magazine in 1863. A man named J. A. Babington wrote from Oxford University under the pen-name of 'Trebla', and if Shakespeare had ever needed a collaborator when he was writing Henry V's Agincourt speech, he need have looked no further than Mr Babington:

'Our game is abused because it permits running with the ball. In our opinion, this forms one of the most striking as well as one of the most attractive features of our game.

'It is said our game is barbarous because it permits brute force to form so important an ingredient. Is it not because of brute force that no nation can face us at the bayonet? And does not brute force form a large element of boating?

'Our game is [said to be] barbarous because it permits hacking, or shinning! For my own part, sir, this is the point above all others

concerning which I am most positive that we are in the right. I do uphold hacking, because it develops that quality of which every Englishman ought to be most proud – his pluck.

'If your readers had seen players appearing in Big Side day after day, either in house matches or in school matches, carrying the ball gallantly through scrimmage after scrimmage, till they could hardly stand, perhaps they would be inclined to admire hacking more than they do at present.

'In all of this, I am not speaking of purely vicious hacking: I am not even speaking of hacking such as our House displayed in a memorable scrimmage some years ago when, for five minutes, both sides ignored the existence of anything but their own hostility and the two best forwards of our house severally hewed their way four times through the enemy's ranks, kicking (I need hardly add) something else than the ball.

'Let unbelievers inquire of those who ought to be the true judges of this – who have worshipped a tarnished cap, and a bit of ribbon, and a certain stoutly built pair of boots, who have struggled on through a long winter's afternoon till the shades of evening closed round their hard won victory – who have known, in the words of our great poet, "to scorn delights and live laborious days."

'They, and only they, can tell what Rugby football is, and what it has been to them. They better than all others can tell, as far as Rugby is concerned, with what justice our greatest general declared that the field of Waterloo was won on the playgrounds of England.'

Not, you may notice, 'the playing fields of Eton'.

Etonians were among the pansies who wanted no part of hacking and scrimmaging and mauling and collaring. They were prepared to do their bit with the bayonet, but as far as they were concerned, it was a question of a place for everything, and everything in its place. In their judgment, a football field was not the place for bayonet drill.

Old Rugbeians and Old Etonians at Cambridge University were just getting warmed up for their slanging match when in 1839 a football club of sorts was formed by a Rugbeian named Albert Pell. It was, almost certainly, the first football club in the world, but there were so many arguments about the rules that the Cambridge University Rugby Club was not formed officially until 1872, three years after a club had been formed at Oxford. Blackheath had formed a club – *the* Club – in 1858, and Guy's Hospital had formed one in 1843.

In 1846, a meeting had agreed a set of rules which were called the Cambridge Rules, but as these eventually formed the basis of what became the Football Association, they did not begin to satisfy the traditionalists. There is not much doubt, either, that the differences between the two sides were influenced profoundly by the Industrial Revolution which was then taking place in Britain. Transport became incomparably easier. Work became

concentrated in the towns and the cities. The population drifted away from the land. Yet mob football had always been played on high days and holidays, and most of it had been played in a rural setting. There was little opportunity for the working man to do that in industrial England.

The clubs met again in 1863 to try to agree a set of rules. The first draft allowed both handling the ball and running with it and it also allowed charging, tripping and hacking. This had the effect of sharpening the divisions. Such a game, it was argued, was all very well for boys, but men who had their livings to earn could not possibly expose themselves to the physical risks

of playing it. The arguments in favour of a dribbling game gained ground. So did the rejection of hacking.

Blackheath tried to hold to the traditional game, but in the end the majority agreed to abolish handling, hacking and running with the ball. The number of players in each team was reduced to eleven, and the clubs agreeing to abide by these rules called themselves the Football Association. Blackheath and other clubs who supported the handling code withdrew and went on doing their own thing for seven more years without acknowledging that the game they were playing was an entirely different game from the

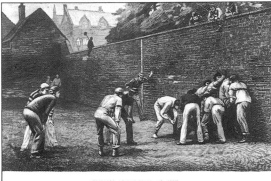

one being played by the Football Assocation.

The irony of these developments was that when the long division was eventually resolved into two parts, the great weight of working-class support was given, not to the traditional working man's game but to the breakaway dribbling code produced by the elegant old boys of the most exclusive school in the world. No doubt the fact that it was physically dangerous to do anything more than kick a ball in a cobbled back street had much to do with this, but Association football did become the game of the masses, and the traditional game preserved most faithfully at Rugby School became the game for the sons of rich or prosperous men.

Far left above The Rules drawn up by Blackheath Football Club in 1862 clearly show that they favoured the traditional elements of the game – handling, hacking and running with the ball. (Below) The 1862 Blackheath team.

Left above Even though the Old Etonians disliked the physical side of the traditional game many would have taken part in the wall game while at school. (Below) An early illustration of the more sedate game of Association football.

For seven years after the formation of the Football Association in 1863, it still did not occur to either side of the footballing argument that the dribbling code had in fact broken away and that there had been a fundamental parting of the ways. The clubs playing the traditional game went on doing so, although more and more of them did abandon the practice of hacking.

Those clubs regarded the Association footballers as parents, brought up on Beethoven and Mozart, might regard their children who listen to the three-chord twangings of pop

since they themselves had always looked upon football as being as much a part of England as summer and winter, they had never felt the need to enshrine it in a national organization. That need did not arise until 1870, when C. W. Alcock was among a group of men who had the idea of arranging a football match between England and Scotland on the Surrey cricket ground at Kennington Oval. England won the match without any difficulty, but it was played under Association rules, and the Scotland team was in no way representative of the strength of football in that country. It was not much more

Above Minutes of the first General Meeting of the Rugby Football Union in 1871.

music – an aberration of youth which, hopefully, will pass away as quickly as possible. It would be stretching things to say that 'the great parent code', i.e. the traditional game, looked benignly on the Football Association, but it certainly regarded the Association as still part of the footballing family and apparently it never considered twirling its moustaches and throwing the infant out of the house with the splendidly Victorian admonition that the Association 'should never darken its doors again'. It would have been rather pressed to do that in any case, because the great parent had never bothered to build a house.

The traditionalists were obviously not well pleased that the Association players should have appropriated the title of 'Football', but

Right The Pall Mall Restaurant where the meeting was held.

Left *A selection of caps awarded to players at Rugby School between 1867 and 1893.*
Above *The inside of the cap awarded to R. Sleight, embroidered as was the custom with the dates and details of the major matches in which he was involved.*
Below *The painting by T.A. Thomas which was commissioned by the RFU to commemorate the development of the game and which now hangs in the museum at Twickenham.*

Right *The international
shirt and cap worn by
players on the first
British overseas tour to
Australia and New
Zealand in 1888.*
Above *An early
international cap
presented to A.G.
Guillemard, who
played in England's
first two matches
against Scotland in
1871 and 1872.*
Below *Post-match
dinners have always
been a feature of
international
encounters.*

than a scratch metropolitan pick-up team. One of the players was known to have crossed the Border to shoot grouse. Another confessed to a liking for Scotch whisky.

Unrepresentative or not, the game caused so much public interest that another match was arranged for the autumn of the same year, again at Kennington Oval. On that occasion, the selectors did try much harder to gather together a more fairly representative Scotland team, but England still won by a goal to nil. It was proposed that a return match should be played the following February in Scotland, but the Scots quite reasonably drew attention to the unsatisfactory selection of the first two teams, and said that in any case they doubted if there were enough good Association footballers in Scotland to give England a game. Despite that, the Scots were urged to take up the challenge by, it is thought, H. H. Almond, who went on to become Headmaster of Loretto and, incidentally, one of the umpires in the subsequent match.

He said: 'No one need be under any misapprehension of the Scots' ability to play under the Association rules. These are only a modification of the great parent code, with the more violent features expunged, and there is probably no better training for them than Rugby play.' A nice put-down, which reads better and better as the years go by. Anyway, a challenge was then published in *The Scotsman* and in *Bell's Life* on 8 December 1870. It read:
'Sir,

There is a pretty general feeling among Scotch football players that the football power of the old country was not properly represented in the late so-called International Football Match. Not that we think that the play of the gentlemen who represented Scotland otherwise than very good – for that it was so is amply proved by the stout resistance they offered to their opponents and by the fact that they were beaten by only one goal – but that we consider the Association rules in accordance with which the late game was played, not such as to bring together the best team that Scotland could turn out. Almost all the leading clubs play the Rugby code, and have no opportunity of practising the Association game even if willing to do so. We therefore feel that a match played in accordance with any rules other than those in general use in Scotland, as was the case in the last match, is not one that would meet with

support generally from her players. For our satisfaction, therefore, and with a view of really testing what Scotland could do against an English team we, as representing the football interests of Scotland, hereby challenge any team selected from the whole of England, to play us a match, twenty-a-side Rugby rules, either in Edinburgh or Glasgow on any day during the present season that might be found suitable to the English players. Let this count as the return to the match played in London on 19th November, or, if preferred, let it be a separate match. If it be entered into, we can promise England a hearty welcome and a first-rate match. Any communications addressed to any one of us will be attended to.
We are, etc.,

A. H. Robertson	West of Scotland F.C.
F. Moncreiff	Edinburgh Academicals F.C.
B. Hall Blyth	Merchistonian F.C.
J. W. Arthur	Glasgow Academicals F.C.
J. H. Oatts	St. Salvator F.C., St. Andrews

This challenge made it clear that the football played in Scotland was the old game, and indeed, the history of football in Scotland went back almost as far as it did in England. Apart from the town and village games which had been played for centuries, Scottish schools had been playing each other at football for at least seventy years, and it is doubtful if any of them had even heard of William Webb Ellis.

The Scottish challenge was not taken up by C. W. Alcock, because the suggested rules were unacceptable to the Association footballers, and so was the number of players. He had said already that 'more than eleven we do not care to play, as with greater numbers it is, in our opinion, that the game becomes less scientific and more of a trial of charging and brute force.'

However, the clubs playing the traditional game in the London area accepted the challenge even though they had little time to form a representative team. Some of their best players were not available, but they agreed to play the match in Edinburgh on Monday 21 March 1871, and eventually they were allowed to play it at Raeburn Place on the ground of the Edinburgh Academicals Cricket Club.

Tactically, the Scots wanted to play the game among the forwards, because that was

R. Munro J. S. Thomson T. Chalmers
J. W. Arthur
A. Buchanan A. G. Colville J. Forsyth J. A. W. Mein R. W. Irvine W. D. Brown D. Drew W. Cross
J. F. Finlay F. J. Moncreiff G. Ritchie
A. C. Ross W. J. C. Lyall T. R. Marshall J. H. L. Macfarlane A. H. Robertson

J. E. Bentley A. E. Gibson F. Tobin D. L. P. Turner F. Stokes J. H. Clayton R. R. Osborne J. H. Luscombe
A. St G. Hammersley W. MacLaren C. W. Sherrard A. Lyon C. A. Crompton
H. J. C. Turner R. H. Birkett J. F. Green
A. Davenport A. G. Guillemard J. M. Dugdale B. H. Burns

Above *F. Stokes,
captain of the first
England team who in
1874, at the age of
twenty-four, was elected
second President of the
RFU.*
Right *The Scottish
team (above) for the
first international and
their English
opponents.*

*The 1890 Calcutta
Cup match at
Raeburn Place as
depicted by* The
Illustrated Sporting
and Dramatic News.

their game. The English, when they arrived after a tiring and uncomfortable overnight journey, thought that there would be no choice in the matter, because the pitch was only 55 yards wide and that did not suit their hopes to use their backs at all. The Scots were not in the least concerned. It was still a strongly held view in that country that passing the ball out from the forwards was almost an act of cowardice.

The game was played for fifty minutes each way, with two umpires, and Scotland won by a goal and a try to a try. The try from which Scotland scored their winning goal was hotly disputed by England and, twenty years later, the umpire who awarded it confessed to doubts himself. It was the same Mr Almond, and he wrote: 'Here let me make a personal confession. I was umpire and I do not know to this day whether the decision which gave Scotland the try from which the winning goal was kicked was correct in fact ... I must say, however, that when an umpire is in doubt, I think he is justified in deciding against the side which makes the most noise.'

That verdict has not yet been written into the laws of the game! It scarcely mattered. The playing of the game was the thing, and a few weeks after the challenge was issued which led to the first-ever international Rugby match, the Rugby Football Union was formed in England. The Scottish Football Union was formed two years later, in 1873. The Irish Football Union was formed in 1874, then the Irish Rugby Union was formed in 1879 and the Welsh Rugby Union in 1880.

These developments confirmed that two separate codes of football had been established, and first Ireland and then Wales joined England and Scotland in playing international matches. But the series between England and Scotland remains the oldest in the world, and ever since 1879 the match has been played for the Calcutta Cup.

This cup was presented to the Rugby Union when the Calcutta Football Club went out of existence in 1877 because most of its members had taken up polo. The club withdrew its remaining funds from the bank in silver rupees, and had them melted down and made into a trophy by Indian craftsmen. England and Scotland first played for it in 1879, when their match in Edinburgh was drawn, and England won it the following year with a decisive victory over the Scots in Manchester.

Long before England played their first match against Wales at Blackheath in 1881, most teams playing Rugby football had been reduced from 20 to 15 a side, although this was not written in the laws until 1893. The clothing worn by footballers on the field of play had also changed out of recognition from the sailor's attire of white or striped shirts, bell-bottomed trousers and small peaked caps that the boys had worn at Rugby School in Tom Hughes's schooldays. Practical experience had taught the players that clothing of that type was much too vulnerable

to scragging.

Accordingly, a much closer-fitting playing kit evolved and it was accurately described in a remarkable interview with a former Welsh player, R.H.B. Summers, which was one of the earliest recordings to enter the BBC sound archives. Summers had played three-quarter for Wales against England in that first match played between the two countries, when Wales were overwhelmed.

'We played in ordinary light walking boots,' he said. 'with a bar of leather nailed obliquely across the sole to help us in swerving; jerseys which fitted closely high up round the neck, so that no fellow could get his fingers in, and dark

blue serge knickerbockers fastened below the knee with four or five buttons.'

He also said that it was hardly surprising that Wales were beaten as badly as they were in their first game against England.

'I had just left school at Cheltenham when I received my invitation to play for Wales. The game was played at the Rectory Field, Blackheath, and we changed at a small, old-fashioned inn nearby. When we got to our changing rooms, we discovered that we were two men short, their invitations apparently having gone astray. However, we picked up two Varsity

men with Welsh qualifications, and they agreed to fill the vacancies on condition that they were allowed to play three-quarter!

'The game was played before a small crowd of Rugby enthusiasts, ranged perhaps three deep round the ground. There were no huge stands or terraced banks in those days. I am not sure that the playing pitch was even roped off. The match was a runaway victory for England by eight goals and six tries to nil, and Lennie Stokes, the England captain, had most to do with our downfall.

'He had a most baffling, swerving run, and his left-footed kicking, which broke our forwards' hearts, astounded us all, for we had never seen a player who was able to kick with his left foot before.

'The Blackheath crowd called Stokes the "something" snipe. The adjective was spelt with a "b", but was not quite BBC. In spite of the odds, we never gave up trying, and at the dinner that night, we were much encouraged when Stokes said: "I have seen enough to know that you Welshmen will be hard to beat in a few years' time, when you get together."'

In that inteview, Summers described the changes in the game that had taken place in the fifty years since he played his first and only

Left *Little separated spectators from players in the early days.*

Far left above *Football dress at Rugby School and (below) more practical outfits for the Cambridge University team of 1878.*

game for Wales.

'In essentials, the game was the same, but the disposition of forces was different. At Cheltenham College, where I learned the game, we made up our fifteen with nine forwards, two half-backs, two three-quarters and two full-backs.

'I believe this formation was almost universal, and was the one used by Wales in the first match against England. Generally speaking, the forwards scrummaged and dribbled, and the two three-quarters were expected to do most of the scoring, usually from a scrum, or squash, as we called it.

'The halves stood near the squash, one on either side, each supported by one of the two three-quarters. The half-back nearest the ball as it came out would throw out a pass to his supporting three-quarter, who ran for the line, trying to evade his opposite number and the two full-backs who converged on him from either side of the field. There was less passing than today, but in my opinion the game was more spectacular, and gave more scope for individual brilliance by the three-quarters.

'There were no wing-forwards as such in those days, but there were work-shy forwards, and we called them skirmishers.' (Today, they are called sea-gulls!) 'Scotland claim to have first introduced a third three-quarter, against Ireland in 1881, but I remember at Cheltenham

several years earlier that we had a forward who was something of a skirmisher, but who could handle the ball well.

'Occasionally, at a signal from the captain he would leave the scrum, and take a pass from the half-back and throw out a long pass to one of the three-quarters, who meantime had moved out towards the touch-line, and so was able to run round the three-quarters who opposed him. There, surely, was the genesis of the idea of the third three-quarter.

'I did not see the introduction of the fourth three-quarter, because I left for India soon after the international match in 1881 and did not return until 1893, when I first saw the formation used by Wales against Ireland at Llanelly, but I understand that it was first introduced by Cardiff, under the captaincy of F. E. Hancock, in 1885.'

And so it was. The development was an accident, because it happened after Hancock had become available again after injury, and rather than leave out the man who had substituted, Cardiff put them both in.

Hancock was not a Welshman. He came from Somerset. However, he was invited to play for Wales for three years in succession between 1884 and 1886 and he accepted. His brother played for Blackheath and England. National qualifications were loose, and went on being loose until after the Second World War.

1879 – a cartoonist's view of the increasingly popular game.

Rugby in Wales was developing rapidly, and within twelve years of their first, overwhelming defeat by England, they won the Triple Crown. They used the new formation of eight forwards and four three-quarters developed at Cardiff, and they included two players, W. J. Bancroft and Arthur Gould, who were among the first of the Welsh Rugby folk heroes.

The Welsh took to Rugby football as if they had invented it. Perhaps they did, because their Gallic ancestors had certainly played a form of football in Europe long before anybody had heard of Rugby School or William Webb Ellis. Rugby in Wales crossed all barriers of class, too. It was a game which was unique in its capacity to offer all men the chance of playing the game at international level whatever their shape or their size, whatever their speed, or lack of it, whatever their agility, whatever their strength, whatever their ball sense, whatever their courage. Indeed, it has often been said that the quickest and most elusive of Rugby players owe the magic in their feet to sheer terror.

The beauty of Rugby for the Welsh was that it was a game which could be played and enjoyed equally by coal miners and poets, and they could relish each other's company as a consequence. The rivalry between the villages in South Wales was intense, and the subtleties of the movements and the subterfuges, as well as the earthy realities of the occasional psychopath in the forwards, became a treasure trove of sporting memories and folk lore. It also became a treasure trove in another sense, because the star players of South Wales found themselves cherished with rewards far more practical than adulation.

England, meanwhile, had been having troubles in more than one direction. They were then much the strongest Rugby-playing country in the world, but the issue of professionalism was causing great concern in the North of England. In addition, the Rugby Football Union had various prickly disagreements with the Scots, and one of these led to the formation of the International Rugby Football Board in 1886.

England had beaten Scotland in 1884, but the Scots had complained that the winning goal should not have been allowed. England did not agree, and said that in any case the Irish referee who had allowed the score was the sole judge of

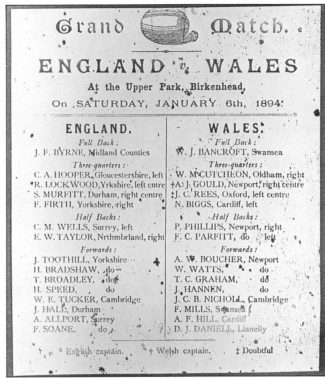

England won this match 24–3 despite the presence in the Welsh side of Gould and Bancroft who had, the previous year, inspired Wales to their first Triple Crown.

fact. Scotland even wanted to put the matter to arbitration, but England rejected the proposal. Eventually, Scotland agreed to concede the match if England would join an International Rugby Football Board on equal terms with the other Unions, but as they were much the biggest Union, England would have none of that either.

In the end, England offered to put the second question to arbitration, and to accept the findings. The other Unions agreed and the matter was then considered by Lord Kingsburgh, the Lord Justice Clerk, and Major F. A. Marindin, the President of the Football Association. They gave their verdict in April 1890 and found so overwhelmingly in favour of England that the Rugby Football Union could have dominated the government of the world of Rugby for all eternity if it had so chosen.

The English Union was given six seats on the new International Rugby Football Board and Scotland, Ireland and Wales were given two each. This meant that England could never be outvoted, and it was only because the Rugby Football Union itself chose to give up two of its seats in 1911 and two more in 1948, when Australia, New Zealand and South Africa were admitted, that the English relinquished their absolute control of the game.

Right *An extract from C. Mathers' record of England's tour to Australia and New Zealand in 1888.*

July & Aug [30 to 1]   30 MONDAY [212-154]   7th & 8th Months 1888

in morning had a look in Exhibition and saw some of Kirkstall Iron there in aft went to see J Pitts had a look round the Shop & found he had got some good stuff at night went to J Roberts & took J Haslam & R Burnett his Wife Sisters been there as well & we had a jolly good farewell & enjoyed ourselves

31 TUESDAY [213-153]

in morning had General Meeting to form a new Committee owing to last Saturday Dr Smith Dr Brooks & J Anderton coming on to the field to play drunk we formed a new Committee R Seddon H E Stoddart S Williams H Eagles & myself was put on in aft Billiards at night I went to J Roberts & we found W Cook in Fitzroy he was doing very well I stayed all night at Tommys.

1 Aug WEDNESDAY [214-152]
Lammas Day

in morning up early & had Breakfast I had slept at Tommys all night the Exhibition was opened this morning so Tommy his Wife & I came into Town to meet Maggie & Bellah to watch the Procession it was very busy in aft we played Melbourne at Rugby & won at night Theatre Monte Cristo

Below *The 1888 tourists. Back row J. Banks, A.E. Stoddart, J.P. Clowes, J. Lawlor, Dr J. Smith, A. Paul, G. McShane. Middle row J. Anderton, A. Penketh, S. Williams, R. Burnett, W.A. Thomas, R.L. Seddon (captain), H. Eagles, T. Kent, C. Mathers, H.C. Speakman, W. Burnett, Dr H. Brooks, W. Bumby, J.T. Haslam, J. Nolan, A.J. Stuart, A.J. Laing.*

The international development of the game.
Above *New York, 1897.*
Far left top *Afghanistan, 1879.*
(Bottom) Yokohama, 1874.
Below *Calcutta, 1875.*

'Boot money' in Rugby football has been given a modern and much more sophisticated significance in recent years by the scandal in which leading players were paid to wear boots made by various leading manufacturers. In the 1880s and 1890s, the illegal practices by which successful clubs bribed leading players to join them brought the newly organized game to its knees and very nearly destroyed it.

In one sense, Rugby football in late Victorian times was the victim of its own success: the building of the railways and the inauguration of public transport meant that any sport which could attract a paying public could develop at a rate never before experienced in the world. Within twenty years of the formation of the Rugby Union, the game had become so popular that clubs had been formed all over the British Isles, and some of them in Lancashire and Yorkshire had become very wealthy. The rivalry between these clubs reflected the intensity of local loyalties, and the Acts of Parliament which gave the working man Saturday afternoon for his leisure created both a playing community and a paying public.

The most successful clubs naturally wanted to retain their status and their support, and it did not take them long to realize that if they relied exclusively upon local recruitment of players, they could have good years and bad years. This did not suit them at all. They wanted good years and even better years, and so, human nature being what it has always been, the clubs went touting for the best players.

In those days, the clubs seeking to recruit playing talent did not bother to approach the toffs who played for the Universities or for the exclusive London clubs. Instead, they concentrated on the working man who needed the money, and went to the mining villages of South Wales. They also went to the back door of star players who turned out for their rivals.

Already, Yorkshire and Lancashire had become by far the strongest counties in England in terms of playing talent. The early England international teams drew heavily upon them, and so it took a great deal of courage for the infant Rugby Football Union to meet head-on the challenge offered by the threat of professionalism. As the various national Unions were to find ninety years later, knowing that illegal practices are going on is one thing;

proving it is another matter entirely. So it was that for some years the Rugby Union knew perfectly well that bribery and corruption were taking root in their Northern clubs, but no one was able to prove it.

The first real chance to do so did not come until 1890 when Cumberland complained that one of Yorkshire's leading clubs had offered one of their players a financial inducement to join them. The Rugby Union appointed a committee of inquiry, and even before the inquiry was held the three members of the committee, William Cail of Northumberland, Arthur Brook of Lancashire, and Frederick Currey were warned that if the accused club was disciplined in any way, all the leading clubs in Yorkshire and Lancashire would part company with the Rugby Union. These threats did not deter them in the least; the committee found in favour of Cumberland, and the club concerned was suspended. The findings were confirmed and approved by the RFU committee.

This caused so much uproar in the North that two general meetings were held in 1891 and special trains were run from Yorkshire to one of them in an attempt to canvas enough votes to pass a resolution allowing the clubs to compensate their players for money which they might have earned if they had been working instead of playing Rugby. These were called broken-time payments.

There was also an attempt to pass a resolution decreeing that annual general meetings of the Rugby Union should be held alternately in London and in the North of England. The proposers of this resolution, which originated in Yorkshire, had a majority in favour of it, but not the 66 per cent majority which the laws required before a change could be made. This, as the Duke of Wellington might have observed, was a damned close-run thing, because if that law had been changed, there is not much doubt that Yorkshire and Lancashire between them would have taken political control of the Rugby Union.

The clubs in those two counties still refused to mend their ways as far as breaches in the amateur code were concerned, and in the next two years they made broken-time payments to their players, and they paid financial inducements to good players to join them. The best-known of these players were two brothers, David and Evan James. They came from Swansea, they were both Welsh

The Rev Frank Marshall, a Northern administrator and staunch supporter of the amateur game.

international half-backs, and they were both such brilliant players that the Northern clubs went fishing for them. This has been a story repeated many times down the years. The difference was that at the end of the nineteenth century the Manchester club Broughton Rangers was able to recruit them and still play as an amateur Rugby club.

But not for long. In 1893, the Rugby Union professionalized the two brothers and yet took no action against their club, Broughton Rangers. This shows the extent of the pressure on the Rugby Union. However, later that year, on 20 September, a General Meeting of the Rugby Union was called in London at which J. A. Millar and M. Newsome, committee members of both the Rugby Union and Yorkshire, proposed that players be compensated for *bona fide* loss of working time.

William Cail, the President of the Rugby Union, and G. Rowland Hill, the Secretary, proposed an amendment saying that the proposition was contrary to the true interests of the game and that the meeting declined to sanction it. Again, the Northern clubs ran special trains to the meeting, but some of their delegates got lost on their way to the Westminster Palace Hotel; meanwhile the Rugby Union had worked very hard to muster all the proxy votes it could. The Northern clubs said sourly afterwards that the Rugby Union had worked too hard, because the individual colleges at Oxford and Cambridge had all voted, instead of the two Universities having a single vote each as they should have done. Even without those college votes, the Rugby Union would still have won, because the amendment was carried by 286 votes to 136, but it is doubtful if the Union would have won without the 120 proxy votes collected by a man named H. C. Steed.

Two years later, the Rugby Union tightened still further its legislation against professionalism, but by then the Northern clubs had decided to break away. On 29 August 1895, 22 of the most powerful clubs in English Rugby decided to form what they called a Northern Football Union, and all the clubs concerned resigned from the Rugby Union. The clubs were Batley, Bradford, Brighouse Rangers, Broughton Rangers, Halifax, Huddersfield, Hull, Hunslet, Leeds, Leigh, Liversedge, Manningham, Oldham, Rochdale Hornets, Runcorn, St Helens, Tyldesley, Wakefield Trinity, Warrington, Widnes, Wigan.

Those clubs contain some of the greatest names in Rugby League football, but if the issue of amateurism was as important as the Rugby Union felt it to be, it was certainly justified in its actions; within three years, the Northern Union had opted for outright professionalism. The departure of those clubs preserved Rugby Union football as an amateur game, but it destroyed the power of English Rugby. From being much the strongest country in the rapidly expanding world of Rugby football, England went into rapid decline.

Within ten years, the number of clubs playing Rugby in England had halved, from 481 to 244, and the poverty of the playing resources which were left opened the way for the other home countries, especially Wales, to enjoy runs of success which would never have been possible if the Rugby Union had been able to keep all its clubs amateur. Having opted for the cleansing spirit, the Rugby Union proved to be so badly shaken by the experience that it acted in a curiously contradictory and conciliatory way when faced with the problem of what to do about the Welsh Rugby Union and about Arthur Gould.

Gould was a famous Newport three-quarter whose admirers not only wanted to give him boot money, they wanted to give him a whole house in which to keep his boots. The player had been one of the stars in the Wales team which, in 1893, had won the Triple Crown for the first time in its history. When, in 1896, local adulation reached the point of giving him a house, the Rugby Union declared crisply 'that the giving of a house is tantamount to the giving of a monetary testimonial', which of course it was. The Rugby Union was both surprised and reassured, after many years of dispute, to find that Scotland shared its view.

Left *David and Evan James of Swansea and Broughton Rangers.*

William Cail, twelfth President of the RFU.

Above *G. Rowland Hill and (right) Arthur Gould, two figures at the centre of the controversy over professionalism.*

The Welsh Rugby Union was even going to contribute £50 towards the Gould testimonial, but withdrew that offer and refused to allow any presentation not authorized by the International Board. England banned its players and clubs from playing against Gould.

Gould took no notice. Instead, in 1897, he took the money.

Wales withdrew from the International Board and from matches against the other Home Unions. However, the Rugby Union, instead of pursuing its vision of amateurism to its logical conclusion, was so badly divided over whether to let the Welsh committee off the hook or whether to insist that the laws were there to be applied, that it called a general meeting and gave the members a free vote.

This resulted in perhaps the most extraordinary proposition that has ever been put at a meeting of the Rugby Football Union. It read: 'That A. J. Gould, having accepted a testimonial in a form that the Committee of the Rugby Union has decided to be an act of professionalism, nevertheless under the exceptional circumstances of the case, this meeting recommends the committee to allow him to play against clubs under their management. (This proposal does not emanate from the committee.)'

It was carried by a large majority. Subsequently the compromisers argued that, awful though it may have been, it was all worth while, because subsequent discussions between the two national committees led to Wales adopting the same laws in relation to professionalism as England.

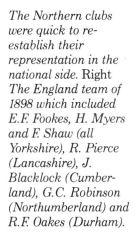

The Northern clubs were quick to re-establish their representation in the national side. Right *The England team of 1898 which included E.F. Fookes, H. Myers and F. Shaw (all Yorkshire), R. Pierce (Lancashire), J. Blacklock (Cumberland), G.C. Robinson (Northumberland) and R.F. Oakes (Durham).*

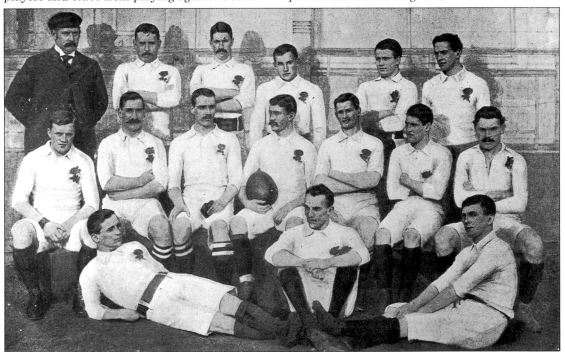

Of all the teams which have played Rugby football down the ages, the one which contributed most to the game in terms of technical advancement and sheer public impact was the 1905 New Zealand All Blacks on their tour of the British Isles.

The New Zealand Maoris had been the eighth wonder of the world in Rugby when they played an incredible total of 74 matches on tour in Europe in 1888 and 1889, and managed to win 49 of those games even though they had to play three or four times a week to pay for their tour. It was a truly remarkable achievement, but it was left standing by what Dave Gallaher and his team of New Zealand All Blacks did in the United Kingdom in 1905 and 1906. They swept through the country like Ghenghis Khan, putting one team after another to the sword. They played Rugby which was so well organized and so marvellously logical and practical that their opponents were overwhelmed and overawed. They had never seen anything like it.

Outside the British Isles, Rugby had been played in Australia since 1829. British wine shippers had taken the game to France and a club had been forme in Le Havre as early as 1872. In South Africa, the Civil played the Military in the first game of Rugby, but for a long time the South Africans played a version of Winchester football practised and preached by the celebrated Canon Ogilvie. He was known as Gog, and the game that the South Africans played was known as Gog's football.

Then a boy called Monro returned from school in England to his home in Nelson, at the top of the South Island of New Zealand, and introduced his fellows to the game. It has been suggested that Monro went to school at Sherborne, but no boy of that name was at Sherborne at the time; others believe that he went to Christ's College. Whatever the truth about his schooling may be, the seed he sowed in New Zealand certainly fell on fertile soil, because as early as 1888 the first British team to tour Australia and New Zealand were astonished to find two teams capable of beating them. Both were in New Zealand.

In the next 17 years, the New Zealanders took up the game and developed it with such enthusiasm that they evolved techniques which were light-years ahead of anything in the United Kingdom. No one outside their country knew what they were doing, of course. The outside world did not discover the brilliance of the New Zealanders' work until 1905. Even then, the immensity of their achievements would not have been appreciated fully if the eyesight and the memory of the technically ignorant British public had been the only record of the way Gallaher and his team played. Fortunately for posterity, Dave Gallaher and his vice-captain, Billy Stead, worked with a journalist to produce a book of the tour which ranks among the best ever written about Rugby football.

The book is called *The Complete Rugby Footballer*, and on page after page is material which is as relevant today as it was when it was written. The 1905 tour by New Zealand was very arduous, but the All Blacks accepted a programme in which they ended with matches against Wales, Glamorgan, Newport, Cardiff and Swansea. No modern team would dream of undertaking a fixture list of such intensity, but stale and exhausted though they were, the only match the All Blacks lost was the international against Wales.

The score in that match was a try to nil, but New Zealanders still come to Cardiff Arms Park to try to take a piece of turf from the corner where the All Black, Bob Deans, went over for what his countrymen will always believe was a perfectly good try. What is more, so did the man who was marking him. Teddy Morgan earned himself undying glory in his own country by scoring the only try of the match, but it was also Morgan who made the cover tackle when Deans went over. 'I thought Deans had scored,' said Morgan, and he repeated that opinion twenty years later, when Cliff Porter's All Blacks were touring the British Isles. Morgan put it in writing, too, because he signed Porter's menu card to that effect at the official dinner.

However, referees in those days were not as fit as they are now, and by the time Scotsman John Dallas arrived, he could not be sure what had happened. Not that the All Blacks complained. They acknowledged that they had played badly. The team were tired, overplayed and suffering from injuries, and in Gallaher's view were much too conscious of preserving their unbeaten record.

That record was built on an understanding of the game, and a mastery of technique, which is astonishing even today. The All Blacks based their game on the most important of the fundamentals: that the essence of Rugby

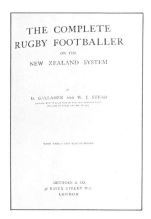

THE COMPLETE
RUGBY FOOTBALLER
ON THE
NEW ZEALAND SYSTEM

BY
D. GALLAHER AND W. J. STEAD

WITH THIRTY-FIVE ILLUSTRATIONS

METHUEN & CO.
36 ESSEX STREET W.C.
LONDON

Above *Richmond entertain the Maoris in 1888.*

Above right *The first All Blacks of 1905.* Right *Action from the tour. Gallaher places the ball for Gillett to attempt a conversion.* Inset *The 1905 fixtures and details of the touring party.*

football is possession of the ball, followed by quick, controlled and accurate passing supported by close backing up of thoroughly fit players, with the object of creating a situation where two attacking players are running against one defender.

Gallaher and Stead stated that the simple act of passing the ball was the most important science in the game. They evolved the classic hip-swing pass which committed a defender before the ball was released and they said

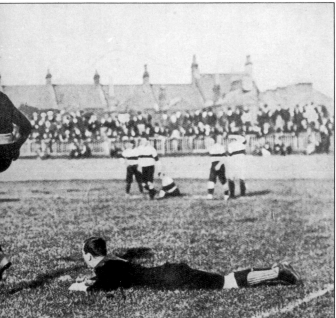

bluntly that a back without pace was a Rugby cripple. They derided a player who could pass off only one hand, or kick off only one foot, as being only half a player. They also developed the loose scrum to the point where it became quite recognizable as the modern ruck, with its deliberate aim of committing the opposition defence in order to leave the attackers with an extra man in attack. Their strictures about pace and fitness were just as firmly applied in their choice of forwards, and they contrasted their

A series of illustrations that reflect the impact made on the British public by the New Zealand tourists.

own methods with what they observed in the British Isles.

'We have noticed shocking neglect in the choice and cultivation of the men of the front rank,' they wrote. 'The prevailing idea in Britain seems to be that anything is good enough for a forward, and that you put in that department all those men who are not thoroughly capable for any other task. Our principle is that every forward should be a potential back and in the team that toured Britain, there was not a man in the pack who could not have fulfilled the duties of a back if the emergency had demanded.'

Gallaher's All Blacks kept a record of the way they scored tries, and the way tries were scored against them. Accidents which produced tries, or oddities of formation which did the same thing, were reproduced deliberately, and added to the repertoire of planned moves which the 1905 All Blacks were the first to use on a really significant scale.

They used the hooker to throw the ball into the lineout, and not the scrum-half or the blind-side wing. This did not become common practice in Britain for another 65 years. They invented the miss move in the backs, the move by which the next player in the line to receive a pass is missed out with a long pass. They used a running full-back. They kept reverse passes to be used as an option all the way down the line, and could do that because their insistence on fitness meant that they invariably had at least one man backing up in support on the inside of the man with the ball.

They used code words as signals for planned moves, something which has only really developed in Europe in the last twenty years, and they adopted the formation of a scrum-half playing with a fly-half, whom they called a first five-eighth. New Zealand teams still use this formation.

They even split the lineout, and threw the ball into the gap. They used this move in the international against Ireland. They broke clean through, and only failed to score because the New Zealand winger put a foot over the dead ball line in trying to run round behind the posts. At that time, it was possible to take a scrum instead of a lineout, which most teams did. But not the All Blacks, and the flexibility of what they did in and from those lineouts confounded most of their opponents.

They were the first to use the lineout as a platform to launch attacks, and they not only scored 33 tries direct from lineouts on tour, but actually knew that they had done so! They also established the principles of blanket support running by all the forwards, and again, it took British and Irish Rugby nearly seventy years to come to terms with that.

'Our forwards,' wrote Mr Gallaher and Mr Stead, 'always seem to be more eager, to follow up better, and to do a far greater amount of work – back work, as it might be called – than the majority of those we encountered on our British tour. In England, it seems to be considered unorthodox for a forward to take part in a passing movement, or to initiate an attack from a lineout, but we believe in our forwards being as quick as the back division in taking the ball.'

The All Blacks also used dummy runs without the ball; they pulled men out of the scrum in defence; they were just as meticulous in the planning of their attacking kicking, and they even had a recipe for the embrocation that they used. Six parts of eucalyptus oil to three parts of whisky and one part of hartshorn! The British public was flabbergasted. It accused the All Blacks of being sustained by magic Maori potions and it was even suggested that the All Blacks' shirts, which were reinforced at the neck with canvas and chamois leather, were made of eel-skin to stop tacklers gaining a fair hold.

The 1905 All Blacks did have an achilles heel, and that was their scrum. They persisted with using a two-man front row, in an attempt to have the loose head whichever side was putting the ball into the scrum, and they used Dave Gallaher himself as what they called a 'rover', in effect a second scrum-half. As a consequence, Gallaher was offside at every scrum, and he clearly stood where he did to obstruct the opposition. These two practices caused no end of bad feeling, and the arguments about the front-row formation led to an All Black being sent off the field when England played New Zealand in front of Royalty at Twickenham in 1925.

Never mind. The fact was that, even in 1925 and after a Great War, the whole of New Zealand still believed in the precepts established by Dave Gallaher as if they were the tablets handed down from Sinai. This was the ultimate accolade to the colossal example set by the 1905 New Zealand All Blacks.

ave Gallaher's All Blacks were not much impressed by the team-work of any of the sides they played in the British Isles, and they were even less impressed by the standard of selection in England, but they did doff their caps to the individual skills of some of the players they met in Wales.

These players had come together in the first few years of the twentieth century to give Wales their first golden era of success in international Rugby. Teddy Morgan, the man who scored the try for Wales that beat the 1905 All Blacks, was one of those players, and so was Rhys Gabe, who played alongside Gwyn Nicholls in the centre. Nicholls was captain of Wales that famous day, and when, late in life, Rhys Gabe was asked what he thought of the Welsh playing stars of his time, he had no doubt of the place that Nicholls occupied.

'He was the perfect centre,' said Gabe. 'I played alongside him for Cardiff as well as for Wales, and only someone who had played alongside him for years, as I did, could appreciate the all-round strength of his play.'

The All Blacks were much impressed with Percy Bush, too. He had proved a rare handful

Percy Bush, Cardiff and Wales.

PERCY F. BUSH. (Capt.)

A great day for Welsh Rugby.

NEW ZEALAND v. WALES AT CARDIFF.—THE COLONIALS BEATEN AT LAST.
THE WELSHMEN SCORE A SINGLE TRY AND KEEP THE "ALL BLACKS" FROM SCORING DURING A FIERCE GAME.

W. M. Llewellyn, the three quarter.   H. T. Winfield, who was brilliant at back.   E. T. Morgan, who scored the try.

A section of the orderly crowd of over 40,000 people.

E. Gwyn Nichols, the Welsh captain, who defended splendidly.

when a British team had toured New Zealand in 1904, and Gabe said: 'He was capable of the most amazing feats of individual brilliance. I once saw him score a try directly from a kick-off.'

Bush won his first cap for Wales in that match against New Zealand, on 16 December 1905, and there is not much doubt that Wales won the game because of the respect that the All Blacks had for the young Welsh fly-half. Gwyn Nicholls worked on this, and decided to feed the ball to Bush all the time to pull the New Zealand defence towards him until the moment came to use him as a decoy and switch the ball in the other direction, where Morgan was waiting to take the ball from Cliff Pritchard and Rhys Gabe. The move worked, and Morgan scored.

Gabe also played for Wales with W. J. Bancroft, the legendary full-back. 'Bancroft played the last of his games for Wales when I played my first, against Ireland in 1901. Bancroft had marvellous speed and dodging powers which he used to tire out the forwards before finding touch. He was a master of the art of place-kicking, drop-kicking and punting and he could kick the ball tremendous distances with either foot.

'Two other great Swansea players were Dicky Owen, a tireless, fearless scrum-half, as full of tricks as a monkey, and W. J. Trew, the best all-round player I ever saw. He was capped for Wales as a wing, centre and stand-off half.'

Owen won 35 international caps for Wales, a record which stood for more than forty years, and Trew was capped 29 times. He played nine internationals at stand-off, his preferred position, six on the wing and 14 in the centre.

W.J. Bancroft, a regular in the Welsh side for twelve years.

A poster announcing the arrival in London of the first All Blacks.

Touch-judge flags from early internationals at Twickenham.

The All Black shirt worn by Taranaki forward W.S. Glenn on the 1905 tour.

Wales won seven Triple Crowns in the years before the First World War, and it was not until the Rugby Union bought and developed a ground at Twickehnham, and made the place their headquarters, that England began to reassert the playing authority they had enjoyed before the breakaway of their Northern clubs.

Before the purchase of the new ground at Twickenham, England had played their matches at Kennington Oval, Crystal Palace, Blackheath, Richmond and various provincial grounds. This nomadic existence did not appeal to the members of the Rugby Union committee, and they began to look for a suitable ground where they could make their headquarters. This ground was found for them in 1907 by a remarkable character called Billy Williams. He was a thoroughly Dickensian figure, who was an active sportsman for most of his life, which lasted 91 years. He was a first-class cricketer, and went on playing club cricket until he was 74. He played full-back for Harlequins. He was something of a wheeler-dealer and he had also been a referee in first-class Rugby.

Billy had become a celebrity when he refereed the match between Surrey and Dave Gallaher's All Blacks in 1905. Like a lot of other people up and down the country, he did not approve of the way Dave Gallaher himself stood out of the scrums and obstructed opponents trying to tackle his scrum-half, and Billy Williams penalized the All Blacks so often that they were restricted to their smallest score against any of the English counties.

Two years after that, he suggested to the Rugby Union committee, of which he became a member himself, that they might like to buy the Fairfield Estate at Twickenham to develop as their new ground. As the site was more than twelve miles from the centre of London, a considerable body of opinion thought that the suggestion was daft, particularly as the heavy clay soil was liable to flooding by the nearby River Crane. Despite these reservations, the Rugby Union went ahead and bought the land for £5,572 12s 6d. It was then a market garden and has often been referred to since as 'Billy Williams's cabbage patch', but there was no more truth in that than there was in the myths about William Webb Ellis. The ground had been used as an orchard, but never as a cabbage patch.

The Rugby Union acquired 10½ acres for their money, and they immediately spent another £1,606 9s 4d to raise the playing area above its existing level. They also set about building two stands, which were known, not as the number one and number two stands, as might have seemed logical, and as they are in New Zealand, but as the 'A' and the 'B' stands. The ends behind the goals were raised with

Pre-Twickenham days. Top *England v Wales at Blackheath, 1892.* Centre *England v Wales at Leicester, 1904.* Bottom *Stoop's invitation to play for England against Scotland at Richmond, 1905.*

37

clinker and ash, and as the new stands could hold 6,000 spectators, and the terracing could accommodate 20,000, the ground capacity was a very respectable 26,000. Seats at the big games cost four shillings each, which was a lot of money in those days.

The first match was played at the ground in October 1909, when Harlequins beat Richmond 14–10, and four months later Twickenham was opened as England's national Rugby ground. The first game that England played there was against Wales, and they began in the best possible way by scoring a try and converting it in the first five minutes. England won 11–6 and that was an event of considerable significance in itself, because it was the first time England had beaten Wales for 12 years. It also heralded a period of remarkable prosperity for England in their home international matches, and Wales did not win their first

Above The Harlequins team to play Richmond in the inaugural match at Twickenham. Standing, left to right: G.R. Maxwell-Dove, J.H. Denison, B.H. Bonham-Carter, G.V. Carey, W.G. Beauchamp, T. Potter, R.E. Hancock, R.O.C. Ward.
Seated: H.J.H. Sibree, D. Lambert, A.D. Stoop (captain), W.A. Smith (president), J.G.G. Birkett, J.G. Bussell, R.W. Poulton. Front: F.M. Stoop, G.M. Chapman.

Right G.V. Carey bursts through the Richmond defence.

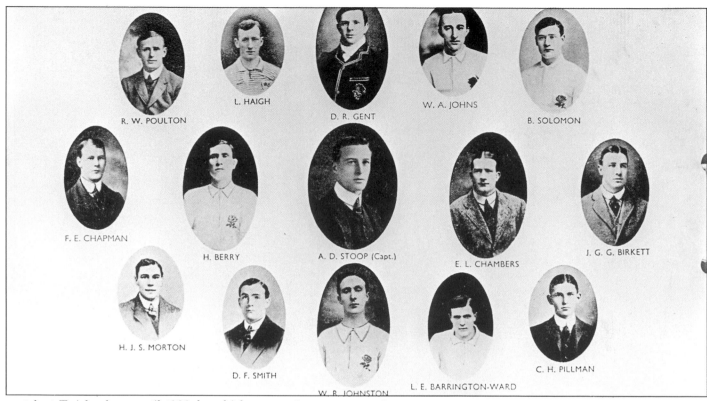

The England team that defeated Wales 11–6 in the first international match played at Twickenham in January 1910.

match at Twickenham until 1933, by which time the entire Welsh nation was convinced that 'HQ', as they called it (pronounced haitch-queue), had a malign Celtic hoodoo on it.

Many years later, an eye-witness named Kenneth Rankin described how England scored their dramatic opening try. 'When Wales came up for the match, England hadn't won for eleven years, and some people were beginning to feel as though we never would. But Adrian Stoop, who was England's captain and fly-half, had other ideas, and decided on immediate audacity.

'When Gronow kicked off for Wales, Stoop caught the ball and ran slightly to the right. Just as everyone was waiting for the usual return to touch, he suddenly slewed off to the left and ran upfield as hard as he could. When

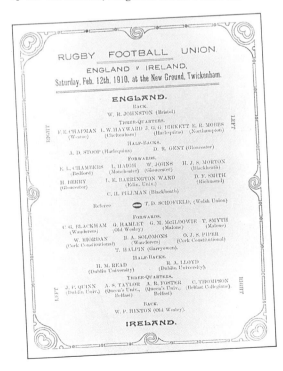

Ronnie Poulton (1889–1915), Oxford University, Harlequins, Liverpool and England.

Far left A programme for the England v Ireland match of 1910. Despite their new home base, England could only hold the Irish to a 0–0 draw

the Welsh defence began to get across and back, he made a short punt. England followed up, out came the ball, there were a couple of quick passes and F. E. Chapman, England's right wing, was over.

'It all happened so quickly that hardly anyone understood it. Lots of people were still getting to their seats and did not properly see it, but from an English point of view, it was a rare experience to have got in the first blow and to watch the puzzled faces and muttering mouths of the Welsh team as they gathered behind their goal-line.'

Beating the other Home Unions at Twickenham was one thing for England, but beating the Overseas Unions was another matter entirely. The South Africans had made their first tour of the British Isles in 1906, and had drawn with England 3–3 at Crystal Palace. However, they had beaten the powerful Welsh team decisively, and had beaten Ireland in Belfast too; the only international match they lost on that tour was to Scotland, by six points to nil in Glasgow.

The South Africans did not make as big an impact on that tour as Dave Gallaher and his All Blacks had the year before, but when South Africa returned to tour again in 1912–13, there was no mistaking the increase in their international stature. They trounced Scotland 10–0 in Inverleith, overwhelmed Ireland 38–0 in Dublin, beat Wales narrowly by 3–0 in Cardiff, and beat England 9–3 at Twickenham. They also beat France 38–5 in Bordeaux to complete a bigger Grand Slam than will ever be possible again because of the reduction in the size of international tours; but of all their wins the victory at Twickenham was the sweetest because it was the first time England had lost a match on their new ground.

One of the players in the England team beaten that day was Ronnie Poulton. Those who watched him play were certain that he was the greatest three-quarter ever to play the game and they held to that opinion all their lives. England did score a try against South Africa, and they owed it to a brilliant run by Poulton in a devastating opening assault. Poulton nearly scored a second try after another dazzling run in that period of early England ascendancy, and the South Africans confessed afterwards that they were lucky to survive.

Poulton later inherited a fortune on condition that he changed his name to Poulton-Palmer; sadly, he did not live to enjoy it, being killed by a sniper's bullet in the Great War. His last words before he died were: 'I shall never play at Twickenham again.'

The South African tourists of 1906–7.

PART TWO

*T*HE INTER-WAR YEARS,
1919 - 1939

Despite the appalling numbers of players killed or wounded in action, Rugby made an enthusiastic recovery after the First World War. This was partly because men who had been through the war returned to their favourite sport with renewed fervour, and were able to guide the younger club members with their pre-war experience, and partly because of the number of mature students at the universities.

A number of men represented their country both before and after the war. The most notable of these was the Scotland forward Jock Wemyss (pronounced Weems) of Gala and Edinburgh Wanderers. He lost an eye in the war, but his colleagues always insisted that he played better with one eye than with two because after the war he could only see well enough to make half the mistakes he used to. Legend has it, too, that when he turned up for his first post-war international, the Scottish Rugby Union were reluctant to give him new stockings, saying that he should have kept the ones he played in before the war. Wemyss stayed in contact with Rugby all his life, becoming a writer on the game and official registrar and keeper of the records of the Barbarians.

The England pack which beat Wales in 1921 had an average age of over thirty even though it included the young Wavell Wakefield

Action from the first Varsity match to be staged at Twickenham in 1921. Wavell Wakefield, third from the right, was in the Cambridge side that lost 5–11.

Revenge for Wakefield as captain of the 1922 Cambridge XV which beat Oxford 21–8. Back row, left to right: D.M. Maxwell, R.K. Melluish. Standing: W.G.B. Mackenzie, A.S. Cohen, J.B. White, D.C. Cumming, W.E. Tucker, D.P. Evans. Seated: F.A. Gardiner, D.J. MacMyn, W.W. Wakefield, R.H. Hamilton-Wickes, T.E. Morel. Front row: A.T. Young, T.E.S. Francis.

Photo : Stearn & Sons, Cambridge.

		D. M. Maxwell		R. K. Melluish		
W. G. B. Mackenzie	A. S. Cohen	J. B. White	D. C. Cumming	W. E. Tucker	D. P. Evans	
F. A. Gardiner	D. J. MacMyn	W. W. Wakefield	R. H. Hamilton-Wickes		T. E. Morel	
	A. T. Young				T. E. S. Francis	

CAMBRIDGE UNIVERSITY RUGBY XV. 1922.
Cambridge 21 points, Oxford 8 points.

(later Lord Wakefield of Kendal) who had a great influence on university and services Rugby. Wakefield, regarded as the father of RAF Rugby, went up·to Cambridge in October 1921 on a special Service course, and he captained the University in 1922. In the 1922-23·season he achieved the remarkable feat of captaining Cambridge to victory over Oxford in the University match before Christmas, and then leading the RAF to victories over the Army and the Navy in the second half of the season. As he was also playing for England at the time, he must have been a busy man.

Wakefield's influence at Cambridge was particularly profound. In his later years he used to pour scorn on those young ignoramuses who proclaimed that coaching was an invention of the 1950s and 1960s. He pointed out that during his captaincy of Cambridge in 1922 he recruited such famous names as John Daniell, Dicky Lloyd, Tommy Vile and Barry Cumberledge to coach his University team. Wakefield's systematic organization of Cambridge Rugby, both on and off the field, began a trend which produced a more scientific approach throughout the game in the British Isles.

Right up to the Second World War the Universities of Oxford and Cambridge continued to turn out sides whose methods were copied by the clubs they defeated. They also produced some great players who served their countries with distinction. Among them were two backs who played together for Cambridge and Wales – Wilf Wooller and Cliff Jones. There was a marked contrast between their respective styles of play. Wooller, a tall man with a long stride, was a thrustful centre who could also kick with immense power. He won 18 Welsh caps between 1933 and 1939 and later captained Glamorgan at cricket. Jones, with 13 caps between 1934 and 1938, was a short and nimble fly-half whose kicking was subtle and accurate. In the same period Oxford had another Welshman of influence in Vivian Jenkins. He won 14 caps for Wales and went on the 1938 Lions' tour of South Africa as a full-back.

A Russian was outstanding at Oxford in the 1930s. He was Prince Obolensky, who had been educated at Trent College where he was renowned as a sprinter. At Oxford, he played on the wing and set out to be as fast on the Rugby field as he was on the running track. To this end he used to spend many mornings sipping coffee

at Elmer Cotton's sports shop in The Turl while he discussed ways of making boots as light as possible. Ultimately he insisted on having boots so thin and light that they would often split during the course of a match; but his theories probably had much to do with the development of the modern lightweight boot. Wearing a pair of light boots, he scored one of Twickenham's most famous tries, for England against the 1935–36 All Blacks (see 'Great Tries, Great Matches').

During the 1920s and 1930s the matches between the three Services came to play a prominent part in the British Rugby calendar. The Army and the Navy had been going strong before the First World War, but the

Below *The strong Navy team which visited Grenoble in 1922 included Kershaw and Davies (front row standing, second and third from left).*
Bottom *Their French hosts.*

THE SERVICES AT WEMBLEY: THE ARMY DRAW WITH THE R.A.F.

1. A GREAT INTERNATIONAL WING THREE-QUARTER, WHO SCORED BOTH THE R.A.F. TRIES: LIEUT. C. N. LOWE JUST BEFORE HIS SECOND TOUCH-DOWN.　2. THE GAME, THOUGH DESPERATELY FOUGHT OUT, WAS PLAYED IN AN ADMIRABLE SPIRIT: A FURIOUS STRUGGLE.
3. CAPT. M. A. GREEN FAILS TO STOP AN AIR FORCE MAN FROM PASSING THE BALL OUT AFTER A SCRUM.
4. AN ARMY MAN BROUGHT HEAVILY DOWN.　　　　　　　5. LT. P. E. C. HONEYMAN TOUCHES DOWN BEHIND HIS OWN LINE.

Both having previously defeated the Navy, the Army and the R.A.F. XV.'s were playing for the Services Championship when they met in the Stadium at Wembley on Saturday last. The score was two tries (6 points) each, the Army narrowly escaping defeat by touching down their second try a few moments before "no side." The 5,000 people who went to Wembley to see this match were completely lost in the vast area of the Stadium, which is estimated to be able to accommodate nearly 130,000 people.

Above *The keenly contested decider in the Services Championship, 1925.*

Above right *'Tuppy' Owen-Smith (Oxford University, St. Mary's Hospital and England), the only South African ever to captain England at Rugby.*

Right *Members of the 1935 Oxford team take a break from training at Eastbourne. Left to right: J.H. Pienaar, H.M. Hughes, C.T. Bloxham, P.C.W. Disney, Prince Alexander Obolensky, K.L.T. Jackson, N.F. McGrath, and C.F. Grieve.*

establishment of the RAF, which grew from the old Royal Flying Corps, led to the setting-up of a three-way Inter-Services Tournament. The standard of Rugby played in this tournament drew large crowds to Twickenham, inspiring them with fresh ideas about how the game should be played.

At the same time the Services played a continuing part in the spreading of Rugby overseas. Army and RAF units were sent to distant parts of the Empire, and wherever they went they tried to play matches and to interest local inhabitants in the game. When the Navy steamed into ports all over the world, they would aim to play a match or two of Rugby while on dry land. The Army and RAF units, and the ships of the Navy, may not have produced Rugby of a high quality, but they played an important part in the spread of the game to parts of the world very far removed from Twickenham and Cardiff Arms Park.

Poster designed by Dame Laura Knight in 1921.

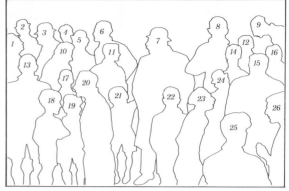

*Some of the great
names in the game as
seen by a
contemporary artist.*

1. G. Rowland Hill
2. Lt Col. W.S.D. Craven
3. C.J.B. Marriott
4. J. Daniell
5. E. Temple Gurdon
6. S.W. Harris
7. Major B.C. Hartley
8. H.C. Harrison
9. E. Loudoun Shand
10. F.C. Potter Irwin
11. V.R. Price
12. C.A. Kershaw
13. B.S. Cumberlege
14. A.T. Voyce
15. J. Birkett
16. G.B. Crole
17. A. Bates
18. C.N. Lowe
19. C. Lewis
20. W.W. Wakefield
21. H. Coverdale
22. R.A. Lloyd
23. W.J.A. Davies
24. A.D. Stoop
25. C.H. Pillman
26. J.E. Greenwood

Right *The Varsity match moved from Queen's Club to Twickenham in 1921.*
Far right *More entertainment for the visitors.*
Below *The shirt worn by the unfortunate All Black Cyril Brownlie, the first man to be sent off in an international. He was dismissed by Welsh referee Albert Freethy during the tourists' win over England at Twickenham during their undefeated tour of 1924–25.*

It was in the 1920s and 1930s that the modern game really developed. This is particularly true of forward formations. The British gradually adopted specialized positional play for their forwards, the South Africans invented the powerful 3-4-1 scrum, and the All Blacks were forced to abandon their traditional scrum formation which had only two men in the front row.

The New Zealanders and South Africans had specialized positions for their forwards many years before the British realized that their first-up-first-down haphazard forming of scrums could not compete with the expertise of the Colonials. When the British got round to specialized forward scrummaging, they adopted a 3-2-3 formation, and this was the norm right up to the Second World War. The outward difference between this formation and the South African 3-4-1 was that in Britain the flank forwards bound on to the No. 8, thus forming a back row of three men, whereas in South Africa the flank forwards bound on to the locks, making a second row of four men and leaving the No. 8 alone at the back.

That was the superficial difference, but there was much more to it than that. In the South African formation the flank forwards were that much further forward for giving support to their own men in attack and for spoiling their opponents if the ball came out on their side of the scrum. Even more important was the fact that the flank forwards, in the South African formation, were shoving directly on to their props, thus producing greater power just where it was most needed.

The New Zealanders were brought up to believe that the wedge produced by having only two men in the front row was the most efficient way of scrummaging. So much so that they were in the habit of using only seven forwards and giving the eighth a roving commission round the fringes of the scrum. This 2-3-2 formation worked well when the All Blacks met British sides using the 3-2-3 arrangement. In 1928, however, when the All Blacks made their first tour of South Africa, they immediately found themselves in difficulties against the more scientifically organized South African 3-4-1 formation. The New Zealanders learned the lesson of that tour, and before long they adopted the 3-4-1 scrum themselves. So, in the course of the 1920s and 1930s, scrummaging moved from the haphazard going down of the

GRAVE IS GAY: WITH THE ALL BLACKS AT TWICKENHAM.

LONDON CALLING! AND NEW ZEALAND ANSWERING — 31 POINTS TO 6.

That hope which "springs eternal" made many of us think that the All Blacks would meet their Waterloo at Twickenham last Saturday, especially as on the previous Wednesday they had only just scraped home against Cambridge University. The contrary, however, was the case. It has now become a custom to say that the New Zealanders "disappoint" unless they overwhelm their opponents at all moments in all departments of the game. We have yet to hear, however, that they themselves are disappointed with their aggregate of hundreds of points to tens since they landed in this country.

(Drawn by Chas. Grave.)

British to the almost universal acceptance of the 3-4-1 system invented by the South Africans.

One of the most controversial positional ploys of the period was New Zealand's use of the rover. He had come into being when the New Zealanders decided they could manage with only seven forwards at scrums. The seven-man formation gave them a surplus player, and it was the use to which they put him that caused the controversy. They reasoned that their seven-man wedge of a scrum was so efficient and got the ball back so quickly that often the ball shot out of the scrum before the

Comment on the New Zealanders' playing methods from The Illustrated Sporting and Dramatic News *following their decisive win at Twickenham in 1924.*

scrum-half, who had put the ball in, could get round to the back of the scrum to pass it out. They therefore got their surplus man, the rover, to put the ball into the scrum while the scrum-half waited at the back of the scrum ready to whip the ball away to his backs.

rover, in not retreating with the ball, was off-side. The matter came to a head when the Lions toured New Zealand in 1930. The Lions' manager, James ('Bim') Baxter of England, spoke out after the Lions' first match, at Wanganui. At the official dinnner he said that

The success of the All Blacks on their 1924–25 tour led to much analysis of their 'system'.

SHOWING THE STRENGTH OF THE "ALL BLACK" SYSTEM: THE "ALL BLACK" HALF (NO. 14) GETS THE BALL OUT TO THE FIVE-EIGHTHS BEFORE THE OPPOSING HALVES CAN INTERFERE, WHILE PORTER (NO. 16), WHO PUT THE BALL IN THE SCRUMMAGE, STANDS READY TO HELP.

SHOWING THE WEAKNESS OF THE ENGLISH SYSTEM: AN ENGLISH SCRUM-HALF COLLARED, WHILE THE "ALL BLACK" WING-FORWARD, PORTER (ON RIGHT), DRIBBLES AWAY, BACKED UP BY RICHARDSON (CENTRE) AND BROWNLIE (EXTREME LEFT).

What other countries objected to was that the rover, having put the ball in, remained at the side of the scrum where he obstructed the opposing scrum-half and prevented him from getting round to spoil his immediate opponent. Not only that: the other countries held that the

the rover was 'not near the borderline but over the borderline. I say he must not only be discouraged; he must be stopped.' Since Mr Baxter was a member of the International Board (New Zealand were not admitted to the IB until 1948) his words carried some weight.

The rover was not seen after 1931.

It was about this time that repeated punting from fly-half became a fashion. Its chief exponent was a South African, Bennie Osler, who demonstrated the tactic to a disapproving public on the Springboks' tour of

the Grand Slam of defeating all four home countries, his methods cannot be said to have been a failure. Even today, however, many people blame Osler for the excessive kicking seen in the modern game.

On that 1931–32 tour Osler had as his

Left *The New Zealanders narrowly won this match against Transvaal but could only draw the Test series on their 1928 tour of South Africa. Bennie Osler (above), and Danie Craven (below left), followed by Boy Louw, were two of the significant figures in the Springboks' dominance of the 1930s.*

the British Isles in 1931–32. From behind a dominating pack of forwards Osler monotonously punted the ball up-field, ignoring his three-quarters. Within reach of his opponents' posts his main ploy was to try to drop a goal. Since those Springboks achieved

scrum-half partner a chunky young man called Danie Craven. Craven is best known nowadays for his work as President of the South African Rugby Board over the last thirty years, but in the 1930s he was highly regarded for his invention of the scrum-half's dive pass. This is the pass in which the player throws his whole body in a dive in the direction of the pass, thus avoiding the attentions of would-be spoilers. Theorists claimed that it was a slower pass than the normal one whipped away off the back foot, but it was certainly a valuable technique for a scrum-half to have in his armoury, and many scrum-halves still find it useful today.

At a time when specialization was in full swing, certainly in South African Rugby, Craven achieved a feat of versatility which may never be overshadowed. Although essentially a scrum-half – he captained the Springboks from this position against the 1938 Lions – he also played in Tests as a centre, a fly-half, and a No. 8 forward. He was picked as a centre for the Fourth Test against the touring Wallabies at Port Elizabeth in 1933 and then, on the 1937 Springboks' tour of Australia and New Zealand, he played at No. 8 in the Second Test at Sydney and at fly-half in the First Test at Wellington.

Although France first played England in 1906, Wales in 1908, Ireland in 1909 and Scotland in 1910, it was not until the early 1920s that they began to make their mark. Before the First World War the French had achieved only one international victory, over Scotland by 16–15 at Colombes in 1911. In the first post-war Five Nations Championship in 1920, however, they quickly showed they were a force to be reckoned with. In that campaign they held England to a score of 8–3 at Twickenham, were beaten only 6–5 by Wales in Paris, held Scotland to 5–0 in Paris, and then achieved their first away victory by defeating Ireland 15–7 in Dublin. In this match they included two of their subsequently most famous backs, Adolphe Jauréguy on the wing and René Crabos in the centre, who both went on to serve on the committee of the Fédération Française de Rugby for many years.

The following year the French went one better, recording two victories, over Scotland at Inverleith by 3–0, and over Ireland by 20–10 in Paris, and in 1922 they ought to have achieved their first win at Twickenham. This was the match for which Harold Day, England's goal-kicker, forgot to pack his boots and had to borrow a pair. Nevertheless he kicked two

The first visit to France by an English team. Rosslyn Park v Stade Français of Paris at Levallois-Perret, 1892.

The French team which lost heavily to England at Twickenham (0–37) in 1911.

penalty goals and then, with the French leading 11–9 in the closing minutes, he made the conversion which condemned France to a draw.

England's try was itself a doubtful score, many people at the ground believing it was scored from an off-side position. There was a skirmish just short of the French line from which the ball was propelled in-goal where it was caught by Tom Voyce, the England forward, who fell on to it. It was not France's lucky day, and they had to wait until 1951 before gaining their first victory at Twickenham.

The French got their first win over Wales in 1928, beating them 8–3 at Colombes, but they

did not win on Welsh territory until 1948. Part of the reason for such long delays was a rupture in relations between France and the home countries which happened in 1931. This split occurred mainly over allegations of rough play and professionalism in the French club championship. The Home Unions asked the French to do away with their club championship, but the French declined, pointing out that without the championship Rugby was unlikely to survive in their country. The Home Unions then stated that there would be no further contacts with the French, at international or club level, 'unless and until we are satisfied that the control and conduct of the game have been placed on a satisfactory basis in all essentials'. The ban lasted until 1939 but the resumption of fixtures, planned for the 1939–40 season, had to be postponed because of the outbreak of the Second World War.

The rupture emphasized the different attitudes to the game on the two sides of the Channel. The outlook in the British Isles was that the game was played strictly for fun and recreation, an attitude underlined in 1933 by the Rugby Football Union's refusal to allow Rugby to be played under floodlights for gate money 'because this is not in the best interests of the game'. In France men played the game for the glory of representing their town and, if possible, their country. From its earliest days French Rugby had always had its club championship, providing a natural outlet for the players' basic need for glory. At the time of the

Manuel Communeau, French captain and a regular member of the French team in the years before the First World War.

In 1919 an Australian XV played an unofficial international against a French team which was considered at the time to be the best ever team selected to represent that country. However, the Australians managed a narrow 3–0 victory in front of a crowd of 20,000.

split the French, with defiance if not truculence, instigated the Fédération Internationale de Rugby Amateur, a body which linked them to several fledgling European Rugby nations. In time the Home Unions were to praise the French for their pioneering work for these other countries.

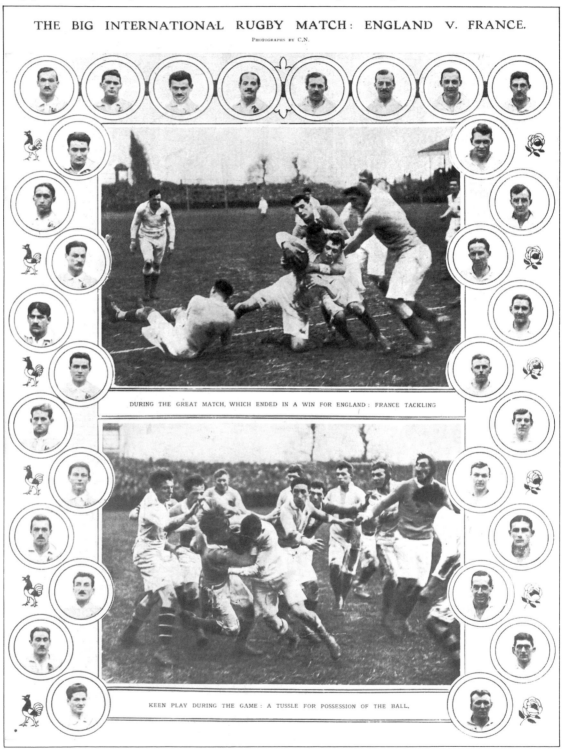

THE BIG INTERNATIONAL RUGBY MATCH: ENGLAND V. FRANCE.

PHOTOGRAPHS BY C.N.

DURING THE GREAT MATCH, WHICH ENDED IN A WIN FOR ENGLAND: FRANCE TACKLING

KEEN PLAY DURING THE GAME: A TUSSLE FOR POSSESSION OF THE BALL.

France provided stern opposition in 1920 but had to wait until 1927 for their first win over England.

For those of us who have lived with the Triple Crown and Grand Slam triumphs of Wales in the 1970s, it is odd to realize that the Welsh did not win a single Grand Slam or Triple Crown in the period between 1919 and 1939. Nor, for that matter, did Ireland. The country which met with most success between the two World Wars was in fact England. They had Triple Crowns in 1921, 1923, 1924, 1928, 1934 and 1937, and Grand Slams in 1921, 1923, 1924 and 1928. Scotland, too, had a reasonably successful time, winning the Triple Crown in 1925, 1933 and 1938, and the Grand Slam in 1925.

Scotland's Grand Slam of 1925 could not have come at a more appropriate moment for them, for their final game, the Calcutta Cup match against an undefeated England team, was the first international ever played at Murrayfield. Scotland had been using the Inverleith ground, and it was here that they opened their 1925 campaign in grand style by defeating France 24–4 before a crowd of 20,000. The Scots scored seven tries that day, and they scored a further six in their second match, against Wales at Swansea. Ian Smith, on the right wing, scored four tries in each of these games.

Ireland put up a great fight at Lansdowne Road before the Scots won 14–8; and so to the Calcutta Cup match with the Triple Crown and the Grand Slam beckoning. The occasion, and the official opening of the new Murrayfield ground, attracted a crowd of over 70,000. They saw a richly exciting match in which the lead changed hands three times. Scotland were trailing 10–11 in the closing stages but with five minutes to go Herbert Waddell, the Scottish fly-half, dropped the winning goal, making the final score 14–11 (a dropped goal was worth four points in those days). This was one of several matches in which Scotland fielded their famous all-Oxford University three-quarter line of I.S. Smith, G.P.S. Macpherson, G.G. Aitken and A.C. Wallace. England's captain was Wavell Wakefield.

THE DOWNFALL OF THE LEEKS : ENGLAND BEATS WALES AT "RUGGER."

PHOTOGRAPHS BY C.N. AND G.P.U.

THE BEST PAIR OF HALF-BACKS ENGLAND EVER HAD : LIEUT. C. A. KERSHAW ("SCRUM HALF") PASSING TO LIEUT.-COM. W. J. A. DAVIES.

THE ENGLISH "SCRUM HALF" (LIEUT. C. A. KERSHAW) THROWING-IN FROM TOUCH AT A LINE-OUT : AN INCIDENT OF THE MATCH.

THE RIVAL CAPTAINS : (L. TO R.) LIEUT.-COM. W. J. A. DAVIES (ENGLAND) AND MR. J. WETTER (WALES).

WHAT IT MEANS "TO GRAPPLE WITH THE FIERCE OLD FRIENDS " : THE "ROUGH-AND-TUMBLE OF A RUGBY MAUL (UNORGANISED SCRUMMAGE).

SCORING THE FIRST TRY FOR ENGLAND : LIEUT. C. A. KERSHAW (WITH THE BALL, IN LEFT FOREGROUND) OVER THE WELSH LINE.

MR. A. M. SMALLWOOD (WITH THE BALL) NEARLY SCORES FOR ENGLAND : COLLARED ON THE TOUCH-LINE CLOSE TO THE CORNER FLAG.

Above *England on their way to the Grand Slam in 1921.*

Left *Welsh supporters enjoy a trip to London.*

Far left *The famous Oxford University and Scotland three-quarter line of Wallace, Aitken, Macpherson and Smith.*

Scotland open their Grand Slam season of 1925 against France at Inverleith.

Wallace scores for Scotland in front of 70,000 spectators at Murrayfield in the match which gave Scotland the Calcutta Cup, the Triple Crown and the Grand Slam.

In order to win their Triple Crown in 1938 Scotland, having already beaten Wales and Ireland at Murrayfield, had to defeat England at Twickenham in front of a crowd of 70,000 which included King George VI. This game is always referred to as Wilson Shaw's match because Scotland's fly-half and captain scored two tries and created another. He was a very fast and sinuous runner with the quickest of eyes for a gap in the opposing defence. Scotland, scoring five tries, won by 21–16, but even Englishmen will tell you this was the best match they ever saw at Twickenham.

Scotland took the lead four times, and England drew level three times. Two minutes from the end Shaw accelerated to the left from a scrum and scored the try which settled the issue. It was a match of many close shaves, not least when Hal Sever, the England wing, was denied a try only because he collided with a goal post. Scotland had to wait until 1984 for their next Triple Crown.

England's Grand Slams of 1921 and 1923 owed much to Cecil Kershaw and W. J. A. Davies at half-back and to such great forwards as Wavell Wakefield and Tom Voyce. Davies had played for England before the First World War, and when he finished playing international Rugby at the end of the 1922–23 season he had never been on the losing side in a Championship match. He played in six victories over Scotland, four over Ireland, and three over Wales. He played in one drawn Championship game,

against France in 1922, and the only losing England side he played in was against South Africa in 1913. He was a trim, elegant fly-half who timed his breaks and his passing to perfection.

In his post-war internationals Davies benefitted much from his intimate understanding with Kershaw, who was his regular partner for United Services, Portsmouth and the Navy. In contrast to his partner Kershaw was a strongly built, robust player who used his strength for sending out controlled passes and for making searing breaks. They are generaly accepted as having been England's greatest pair of half-backs.

Wakefield, who had a considerable reputation as a sprinter and quarter-miler, played both lock and loose forward for England and went on to win 31 caps. Voyce, a dynamic loose forward from Gloucestershire, played 27 times for England.

Wakefield took over the captaincy from Davies for the 1924 campaign amid fears that England could not possibly do so well without the long-established partnership of Kershaw and Davies at half-back. Yet England beat Wales 17–9 at Swansea, Ireland 14–3 at Ravenhill, Belfast, France 19–7 at Twickenham, and Scotland 19–0, also at Twickenham. To this day it remains a very rare feat for any country to win the Grand Slam two years running. Wales did it in 1908 and 1909, England in 1913 and 1914 and in 1923 and 1924. But that is all.

A band of Scottish supporters arrive in London for the international in 1936.

Top *Spectators make their way to Twickenham for the England v Wales match, 1929.*

Above *Owen-Smith, the English captain, encourages his team at a training session, 1937.*

With neither Wakefield nor Voyce now in the side, England were given a tough passage on their way to their sixth Grand Slam, in 1928. In wind and rain they beat Wales by no more than 10–8 at Swansea. Ireland were defeated 7–6 at Lansdowne Road, again in dreadful conditions. The sun shone for England's victory by 18–8 over France at Twickenham, but the Calcutta Cup match, also at Twickenham, resulted in a meagre win for England by 6–0. Still, they all count, and the glory is everlasting.

A wash and brush-up at half-time for the England team who were defeated by Wales in the notorious mud of Cardiff Arms Park, 1922.

Wavell Wakefield in 1926.

Although the first seven-a-side tournament was held as long ago as 1883 at Melrose in the Scottish Borders, the idea did not really catch on in other countries until the 1920s and 1930s. The staging of the first Middlesex Sevens in 1926 at Twickenham played a major part in popularizing the seven-a-side game, and it comes as no surprise to find that Wavell Wakefield and Bill Ramsay (later Sir William) were on the sub-committee which organized the first Middlesex competition. Nor is it surprising to discover that the Middlesex committee meeting which resolved to stage the Sevens was held in a pub, the Cock Tavern in London. Much Rugby business in those days was done in pubs, and still is.

The original motive for holding the first Sevens tournament at Melrose was that the club was short of money. It was hoped, and proved, that such a tournament would get Melrose over an awkward financial period. The aim of the Middlesex committee was entirely different. They wanted to make their tournament a fun event, ending the season in a cheerful social atmosphere, with the proceeds going to charity. Although the price of admission to Twickenham in 1926 was only one shilling, and stand seats cost only five shillings, that first Middlesex tournament raised more than £1,600 for charity.

In each of the first four years of its existence, the Middlesex Sevens was won by Harlequins; a notable ever-present in those winning teams was Wavell Wakefield. Then it was the turn of London Welsh to win for two years running, with Wick Powell as their scrum-half. Blackheath followed with, among their backs, such internationals as Carl Aarvold, later Recorder of the City of London, and John Tallent, destined to become chairman of the Four Home Unions Tours Committee.

Sale, a guest side, won in 1936 with Wilf Wooller and Claud Davey of Wales and Ken Fyfe of Scotland among their backs, and Wooller again apeared in the winning side in 1939, this time playing for Cardiff along with Les Spence and 'Wendy' Davis. Thus was the trend set which would annually attract crowds of 50–60,000 and raise vast amounts of money for charity. It was to become the biggest Sevens tournament in the world with something like 300 clubs taking part in the preliminary rounds.

Countless other Sevens tournaments soon sprang up, but none achieved the status of the Middlesex event. One which was to have considerable influence, however, was the Rosslyn Park Schools Sevens, held for the first time in 1939 at the Old Deer Park, which was Park's ground until London Welsh took it over in 1957. Nowadays staged on Park's ground at Roehampton, the Schools Sevens cater for something like 250 schools and involve about 450 matches. For many boys the Schools Sevens represent a first opportunity of playing Rugby away from the school environment. They give schoolboys a wider perspective of what the game has to offer, and what started in 1939 as a tournament for 16 schools has become an important national, and indeed international event, encouraging boys to stay on in Rugby after their schooldays are over.

The following year, London Irish in action against Westminster Bank.

Blackheath on their way to victory over London Welsh in the 1930 final of the Middlesex Sevens. This was the first year that the Harlequins had failed to win.

GRAVE IS GAY: AT THE SEVEN-A-SIDE RUGBY MATCHES.

The exertions of Sevens as seen by The Illustrated Sporting and Dramatic News, *1927.*

SHORT–TIME, SMALL–TEAM RUGBY: THE HARLEQUINS WIN AGAIN AT TWICKENHAM.

The Seven-a-Side Rugby Tournament organised by the Middlesex County Rugby Union on behalf of the King Edward Hospital Fund was brought to a conclusion before some 10,000 spectators last Saturday at Twickenham. The Harlequins were again successful, running away with the game from Blackheath in the final. In the semi-finals the 'Quins had beaten Richmond and Blackheath the Old Cranleighans.

(Caricatures by Chas. Grave.)

The most famous try of the inter-war period was Obolensky's against the touring All Blacks at Twickenham in January 1936. Prince Alexander Obolensky was the son of an officer in the Czar's Imperial Horse Guards who had brought his baby son to England to escape from the Russian Revolution. On this day at Twickenham Obolensky had already scored one orthodox try with a fast run up the right touchline when, shortly before half-time, England launched another three-quarter

Prince Obolensky at full speed for Rosslyn Park during the last match that he was ever to play.

movement towards the right. When Obolensky was about to get the ball, he saw that the All Black cover was racing across to cut him off. He therefore checked his stride, took the pass, and turned inwards.

It was a classic example of how to open up a channel in the defence by wrong-footing the opposition. Obolensky, a swift and graceful sprinter, continued his inward course at great speed and crossed the New Zealand line not far from the left corner flag. England won 13–0, the first time an All Black side had ever been

defeated on English soil. Obolensky joined the RAF in the Second World War and was killed when his Hurricane fighter crashed on landing. He was the first Rugby international to lose his life in the war.

One of the oddest happenings in an England match is sometimes remembered as the Case of the Flying Hooker. On the morning of the Wales–England match at Cardiff in January 1930, the England hooker, Henry Rew of Exeter, withdrew from the side at such short notice that Sam Tucker of Bristol had to be flown over the Severn estuary to Cardiff. He arrived at the ground only minutes before the kick-off but played so well that he retained his place in the team for England's three remaining matches. More than that, he captained England against France and Scotland with Rew as one of his props. That Welsh match is also notable for the fact that England fielded nine new caps yet still combined well enough to achieve a remarkable 11–3 win.

For many years Twickenham was England's lucky ground. Opponents were constantly frustrated either by their own shortcomings in attack or by England's last-ditch defensive efforts or by mistakes by referees or by sheer luck. Although the first international was played at Twickenham in 1910, Scotland did not win there until 1926, Ireland until 1929, Wales until 1933, and France until 1951.

Ireland's 6–5 victory in 1929 is looked upon as one of the finest in Irish Rugby history. Although Eugene Davy, the Irish fly-half, scored a try after only two minutes from a fumble by the England full-back, Ireland had to fight against adversity because their captain and centre, George Stephenson, suffered rib damage early in the first half. This was long before the days of substitutes, so Stephenson battled on but was far from his normal self. Two minutes after half-time England scored a try and converted it for a lead of 5–3 (a try was worth only three points in those days) and another English victory was on the cards. However, the Irish, and especially that robust forward Jamie Clinch, worked wonders in defence, and eventually Ireland had a scrum not far from the English line. Mark Sugden, the Irish scrum-half, slipped away on the blind side and, dummying his way through, scored the winning try. In their elation the Irish suporters threw their seat cushions into the air or had pillow fights with them. Later the occasion became known as Twickenham's Battle of the Cushions.

The Welsh win in 1933 made a local hero of Ronnie Boon, the Cardiff wing three-quarter, who scored all Wales's points in their 7–3 victory with a try and a dropped goal. The Welsh forwards, led by the formidable Watcyn Thomas, were in rampaging form. Wales had seven newcomers in their side, including Vivian Jenkins at full-back and Wilf Wooller in the centre.

ground gave way, and thousands of spectators spilled over the turf.

Scotland led 11–0 at the interval, but Albert Jenkins then dropped two goals for Wales who started applying almost continuous pressure. The pressure was relieved when the crowd surged back on to the pitch, and a hold-up of 12 minutes allowed the Scots to recover their breath and their composure. During the hold-up they threatened to abandon the match, but in the end Sloan, one of their wings, scored a try, touching down amid spectators sitting in

WALES'S FIRST WIN AT TWICKENHAM: A TENTH-GAME VICTORY.

A lineout during the England v Wales match of 1933. 60,000 spectators saw the Welsh win 7–3 to record their first victory at Twickenham.

Cyril Brownlie, sent off for allegedly striking Voyce at Twickenham in 1925.

Rugby, despite its generally admirable record, has not been completely free of unsavoury behaviour on the part of the crowds. The 1921 game between Wales and Scotland at Swansea is remembered as the Riot Match. Play was held up on several occasions while mounted and other police cleared spectators from the playing area, and the players were forced to leave the field. The crowd numbered about 50,000, and the WRU were blamed for not closing the gates earlier than they did. The barriers on the cricket pavilion side of the

the Welsh in-goal area and making the final score 14–8 to Scotland. It was Scotland's first victory in Wales for 29 years. The hold-ups in play meant that the Scots did not have time to change before leaving the ground to catch their train. They picked up their clothes, rushed to the bus, and did their washing and changing on the train.

Twickenham was stunned by the sending-off of Cyril Brownlie, the New Zealand forward, early in the game between England and the touring All Blacks on 3 January 1925. It was the

Freddie Turner (top) and Louis Babrow – both try scorers for the Springboks in their decisive win at Eden Park in 1937.

Above right Boy Louw in possession during the First Test match against Australia in 1937 which South Africa won 9–5.

first time a player had ever been sent off in an international match. There had already been some skirmishing between the two packs, and the referee, Albert Freethy of Wales, had issued two general warnings. When there was another skirmish, the referee ordered Brownlie from the field.

The England captain, Wavell Wakefield, is said to have pleaded with the referee to change his mind, and there was a general feeling that Brownlie was unlucky to have been singled out. The All Blacks made light of their handicap of having to play with only 14 men for most of the match and emerged victorious by 17–11. They thus completed their tour of the British Isles with the astonishing record of having played 30, won 30.

Probably the greatest match of the interwar period, at least in terms of its significance in world Rugby, was the clash between the All Blacks and the Springboks in the Third Test at Eden Park, Auckland on 25 September 1937. The Springboks had toured New Zealand only once before, in 1921, and the Test series had been shared. The All Blacks had toured South Africa only once, in 1928, and that series also had been shared. Then, in the 1937 series of three Tests in New Zealand, the All Blacks had won the First Test 13–7 and the Springboks the Second 13–6.

The Third and decisive Test drew a record crowd of 58,000, and although the New Zealand spectators were to be disappointed in terms of the result, they were not disappointed with the

style of Rugby played by the Springboks. The South African forwards, including such formidable men as Boy Louw, Jan Lotz, Philip Nel and Ferdie Bergh, got well on top, enabling Danie Craven to send out a stream of accurate passes, and the fly-half, Tony Harris, later a Test cricketer, made full use of his centres, Louis Babrow and Flappie Lochner.

Babrow and Bergh, from a cross-kick by Babrow, scored tries in the first half, one of which was converted by the very experienced full-back, Gerry Brand. Babrow scored another try soon after the interval, and two more dashing tries followed from Dai Williams and Freddie Turner, the wing three-quarters. The All Blacks could manage no more than two penalty goals by Dave Trevathan, so the final score was 17–6 to the Springboks, a result which allowed them to consider themselves the best team in the world at that time.

While that 1937 series was still in the balance the All Black centre, Jack Sullivan, later to become Chairman of the NZRU, scored the classic interception try in the Second Test at Lancaster Park, Christchurch. He had already scored one try when he made his interception deep in his own half. Pursued by Dai Williams, Sullivan kicked the ball over the head of Gerry Brand, got a foot to the ball when it landed, booted it again, and just won the race with Williams for the touchdown. New Zealand led 6–0 at half-time, but the crowd's elation died down later as the Springboks went on to win 13–6.

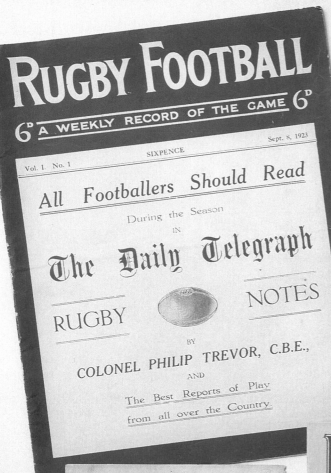

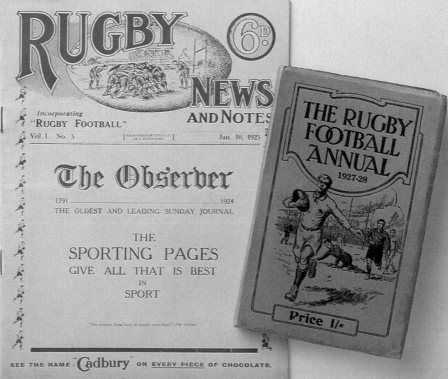

Reading matter for the Rugby enthusiast of the 1920s.

WILLS'S CIGARETTES.

C. D. AARVOLD.

Wills for Quality
· RUGBY ·
INTERNATIONALS
A SERIES OF 50
1
C. D. Aarvold.
Durham School, Cambridge University, Headingley and England.
C. D. Aarvold is one of the most adaptable outsides of modern times. He played for Cambridge against Oxford at right centre-threequarter in 1925 and in 1928 when captain; in 1926 he was placed at full-back, and in 1927 on the right wing. First appearing for England in 1928 as right centre against New South Wales, he retained that position throughout the international tournament, but at the end of the season he was tried on the right wing. Standing over 6 ft. in height, he is very fast, and has a wonderful eye for an opening.
W.D.& H.O.WILLS
ISSUED BY THE IMPERIAL TOBACCO CO. (OF GREAT BRITAIN & IRELAND), LTD.

WILLS'S CIGARETTES.

R. COVE-SMITH.

Wills for Quality
· RUGBY ·
INTERNATIONALS
A SERIES OF 50
3
R. Cove-Smith.
Cambridge University, Old Merchant Taylors', Middlesex and England.
Cove-Smith, one of the hardest-working of second row forwards has been happily described as a man who gives backbone to a scrummage. He was a member of the Cambridge University XV. in 1919-20-21, and holds twenty-nine English caps. He led his University side in 1921, and was England's captain in 1928 and for two matches in 1929. Though a busy medical man, and unselfishly devoting much spare time to social service, he was so fit in the 1928-9 season that he played in four important matches within a period of nine days.
W.D.& H.O.WILLS
ISSUED BY THE IMPERIAL TOBACCO CO. (OF GREAT BRITAIN & IRELAND), LTD.

WILLS'S CIGARETTES.

R. H. SPARKS.

Wills for Quality
· RUGBY ·
INTERNATIONAL
A SERIES OF 50
8
R. H. Sparks.
Plymouth Albion, Devon and England.
Devon County and Plymouth Dockyard, famous nurser of forwards, have produced few more typically sturdy than R. H. Sparks. Capped 1928 he "linked" with J. Tucker and E. Stanbury partnership making England scrummage formidable to opponents. A skilful hooker he uses every ounce of his weight in the tight and does regard work in the tight as only part of his job; with mass of dark curly hair making him conspicuous, he is alway on the ball in the open and in defence he will go down fearlessly to the fiercest rush.
W.D.& H.O.WILLS
ISSUED BY THE IMPERIAL TOBACCO CO. (OF GREAT BRITAIN & IRELAND), LTD.

WILLS'S CIGARETTES.

E. STANBURY.

Wills for Quality
· RUGBY ·
INTERNATIONALS
A SERIES OF 50
9
E. Stanbury.
Plymouth Albion, Devon and England.
When E. Stanbury describes a football match he often uses the expression "good and hearty," and one might well adopt that phrase to sum up Stanbury's own play. Always good-humoured, he is a splendid West Country forward. From 1926, when capped against Wales, he has been invariably a first choice for the front row of the scrummage. He is a player whose 13 st. is felt in the scrum, and whose skill and sense of position are seen anywhere on the field. His goal-kicking has gathered many points for country, county and club, and he is one of the most popular players in England.
W.D.& H.O.WILLS
ISSUED BY THE IMPERIAL TOBACCO CO. (OF GREAT BRITAIN & IRELAND), LTD.

WILLS'S CIGARETTES.

J. S. TUCKER.

Wills for Quality
· RUGBY ·
INTERNATIONALS
A SERIES OF 50
10
J. S. Tucker.
Bristol, Gloucestershire and England.
Tucker, known everywhere as "Sam," is an ideal front row forward and one of the best hookers who have played for England. First capped in 1922, he has pushed his 13¼ st. weight in 22 international matches. During the season 1928-9 he appeared against Wales and Ireland, and then, regaining his place, played well in the match with France. A hard-working honest forward, he does not merely content himself with hooking, but contributes his fair share in the open and is particularly useful at the line-out.
W.D.& H.O.WILLS
ISSUED BY THE IMPERIAL TOBACCO CO. (OF GREAT BRITAIN & IRELAND), LTD.

WILLS'S CIGARETTES.

G. S. WILSON.

Wills for Quality
· RUGBY ·
INTERNATIONAL
A SERIES OF 50
14
G. S. Wilson.
Manchester, Lancashire and England.
A great capture for the Rugby game was made when G. S. Wilson, a convert from Soccer, joined the Tyldesley club. Then by way of Manchester and Lancashire, he graduated to an English cap against Wales in Jan. 1929. as left wing threequarter. Success in that position proved Wilson's versatility, for his early promise had been shown as a centre. He is a clever player, deceptively fast, with a well-judged swerve and a trick of suddenly checking his run. Wilson laughs his way through the hardest game, and by his brilliant opportunism helped Lancashire into the final of the 1928-9 championship.
W.D.& H.O.WILLS
ISSUED BY THE IMPERIAL TOBACCO CO. (OF GREAT BRITAIN & IRELAND), LTD.

WILLS'S CIGARETTES.

A. T. YOUNG.

Wills for Quality
· RUGBY ·
INTERNATIONALS
A SERIES OF 50
15
A. T. Young.
Cambridge University, Blackheath, Kent, The Army and England.
Known as England's "little man" (he is 5 ft. 5 in. in height) Young is the most daringly original scrum-half in the modern game. A Cambridge blue in 1922-3-4, and capped in 1924, he played for England till 1928-9, dropping out occasionally. He is sportingly artful, and has scored many tries through stealing away on the blind side of the scrum. His sense of position is valuable in defence, and it was said of him by one of the tourists from New South Wales, "whenever a Waratah kicked a blade of grass, there was Arthur Young behind it."
W.D.& H.O.WILLS
ISSUED BY THE IMPERIAL TOBACCO CO. (OF GREAT BRITAIN & IRELAND), LTD.

WILLS'S CIGARETTES

W. V. BERKLEY.

Wills for Quality
· RUGBY ·
INTERNATIONALS
A SERIES OF 50
18
W. V. Berkley.
Oxford University, London Scottish and Scotland.
Berkley is the giant of the Scottish pack. Born in England and at school at Fettes, he played for Oxford against Cambridge in 1924-5-6, and made his first appearance for Scotland in the 1926 match with France. Afterwards he went abroad, but having played for the London Scottish in 1929, was included in the Scotland pack meeting France, and retained his place against Wales and Ireland. Berkley is a hefty player, whose weight proves useful in the scrummage, and he is a keen supporter of Bannerman when a typical Scottish forward rush develops.
W.D.& H.O.WILLS
ISSUED BY THE IMPERIAL TOBACCO CO. (OF GREAT BRITAIN & IRELAND), LTD.

G. P. S. MACPHERSON.

Wills for Quality
RUGBY
INTERNATIONAL
A SERIES OF 50
23
G. P. S. Macpherson.
Edinburgh Academicals, Oxford University, London Scottish and Scotland.
Macpherson, a Highlander from Inverness-shire, was educated at Edinburgh Academy, Fettes and Oxford. Though capped for Scotland in 19__ he did not gain his Oxford blue as a Senior till the following season. He was Oxford's captain in 1923. The continuity of his appearances for Scotland has been broken by absence while studying at an American University. A brilliant attacking centre, he has scored many tries and cleared the way for still more with his great wing partner, Ian Smith. His "jinking" sidestep makes Macpherson particularly hard to stop.
W.D.& H.O.WILLS
ISSUED BY THE IMPERIAL TOBACCO CO. (OF GREAT BRITAIN & IRELAND)

Wills for Quality

RUGBY INTERNATIONALS

A SERIES OF 50

27

Ian S. Smith.

Oxford University, Edinburgh University and Scotland.

Ian Smith advanced from Winchester—where they do not play Rugby—to become an Oxford blue in 1923, receiving his first cap for Scotland in 1924. One of the fastest modern right wing threequarters he is well-named the "Flying Scotsman." Among his scoring feats are four tries out of six against Wales and four out of seven against France in 1925–6. It was feared after 1927–8 that an injury had closed Smith's career, but he returned, scoring two splendid tries against England. Good judges place him second to E. H. Liddell, the Olympic runner, for pace.

W.D. & H.O.WILLS

ISSUED BY THE IMPERIAL TOBACCO CO. (OF GREAT BRITAIN & IRELAND), LTD.

WILLS'S CIGARETTES

IVOR JONES.

Wills for Quality

RUGBY INTERNATIONALS

A SERIES OF 50

33

Ivor Jones.

Llanelly and Wales.

Ivor Jones is a player who, at the age of 28, refutes by his liveliness the idea of his being a veteran. Tall and fit, he continues to put up a great game as a back row forward, though he first appeared for Wales as long ago as 1924. He was originally a full-back, but since 1922 has been a brilliant winger, fast in the open, dangerous near the goal line, and a skilful dribbler. His command of the game extends to remarkably accurate goal-kicking. Jones has been captain of the Welsh XV. and last season he led the forwards.

W.D. & H.O.WILLS

ISSUED BY THE IMPERIAL TOBACCO CO. (OF GREAT BRITAIN & IRELAND), LTD.

WILLS'S CIGARETTES

W. C. POWELL.

Wills for Quality

RUGBY INTERNATIONALS

A SERIES OF 50

36

W. C. Powell.

London Welsh, Middlesex and Wales.

Powell, a powerful determined player, is a tower of strength for Wales, while Middlesex have lost no county championship match in which he has played. The Welsh authorities think so highly of his defence that with another scrum-half in favour, they have placed him on the wing to mark a dangerous flier. Scrum-half is Powell's true position, and whether attacking or spoiling his opposite number, he is a great player and a master of the unexpected reverse pass. Powell, at one time in the Welsh Guards, is now an architect. He collected his thirteenth cap at the age of 25.

W.D. & H.O.WILLS

ISSUED BY THE IMPERIAL TOBACCO CO. (OF GREAT BRITAIN & IRELAND), LTD.

WILLS'S CIGARETTES

CECIL PRITCHARD.

Wills for Quality

RUGBY INTERNATIONALS

A SERIES OF 50

37

Cecil Pritchard.

Pontypool and Wales.

Pritchard, who played for Blaenavon before joining Pontypool, plays a quick, keen game, works hard in the scrummage, and seems always to be on the ball. He gained his first cap against England in 1928, and has been a regular member of the Welsh pack ever since. Pritchard comes of a well-known family of Rugby players and is a wonderfully accurate goal-kicker. In April, 1926, he scored 21 points for Pontypool against Edgware by converting 6 tries, kicking 2 penalty goals and obtaining 1 try himself.

W.D. & H.O.WILLS

ISSUED BY THE IMPERIAL TOBACCO CO. (OF GREAT BRITAIN & IRELAND), LTD.

WILLS'S CIGARETTES

J. E. ARIGHO.

Wills for Quality

RUGBY INTERNATIONALS

A SERIES OF 50

40

J. E. Arigho.

Lansdowne and Ireland.

Arigho is a dashing left wing threequarter who knows the way to the goal-line. He was criticised after his first appearance at the age of 20, for Ireland against France at Belfast in 1928, as a player who required space in which to move, but as he scored two tries in that match followed by one try against England at Dublin, and two crossings of the Welsh line at Cardiff, he also scored off the critics in his first international season. He gave valuable service in attack and defence during the 1928–9 season his play holding out hopes of numerous additions to a stock of seven Irish caps.

W.D. & H.O.WILLS

ISSUED BY THE IMPERIAL TOBACCO CO. (OF GREAT BRITAIN & IRELAND), LTD.

WILLS'S CIGARETTES.

G. R. BEAMISH.

Wills for Quality

RUGBY INTERNATIONALS

A SERIES OF 50

41

G. R. Beamish.

Royal Air Force, Leicester and Ireland.

Good judges of Rugby football have described George Beamish as Britain's best forward and certainly he is a splendid player, one who uses his strength and his knowledge of the game with equal effect. Educated at Coleraine Academy, Beamish, who is now a Flight-Lieutenant in the Royal Air Force, is of magnificent physique standing over 6 ft. and weighing more than 14 st. Although first capped for Ireland in 1925, the effects of breaking a leg kept him out of international football till 1928. He is one of Leicester's outstanding players and has given valuable service to the R.A.F. fifteen.

W.D. & H.O.WILLS

ISSUED BY THE IMPERIAL TOBACCO CO. (OF GREAT BRITAIN & IRELAND), LTD.

WILLS'S CIGARETTES

E. O'D. DAVY.

Wills for Quality

RUGBY INTERNATIONALS

A SERIES OF 50

45

E. O'D. Davy.

Lansdowne and Ireland.

A University College, Dublin, man, Davy, who was born on July 26th, 1904, is the holder of 18 Irish caps. His strong play at stand-off half in partnership with M. Sugden has proved of great value on many occasions. In his best form, he is a thrustful player, and, in defence, a good tackler. His opportunism in being up to score an early try laid the foundation for Ireland's great victory over England at Twickenham in 1929. He acted as captain in the absence of G. V. Stephenson, when Ireland met Scotland in Feb. 1929 at Dublin.

W.D. & H.O.WILLS

ISSUED BY THE IMPERIAL TOBACCO CO. (OF GREAT BRITAIN & IRELAND), LTD.

WILLS'S CIGARETTES.

J. D. CLINCH.

Wills for Quality

RUGBY INTERNATIONALS

A SERIES OF 50

44

J. D. Clinch.

Dublin University, United Services, Army, Hampshire, Wanderers and Ireland.

Jamie Clinch may be a veteran in the sense that he first played for Ireland in 1923, but when his country defeated England at Twickenham in 1929, he was just about the best forward on the field. He is that unusual type, the defensive wing forward, one who possesses a wonderful instinct for being in the right place at the right moment. His tackling and his kicking for touch are always effective, and he is by no means neglectful in hard attack. He holds twenty-one Irish caps, and toured South Africa with the British team in 1924.

W.D. & H.O.WILLS

ISSUED BY THE IMPERIAL TOBACCO CO. (OF GREAT BRITAIN & IRELAND), LTD.

WILLS'S CIGARETTES

G. V. STEPHENSON.

Wills for Quality

RUGBY INTERNATIONALS

A SERIES OF 50

48

G. V. Stephenson.

North of Ireland, Middlesex and Ireland.

Ireland's captain, who was educated at Haileybury and Queen's University, Belfast, holds the wonderful record of having played in thirty-eight matches for his country. Capped against France in 1920, he made thirty-seven consecutive international appearances before an injury compelled him to stand down in 1929. A classic centre, brilliant in attack, and an inspiring leader, George Stephenson, like his brother Harry, also an Irish cap, is a beautiful runner, deceptively fast. He played for London Hospital, and helped Middlesex to win the English county championship in 1929.

W.D. & H.O.WILLS

ISSUED BY THE IMPERIAL TOBACCO CO. (OF GREAT BRITAIN & IRELAND), LTD.

Great names of the Twenties.

67

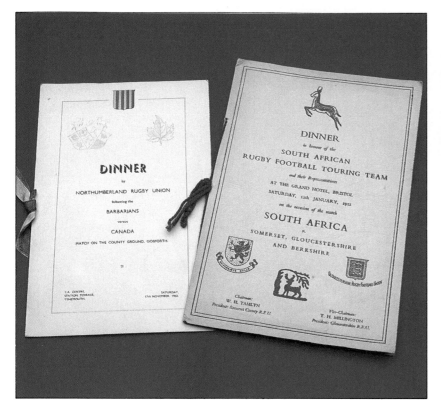

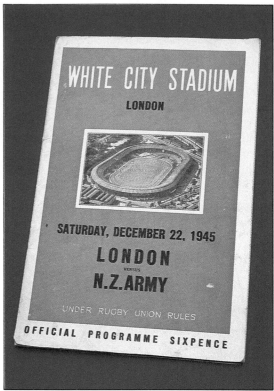

Above *Hospitality at The Grand Hotel, Bristol for the first post-war Springboks, and at the T.A. Centre, Tynemouth for the Canadians in 1962.*
Above right *The New Zealand Army were on hand to offer stern opposition during the 1945-6 season.*
Right *The touch flag carried at the Ireland v England match of 1932 in Dublin. England won 11–8 and shared the Championship that year with Ireland and Wales.*

Although a more forceful example was set by South Africa and New Zealand, the domestic structure of English Rugby continued throughout the 1920s and 1930s to be based on friendly club games. Oxford and Cambridge, of course, had their highly competitive Varsity matches, and the County Championship was taken seriously in some parts of the country – and less so in others. However, there was nothing to compare with the local club leagues and inter-provincial competitions of South Africa and New Zealand.

When teams from overseas visited England, they may have felt a certain amount of envy for the happy-go-lucky atmosphere of English club Rugby. But the strength of the game in South Africa and New Zealand derived from its domestic pyramid: at the base were the local club leagues, which provided players for the provincial sides, and they in turn supplied the national team. It is surprising that such a logical system was not copied, especially since the All Blacks of 1905 and 1924 and the Springboks of 1906, 1912 and 1931 had proved such formidable opponents. The English, however, preferred to go along in their own haphazard way.

The Currie Cup in South Africa and the Ranfurly Shield in New Zealand created enormous public interest as the provinces held their annual battles for supremacy. The English County Championship was small beer by comparison, even though it was enthusiastically followed by supporters in those counties where it was played on Saturdays, as opposed to mid-week, and taken seriously. This enthusiasm is reflected in the success achieved by counties from the South-West and the North in the 1920s and 1930s. In that period Gloucestershire won the title seven times and were twice runners-up. Lancashire and Yorkshire each won it twice, and Somerset and Cumberland once each. Lancashire were three times runners-up.

The England team which were to defeat Wales 11–9 at Twickenham in 1927.

A.T. Voyce with England colleagues A.F. Blakiston (left) and E.D.G. Hammett.

Far right *Programme for the 1929 County Championship final. After a drawn match at Twickenham, Middlesex won the replay at Blundellsands.*

Below right *A report in* The Evening News *of the centenary match played at Rugby School in 1923.*

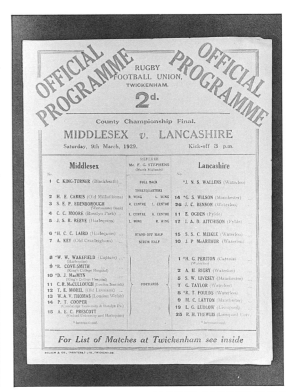

Of the English club game in those days it was said that while the English played Rugby to keep fit, the South Africans and New Zealanders got themselves fit to play Rugby. Contemporary accounts show that club Rugby in England really was fun. The night after a big club match the pubs, restaurants and night-clubs in the West End of London were filled with Rugby men rejoicing or drowning their sorrows.

Easter tours flourished, and the Barbarians' tradition of playing golf on the Easter Sunday between matches was copied by players of clubs great and small. Regardless of their ability on the field, players rushed from their offices to take a break in the hospitable climate of the West Country or in South Wales. In 1925 the Barbarians etablished on a regular basis their four-match tour of South Wales, playing Penarth on Good Friday, Cardiff on the Saturday, Swansea on the Monday, and Newport on the Tuesday, an arrangment which was to last until the 1980s.

A large number of Old Boys clubs was formed in the 1920s and 1930s in England, and these brought a special brand of humour, wit and revelry to the social side of the game – and not only on Easter tours. Some Old Boys clubs

SHEER LOVE OF IT.

The Rugby football players who saw England and Wales beat Scotland and Ireland in Rugby Close yesterday speak of the game as a thrilling encounter that was crowded with incidents of magnificent and inspired effort. Why did every man on the field go "all out" and all but burst his sides? Why were half-a-dozen men hurt as in a Hospital Cup-tie? Why did the crowd, who were chiefly English, shout with excitement at the end—when Scotland and Ireland might still draw level again?

It is queer, but it is true, that these men did not play for cups, medals, caps; they hadn't any "old scores" to pay off. They were just playing the game on its birthday and did their best out of sheer love for the game; and then the game took hold of them and Rugby Close saw one of the fastest and most exciting ten minutes it has ever seen.

managed to achieve and maintain a high standard of play – clubs such as Old Merchant Taylors, Old Millhillians and Old Cranleighans – and they had regular fixtures with the Baths, the Coventrys and the Newports of the British Rugby world.

In the 1920s the All Blacks and Springboks began a series of meetings to establish who was the supreme nation in the Rugby-playing world. The Springboks first toured New Zealand and Australia in 1921, and the All Blacks played their first Test series in South Africa in 1928. On each of these tours the Test series was shared. But when the Springboks returned to New Zealand in 1937, they won the Tests 2–1.

These and other major tours were important for two main reasons. Firstly, the tourists attracted huge crowds of spectators, producing gate receipts which enabled the host country to expand and develop its own game. Secondly, the tourists brought with them fresh ideas and new methods of playing which rubbed off not only on the men they played against but also on those who watched their games.

In New Zealand in 1921 the All Blacks won the First Test 13–5 at Carisbrook, Dunedin. The Second Test, at Eden Park, Auckland, went to the Boks by 9–5. The Third, played in continuous heavy rain at Athletic Park, Wellington, ended in one of those rare results, a 0–0 draw. One unusual feature of this series was that the All Blacks included a forward, Ned Hughes, who was 40 years old.

The All Blacks had a shock when they went to South Africa in 1928. Largely because of the power of the Springboks' 3-4-1 scrum formation – and the Boks' decision to opt for scrums rather than line-outs when the ball went out of play – the New Zealanders were beaten 17–0 at Durban in the first of the four Tests, New Zealand's heaviest defeat to date. The All Blacks recovered to win the Second Test 7–6 at Ellis Park, Johannesburg, but the Boks took the Third Test 11–6 at the Crusader Ground, Port Elizabeth. The home side were generally expected to win the Fourth Test at Newlands, Capetown, but the All Blacks won it 13–5, thus squaring the series. It is worth noting, in view of later developments, that the All Blacks had to tour South Africa without their great full-back, George Nepia, because he was a Maori.

Many old-time New Zealanders will tell you that the side the Springboks took to New Zealand in 1937 was the best all-round Rugby team there has ever been. It was a surprise when the All Blacks won the first of the three Tests 13–7 in Wellington, but the Boks proved

Programme which showed the differences in the formation of the two teams.

Above right *The invincible All Blacks with the Cardiff team before their match in 1924.*
Above *Dennis Hunt plunges over to score in Swansea's 11–3 win over the 1935 All Blacks.*

Below *The British Isles team leaves for South Africa, 1924.*
Below right *The British team to tour South Africa in 1938.*

far superior in the other two, winning 13–6 in Christchurch and 17–6 in Auckland. The First Test was the only defeat suffered by the Springboks on their 1937 tour. Their record was: played 17, won 16, lost 1, points for 411, against 104. They also scored 342 points in nine games in Australia.

In terms of results the most successful touring side of the inter-war period was the 1924–25 All Blacks in the British Isles. Their record speaks for itself: played 28, won 28, points for 654, against 98. They did not play in Scotland, but they did go to France, winning both their games there and scoring 67 points to 14. If you combine the record of the 1924 All Blacks with that of their 1905 predecessors, it is no wonder that the British looked upon New

Zealand Rugby with awe. In 60 matches those two All Black touring teams scored 1,484 points and had only 137 points scored against them. Moreover, they averaged six tries per match.

The All Blacks toured the British Isles again in 1935–36 but were less successful, losing three and drawing one of their 28 games. In their internationals they beat Scotland 18–8 and Ireland 17–9 but were defeated 13–12 by Wales and 13–0 by England. This relative lack of success has been blamed on two factors. Firstly, on the 1905 and 1924 tours they were using a rover, a position which was later deemed illegal. Secondly, the 1935 side were in the process of adapting to a fresh scrum formation to replace the two-man front row which they had previously favoured. The International Board now insisted that a front row be made up of three men.

The Springboks made only one tour of the British Isles between the World Wars, and that was in the 1931–32 season. They beat all four home countries and lost only one of their 26 games. This was at Leicester where the Midland Counties, inspired by George Beamish, a vigorous Irish international forward, defeated them 31–20. In most of their matches the

scientifically applied weight and strength of their 3-4-1 scrum formation proved too much for their opponents, and all the home countries, indeed the whole Rugby world, adopted this formation in later years, largely as a result of this tour. The South Africans' style of play was not popular, however, because of the excessive kicking of their fly-half and captain, Bennie Osler.

The title of Lions was bestowed for the first time in 1924 on the team which toured South Africa. It was a much less cumbersome expression than their official title, the British Isles Rugby Union Team. They did not win any of their four Tests on that tour. They went to South Africa again in 1938 and, after losing the first two Tests in Johannesburg and Port Elizabeth, they won the Third 21–16 in Capetown. The 1938 Lions had to travel without several outstanding players, including Wilson Shaw of Scotland and Cliff Jones and Wilf Wooller of Wales among the backs, and Tom Huskisson, the England lock. The party of 29 included four Englishmen who had not played for their country.

The only other Lions tour in the inter-war period was in 1930 when they went to New Zealand and Australia. This was the tour on which the Lions' manager, Bim Baxter, who was a member of the International Board, outspokenly stated his objection to the rover, thus hastening his disappearance from the game. The Lions won the First Test of the four-match series 6–3 at Dunedin, but they were beaten 13–10, 15–10 and 22–8 in the others. George Nepia played brilliantly at full-back for the All Blacks in this series. He subsequently played Rugby League in England for Streatham and Mitcham but was later reinstated as an amateur in New Zealand, playing his last first-class match in 1950 at the age of 45. For someone who played Test Rugby at the age of 19, this was indeed the close of a long innings.

Like the All Blacks, the Wallabies made their first tour of South Africa in the inter-war period. They went there in 1933 and gave a good account of themselves in losing the five-match Test series by no more than 2–3. No full Australian side visited Britain in the period, but a New South Wales team, known as the Waratahs, made a full-length tour in 1927–28 and were accorded international matches against all the four home countries and France. They lost to England and Scotland but defeated Ireland, Wales and France. Incidentally, a waratah is not an animal, the conventional choice of emblem, but a plant with 'heads of showy crimson flowers'.

A full Wallaby tour was to have taken place in the 1939–40 British season, and in fact the boat carrying the team arrived on schedule. However, the Second World War broke out shortly afterwards and no games were played. Some of the Australian tourists remained in Britain to help in the war effort.

Harlequins and London Scottish on their way from the dressing room before their match in 1939.

More Rugby during the 'phoney war' of 1939 – Army Ordnance Corps v New Zealand Anti-Tank Brigade.

Far left Australian captain V.W. Wilson (with ball) playing for Rosslyn Park in November 1939. His unfortunate team had arrived in England the day before war was declared and was disbanded without a match being played.

Reading overcome transport difficulties for their away match with Rosslyn Park, September 1940.

Right *London District Anti-Aircraft XV on the attack against Middlesex, 1940.*
Far right *Unofficial international between England and Scotland at Wembley, 1942.*

Right and far right *Action from the match arranged between a New Zealand XV and Rosslyn Park, 1943.*

PART THREE

THE POST - WAR YEARS,
1945 - 1968

From the outbreak of war on 3 September 1939 until VJ Day in August 1945, Rugby players, in common with other sportsmen, were more concerned with the life-and-death matter of war against the Germans and the Japanese. However, unlike in the First World War, Rugby remained alive in the Schools, Universities and Services, and in many clubs which, thanks to dedicated committee men, managed to keep their flags flying.

Haydn Tanner, a Welsh international both before and after the war.

Above right *Many clubs desperately needed ticket money to repair war damaged grounds.*

On such grounds as Richmond, Cardiff Arms Park, Newport, Swansea, Inverleith, Wembley, Murrayfield, Leicester and Old Deer Park, Rugby flourished in an *ad hoc* fashion. Services internationals were played and, for the war period, there was a *détente* between the two codes of Rugby Union and Rugby League which allowed spectators the great pleasure of seeing such wonderful players as Bleddyn Williams and Haydn Tanner playing together with stars of the other game such as Gus Risman and W.T.H. Davies. In 1945 the four Home Unions reconvened and 16 Victory internationals were played, for which no caps were given. The concession to Rugby League players was suspended, apart from those playing in the Services.

Twickenham remained the great cathedral of British Rugby, elegant and lavish but slightly remote and inhibiting by Celtic standards. Its changing-rooms were unnervingly large, with proper baths, and many visitors found it a nerve-wracking experience to run out onto the pitch, beneath those fortress-high stands. Fortunately for Welsh feelings of inadequacy, a mood of reform was in the air. In 1952 the Welsh Rugby Union appointed Mr Ken Harris as its treasurer. He was a far-sighted and brilliant administrator, and it was he more than anybody who was to create the new stadium, which

nowadays compares with any Rugby ground in the world.

At the time he faced a daunting task because, while Twickenham had suffered damage from a bomb blast, the only international ground to be well and truly blitzed was Cardiff Arms Park. On 2 January 1941, a German land-mine exploded in the in-goal area of the river end, wrecking part of the South Stand and the West Terrace and almost completely demolishing the North Stand, which had been opened only seven years before. The Welsh Rugby Union had borrowed heavily to build it and in 1945 the overdraft of the Union stood at the then massive sum of £40,700. Because of the damage, none of the Services internationals could be played at Cardiff, which would have helped to reduce the debt. However, at the end of the war the War Damages Commission paid for the repairs and the North Stand was recommissioned in March 1949. (For the recent history of the ground, see Part Five: 'Same Religion, Different Cathedrals'.)

In the meantime Twickenham, Lansdowne Road and Murrayfield were not neglected; they were all improved and they now boast handsome new stands. Thanks to spadework done in the 1960s, which was a difficult financial period for Rugby football, the four Home Unions can hold their heads high in the facilities that they provide for international Rugby in the British Isles.

The first international Rugby player to lose his life in the Second World War was the legendary Prince Obolensky, who was killed in a training flight on 29 March 1940. Many others were to die, be maimed or imprisoned during those grim years. It was fitting, therefore, that British Rugby, faced with the task of re-igniting the full enthusiasm of club and international Rugby at the end of hostilities, had available no less a touchpaper than the New Zealand Army team. 'The Kiwis', as everyone called them, were largely drawn from the famous Second New Zealand Division commanded by Lt-Gen Sir Bernard Freyberg, VC, known to his face by all ranks as 'Tiny'.

The team prospered under the bright-eyed captaincy of Charlie Saxton, the man who coined the phrase 'Position, possession and pace'. Like all New Zealanders, he believed that the forwards were the key to the game, but that position and possession were essential to creating the score; pace was only his third

T.K.M. Kirby converts for Cambridge in their match against London Scottish, 1945.

Top *Lt-Gen Sir Bernard Freyberg VC in the Western desert.*

Above *Charlie Saxton, captain of the New Zealand Army team in 1945.*

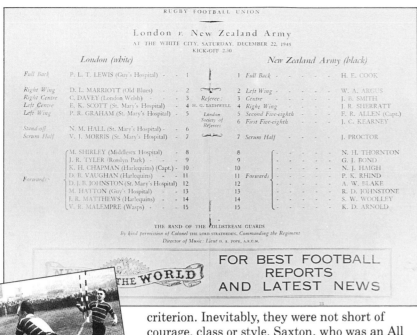

THE WORLD

FOR BEST FOOTBALL
REPORTS
AND LATEST NEWS

W.G. Argus scores for the Kiwis against Neath.

Bath lose their stands and changing-rooms to the bombing. But the flag still flies and the supporters are in good heart.

criterion. Inevitably, they were not short of courage, class or style. Saxton, who was an All Black in 1938, was surrounded by other players who were to become legends – men such as Bob Scott, John Smith and Fred Allen.

The Kiwis swept through the UK, rekindling enthusiasm amongst players and spectators alike, and they more than anybody re-established our taste and appetite for

international Rugby. The Kiwis, although not the All Blacks, were their spitting image in determination and competitive spirit. They played 27 matches in the British Isles, winning 23, losing 2 and drawing 2. They beat England and Wales and lost only to Scotland and Monmouthshire, and they drew with Leinster and Newport. They re-crossed the Channel to beat France twice.

The immediate post-war period was one of accelerating growth for British Rugby. It was still the game of the Public and Grammar Schools, the London Old Boys' teams, the Hospitals and the Universities, and it was supported and nourished by a strong national network of clubs. Rugby, for its followers, became the panacea for rigorous post-war austerity, when everything was on ration including sweets, clothing, food and even bread, which had not been rationed during the war. Petrol rationing continued until 1950, and not until 1954 was rationing lifted from all types of food.

There was no shortage of young men eager to get back into the game and no shortage of up-and-coming youngsters. It was also a boom-time for spectators. A record crowd of 48,500 turned up to see Cardiff play Newport in 1951, and the takings at such games provided an important financial stimulus.

In 1945, British clubs were given formal permission to renew fixtures against the French, who had been expelled from the Five Nations Championship in 1931 for professionalism. Although the Four Home Unions had decided in July 1939 that fixtures could be resumed, beginning with a game against England at Twickenham on 24 February 1940, the French then had to wait seven long years before they were re-introduced to the Championship. Their first match was against Scotland at Stade Colombes, Paris, on 1 January 1947, and France won it by 8 points to 3.

At the next game, in Dublin on 25 January, the French took the field, led by their great flanker Jean Prat, to a wave of Irish sympathy. The home crowd looked on them as the representatives of starving Europe. But not for long. Soon the sympathetic silence gave way to gales of Irish laughter as the crowd absorbed the spectacle of forwards like Soro, Moga and Basquet, who between them weighed over 50 stone. France won this match 12–8, but then lost to Wales 3–0 and to England 6–3.

The years ahead showed the wisdom of bringing the French back into the fold. In 1953–54 they shared the Championship for the first time; in Paris in 1954 they beat the All Blacks for the first time, and in 1959 they won the Championship outright for the first time, under the ferocious and intelligent leadership of Lucien Mias, who was the first French captain to bring real discipline and order to a French team. He was a doctor from the Pyrennean town of Mazamet, and it was his keen Rugby brain which inflicted on South Africa their first defeat in a Test series since 1896. It was a dour series; they drew the First Test at Newlands, a drop goal by Danos being matched by a try by Lochner. In the Second test at Ellis Park, Lacaze kicked a penalty and dropped a goal and Martine scored another drop-goal. These scores, against a try by Fourie converted by Gerber, brought them a famous victory by 9 points to 5. Their heroes in the forwards were Roques, who got his first cap at 34 years of age, Mias, Barthe and Moncla.

From here on the French were (together with the Welsh) the most dangerous force in European Rugby over the next two decades. Their unorthodox flair, brilliant handling and their ability to innovate made them a consistently exhilarating side to watch and play against. In 1964, under another powerful captain, Michel Crauste, they beat the Springboks 8–6 at Springs in the only Test of a short six-match tour. In 1967 they lost a four-Test series in South Africa, when the Springboks won 2, lost 1 and drew 1. They were

Guy Basquet introduces his team before the drawn game with Ireland in 1950.

Sensational defeat for France against Rumania, 1962.

Far right Danos (left), Barthe (centre) and Mias (right) hold off the Scottish forwards in France's 9–0 win on their way to their first International Championship, 1959.

Right Lacroix, protected by Moncla and Crauste, gets the ball away during New Zealand's 32–3 win at Christchurch, 1961.

Below On the same tour Saux listens to Celaya (left) and Bouguyon during the Auckland Test.

far less effective in New Zealand, however. In 1961 and 1968, they lost their Test series 3–0. In 1961 they won their test in Australia, but lost in 1968.

In the Five Nations tournament France won the Championship outright in 1961, 1962, 1967 and 1968, the year they also won the Grand Slam for the very first time. From 1947 to 1968 they produced some truly magnificent players: among the forwards were Mias, Prat, Soro, Moga, Celaya, W. Spanghero, Dauga, Cester, Basquet and Moncla. They also had

The French side to tour South Africa in 1961. Back row, left to right: Jean De Grégorio, Pierre Lacroix, Amédée Domenech, Michel Crauste, François Moncla, Michel Celaya, Gerard Bouguyon, Jean-Pierre Saux. Front row: Henri Rancoule, Guy Boniface, Alfred Roques, Michel Vannier, Pierre Albaladéjo, Jacques Bouquet, Jean Dupuy.

Claude Lacaze has his kick charged down in the match against England in Paris, 1964.

Guy Cambérabéro sets up another attack in France's 14–9 win over England in 1968, the year of their first Grand Slam.

some magical backs in Dufau, Villepreux, Dourthe, Dupuy, Gachassin, Darrouy, Albaladejo, Trillo and G. Cambérabéro, to mention but a few. They had a marvellous sharpness of mind and movement, and by their deeds and talents they demonstrated the magnificent heights to which French Rugby can aspire. On and off the field they had colour, courage and style, they were prepared to run and take risks, and at their best they were, perhaps, the very best of all.

The chroniclers of the game in the immediate post-war days were men such as O.L. Owen of *The Times,* who became the historian of the Rugby Football Union and wrote the history of the RFU in 1955. He was the doyen of them all and was highly respected, as were Dai Gent, J.P. Jordan, Tony Goodrich, H.L.V. Day, Pat Marshall, Roy McKelvie, Geoff Nicholson, Vivian Jenkins, E.W. Swanton, J.B.G. Thomas in Wales, Paul MacWeeney in Ireland, Terry McLean of New Zealand and Ace Parker and Reg Sweet of South Africa. Later in the Fifties and Sixties came Burt Toft, Terry O'Connor, John Reason and David Frost. Uel Titley succeeded O.L. Owen and collaborated with Ross McWhirter (who was sadly killed in a dastardly bombing) to write the centenary of the RFU in 1970.

They were all remarkable characters, remembered by all those who knew them and their writings, which above all clearly illustrated their love for the game. Their idiosyncrasies were legend. Uel Titley once said: 'I never use a player's Christian name unless I have been introduced to him.' Tony Goodrich, when asked why he did not bother to talk to or interview the players, replied: 'The readers of the *Telegraph* do not want to hear the opinions of the players, they want only to read my own dispassionate comments.'

Others weighed in occasionally, like Ivor Brown, the drama critic of *The Observer* who, in the late 1940s, wrote that 'Twickenham is the last fortress of the Forsytes.' Alec Waugh, in a book called *On Doing What One Likes,* wrote: 'An International at Twickenham is more than just a spectacle. It is an immense family party. It is the gathering of the clan.' The war claimed Peter Lawless, who was killed as a War Correspondent. He wrote a marvellous book entitled *Rugger's An Attacking Game,* which encapsulated the whole ethos of Rugby. He was lovely humorous writer, and between the wars he wrote a magnificent parody of the Shakespearean soliloquy, when England

T.P. McLean and (top) Ace Parker.

J.D. Thorne tries to prevent the ball going into touch during England's narrow win (6–5) over France in 1963.

Action at the lineout in the All Blacks' decisive win over England (23–11) during their undefeated tour of 1967 under Brian Lochore.

P. CRANMER

5
P. CRANMER
(Oxford, Richmond and England)
Peter Cranmer began his Rugby at St. Edward's School, where he played in the centre position. His rise to fame was meteoric, for he obtained both his Blue for Oxford and his international cap for England the season after he left school. He is one of the most brilliant international footballers of the present day, his chief attributes being quickness off the mark and straight running. His defence is equally as good as his attack, his kicking being particularly effective. Our illustration shows the Richmond colours.

W.A. & A.C. CHURCHMAN
ISSUED BY THE IMPERIAL TOBACCO CO.
OF GREAT BRITAIN & IRELAND, LTD.

CHURCHMAN'S CIGARETTES

J. HEATON

RUGBY
INTERNATIONALS
A SERIES OF 50

9
J. HEATON
(Liverpool University and England)
Although only 21, Heaton has appeared in more than 15 county matches for Lancashire —a record, at such an age, that would be hard to beat. He played for his University, of which he was captain, while still in his teens, and in the 1931-'32 season scored 52 tries and kicked more than one hundred goals. He is a centre-three-quarter, and learned his football at St. Helens, a Rugby League stronghold. His ability to cut through, combined with his speed and opportunism, earned him his first cap for England in 1935. He is here shown wearing the Liverpool University colours.

W.A. & A.C. CHURCHMAN
ISSUED BY THE IMPERIAL TOBACCO CO.
OF GREAT BRITAIN & IRELAND, LTD.

CHURCHMAN'S CIGARETTES

D. A. KENDREW

RUGBY
INTERNATIONALS
A SERIES OF 50

10
D. A. KENDREW
(Woodford, the Army, Leicester and England)
"Joe" Kendrew (here shown in the Leicester colours) was first capped for England in 1935, when he played against Ireland and Wales. He next appeared in the national sides of 1935 against Ireland and Scotland. The following season he injured a knee in one of the Trial games, and only played once, but was captain of the English side against Wales and Ireland in 1935. He injured a shoulder in the Army and Navy match that year (he is in the Leicester-shire Regt.), and was unable to play against Scotland. He is a member of the British team that toured New Zealand and Australia in 1930.

W.A. & A.C. CHURCHMAN
ISSUED BY THE IMPERIAL TOBACCO CO.
OF GREAT BRITAIN & IRELAND, LTD.

CHURCHMAN'S CIGARETTES

W. H. WESTON

RUGBY
INTERNATIONALS
A SERIES OF 50

15
W. H. WESTON
(Northampton and England)
W. H. Weston is comparatively small for a forward, but what he lacks in "ounces and inches" he makes up with determination and grit. He was capped twice in 1933, twice in 1934 and three times in 1935, as a wing-forward who specializes in blind-side work. His father played for England against Scotland in 1901; an interesting and rather rare example of both father and son representing their country at Rugby football. W. H. Weston (here shown wearing the Northampton colours) was one of the bulwarks of the East Midlands side of 1934 which won the County Championship for the first time.

W.A. & A.C. CHURCHMAN
ISSUED BY THE IMPERIAL TOBACCO CO.
OF GREAT BRITAIN & IRELAND, LTD.

CHURCHMAN'S CIGARETTES

J. H. BEATTIE

RUGBY
INTERNATIONALS
A SERIES OF 50

16
J. H. BEATTIE
(Hawick and Scotland)
J. H. Beattie, although approaching the "veteran" stage, is still one of the finest forwards in the four Unions. In fact, his best ever was against Wales in 1935, when he stood out above all the forwards playing, and appeared to be in practically every movement that took place. A second-row forward, he is quick to break away from the scrum, when he becomes a very difficult man to stop. He gained the first of his 19 caps for Scotland in 1929, when he played in two matches. He was only chosen once the following season, and has only missed one game for Scotland since. He is shown wearing the Hawick colours.

W.A. & A.C. CHURCHMAN
ISSUED BY THE IMPERIAL TOBACCO CO.
OF GREAT BRITAIN & IRELAND, LTD.

CHURCHMAN'S CIGARETTES

R. C. S. DICK

RUGBY
INTERNATIONALS
A SERIES OF 50

19
R. C. S. DICK
(Cambridge, Guy's Hospital and Scotland)
R. C. S. Dick was one of Scotland's "finds" in 1934. A neat and polished footballer, he is a dangerous centre, and a strong and firm believer in straight running. He learned his Rugby football at Sherborne School, and was awarded his Blue for Cambridge in the 1933-'34 season. During that year he helped Clare to win the Inter-College Cup for the first time. Dick was capped that season three times, and was also in all three Scottish sides in 1935, in spite of the fact that an injury had kept him out of football for the first half of the season. He is shown wearing the Guy's Hospital colours.

W.A. & A.C. CHURCHMAN
ISSUED BY THE IMPERIAL TOBACCO CO.
OF GREAT BRITAIN & IRELAND, LTD.

CHURCHMAN'S CIGARETTES

K. C. FYFE

RUGBY
INTERNATIONALS
A SERIES OF 50

21
K. C. FYFE
(Cambridge and Scotland)
K. C. Fyfe is one of those footballers who have real football brains as well as speed and determination. He made a great reputation for himself while at Oundle, and obtained international honours in his first season of big football (1932-'33). In that season he was given his Blue at Cambridge (whose colours are illustrated), and was capped twice for Scotland. The following year he played only once for his country owing to a leg injury, but was chosen for all three games in 1935. He has played three times for Cambridge against Oxford, and scored three tries in 1934. Fyfe, who is 5 ft. 10 ins. in height and 21 years of age, is a good golfer.

W.A. & A.C. CHURCHMAN
ISSUED BY THE IMPERIAL TOBACCO CO.
OF GREAT BRITAIN & IRELAND, LTD.

CHURCHMAN'S CIGARETTES

W. R. LOGAN

RUGBY
INTERNATIONALS
A SERIES OF 50

26
W. R. LOGAN
(Edinburgh Wanderers, University and Scotland)
W. R. Logan, scrum half-back, plays a characteristic hard game, and is a past master in both defence and attack. He was captain of his school, Merchiston, for three seasons, and is in command of his club side, Edinburgh Wanderers, in whose colours he is shown. He first played for Scotland in 1931 against England (his only international match of that year), and in 1932 was in the sides against Wales, Ireland and the South African touring side. Since then he has played in every game for Scotland, and has 13 caps to his credit.

W.A. & A.C. CHURCHMAN
ISSUED BY THE IMPERIAL TOBACCO CO.
OF GREAT BRITAIN & IRELAND, LTD.

CHURCHMAN'S CIGARETTES

E. C. DAVEY

RUGBY
INTERNATIONALS
A SERIES OF 50

32
E. C. DAVEY
(Swansea, Sale and Wales)
Claude Davey was captain of the Welsh team in two years in 1934 and for all three in 1935, and it is noteworthy that Wales lost only one match under his command—against Ireland, in 1935, when his country won the International Championship. Davey usually played as a centre, but recently showed an aptitude for the wing position. Quick off the mark and one of the best tacklers in the game, but prone to individualism in attack. He was first capped in 1930, against France, and together has represented his country 17 times. Our photo shows Davey wearing the Welsh colours.

W.A. & A.C. CHURCHMAN
ISSUED BY THE IMPERIAL TOBACCO CO.
OF GREAT BRITAIN & IRELAND, LTD.

CHURCHMAN'S CIGARETTES

RUGBY INTERNATIONALS
A SERIES OF 50

34
V. G. J. JENKINS
(Oxford, Bridgend and Wales)

V. G. J. Jenkins, here shown wearing the Bridgend colours, played three times for Oxford against Cambridge in the centre position in 1930, '31 and '32. Jenkins, however, fills the full-back position for Wales. He first received international recognition in 1933, when he played in two games, and represented his country a similar number of times the two following seasons. Against Ireland in 1934, by his backing up, he achieved the rare distinction of a full-back scoring a try. He is very cool and safe, a deadly tackler, a splendid dropkick and converter of tries. Jenkins, who is 23 years of age, is 6 ft. tall and weighs 14 stone.

W. A. & A. C. CHURCHMAN

ISSUED BY THE IMPERIAL TOBACCO CO.
(OF GREAT BRITAIN & IRELAND), LTD.

V. G. J. JENKINS

CHURCHMAN'S CIGARETTES

CLIFF W. JONES

RUGBY INTERNATIONALS
A SERIES OF 50

35
CLIFF W. JONES
(Cambridge and Wales)

Cliff Jones, with six caps, is the most brilliant stand-off half of recent years. A very elusive runner, he has a trick of showing the ball to the opposition while almost standing still, and even then getting his would-be tackler on the wrong foot. A good kick and a plucky player, in spite of his lack of inches. A product of Llandovery, he was given his first Blue at Cambridge in the 1933-34 season, when he played for Wales in all three matches. His fine play in the 'Varsity match of 1934 was mainly responsible for Cambridge's victory, and he was a tremendous thorn in the side of England at Twickenham in 1935. He is shown wearing the Cambridge colours.

W. A. & A. C. CHURCHMAN

ISSUED BY THE IMPERIAL TOBACCO CO.
(OF GREAT BRITAIN & IRELAND), LTD.

CHURCHMAN'S CIGARETTES

RUGBY INTERNATIONALS
A SERIES OF 50

37
J. IDWAL REES
(Cambridge, Swansea, Edinburgh Wanderers and Wales)

Idwal Rees (here shown in the Edinburgh Wanderers colours) was one of the best centres in the four Unions in 1934, when he was capped three times for Wales. The following season he was not chosen to play against England, although he played against Scotland (on the wing), and had to drop out of t'e national side against Ireland at the last minute owing to an injury. He was awarded his Blue for Cambridge in 1931 and '32, and has also played for Swansea. The groundwork of his football was learned at Swansea College. Now he is a master at Fettes College: hence his association with Edinburgh Wanderers.

W. A. & A. C. CHURCHMAN

ISSUED BY THE IMPERIAL TOBACCO CO.
OF GREAT BRITAIN & IRELAND), LTD.

J. IDWAL REES

RUGBY INTERNATIONALS
A SERIES OF 50

38
A. SKYM
(Llanelly, Cardiff and Wales)

A. Skym (here shown in the Cardiff colours) first played for Wales in 1928, when he took part in all four international matches, including France. He did not play in any of the games the following year, but was in every Welsh side up to the end of 1933. Thus, with one cap to his credit in 1935 (against England), he has played 20 times for Wales. As this record suggests, Skym, who is a policeman, is one of the best forwards Wales has had in recent years. He used to pack in the front row, but Cardiff made a wing-forward of him in 1934-'35, and he played in that position for Wales. Captained Cardiff.

W. A. & A. C. CHURCHMAN

ISSUED BY THE IMPERIAL TOBACCO CO.
(OF GREAT BRITAIN & IRELAND), LTD.

A. SKYM

CHURCHMAN'S CIGARETTES

W. WOOLLER

RUGBY INTERNATIONALS
A SERIES OF 50

40
W. WOOLLER
(Sale, Cambridge and Wales)

In 1933, while still at Rydal School, Wooller was chosen by Wales to play in all three international matches, and acquitted himself well. In the following season, however, although obtaining his Blue for Cambridge (whose colours we illustrate), he was out of form and did not appear in any of the national sides. In 1934-'35 he played brilliantly both for his University and for Wales (in all three games). A very powerful centre, with a devastating stride, he can kick like a mule. He played once for Wales on the wing. A good cricketer, he got his Blue for Cambridge as a bowler in 1935.

W. A. & A. C. CHURCHMAN

ISSUED BY THE IMPERIAL TOBACCO CO.
(OF GREAT BRITAIN & IRELAND), LTD.

CHURCHMAN'S CIGARETTES

RUGBY INTERNATIONALS
A SERIES OF 50

41
A. BAILEY
(Lansdowne and Ireland)

Aidan Bailey was capped for Ireland in 1934 against Wales, when still a schoolboy, and played in all three international games the following year. He gave a most promising display on his début. He gained confidence with experience, so much so that in his fourth international match, when Ireland beat Wales, his deadly tackling was the chief thorn in the Principality's side. He is quick off the mark and has a long stride, so that he is often back in defence to tackle a man on the opposite side of the field. He is equally good at centre-threequarter and stand-off half-back. We illustrate the Lansdowne colours.

W. A. & A. C. CHURCHMAN

ISSUED BY THE IMPERIAL TOBACCO CO.
(OF GREAT BRITAIN & IRELAND), LTD.

A. BAILEY

RCHMAN'S CIGARETTES

RUGBY INTERNATIONALS
A SERIES OF 50

42
C. E. St. J. BEAMISH
(R. A. F., Harlequins, Leicester and Ireland)

Charles Beamish provides yet another instance of a family with "rugger in its blood," for he has three brothers in the game, one of whom, George Beamish, first played for Ireland in 1925 and was capped 25 times. George was also captain of the Leicestershire and East Midlands XV which recorded the only win against the "Springboks" in their 1931-'32 tour. Charles, a forward like his brother, played for Ireland twice in 1933 and twice in '34. He has captained the R.A.F., and has played for the Harlequins and Leicester (whose colours we illustrate). Equally good in the back or front row of the pack, he well deserved his three caps in 1935.

W. A. & A. C. CHURCHMAN

ISSUED BY THE IMPERIAL TOBACCO CO.
(OF GREAT BRITAIN & IRELAND), LTD.

C. E. St J. BEAMISH

CHURCHMAN'S CIGARETTES

RUGBY INTERNATIONALS
A SERIES OF 50

49
J. RUSSELL
(University College, Cork and Ireland)

An interesting story told about this player is that less than five years ago he had no knowledge of the Rugby game, and the only football he played was Gaelic, a cross between Rugby and Soccer. One day he was persuaded to play Rugby and within a few weeks he was the best forward in the college. To-day he is one of the best forwards in international Rugby. Packing in the second row, he is very fast in the open. He was first capped for Ireland in 1931, when he took part in all four games. He played against S. Africa in 1932, and in every match during 1933, '34 and '35. His club Rugby is with University College, Cork, in whose colours he is shown.

W. A. & A. C. CHURCHMAN

ISSUED BY THE IMPERIAL TOBACCO CO.
(OF GREAT BRITAIN & IRELAND), LTD.

J. RUSSELL

CHURCHMAN'S CIGARETTES

J. A. SIGGINS

RUGBY INTERNATIONALS
A SERIES OF 50

50
J. A. SIGGINS
(Belfast Collegians and Ireland)

J. A. Siggins has played for Ireland in every international match since 1931, but his best season was undoubtedly 1934-'35, when, by his leadership and personal prowess, he captained the Irish XV that won the International Championship outright for the first time since the 1898-'99 season. One of Ireland's heaviest forwards—he weighs over 15 stone—he is magnificent in the loose, while his coolness and tactical play make him a capable leader. Siggins, who is a reliable place-kick, has a total of 17 international appearances to his credit. We illustrate the Belfast Collegians colours.

ISSUED BY THE IMPERIAL TOBACCO CO.
OF GREAT BRITAIN & IRELAND), LTD.

Great names of the Thirties.

Centenary Celebrations.
Right *Programmes to celebrate the RFU Centenary and the first international.*
Below *Centenary dinners for the RFU (1971), the Welsh RU (1981) and the Varsity Match (1981).*

88

were the result of the coming together of magnificent players under the leadership of John Gwilliam, who was the first captain since the war to instil team discipline, doing so with a fatherly and schoolmasterly approach which often baffled the hard cases in the side. The Gwilliam era was blessed by players of the calibre of Rex Willis, Cliff Morgan, Bleddyn Williams, Lewis Jones, Don Hayward, Dai

In 1957 England hit their high spot of the decade. Under the chirpy and fierce captaincy of Eric Evans, they won a narrow victory over Wales by a penalty goal to nil, then carried all before them to win the Grand Slam for the first time in 29 years. Many would say that it was Evans's pep-talk rhetoric which persuaded England into winning everything, but he had some pretty devastating players both up front

John Kendall-Carpenter and (below) Eric Evans.

Davies, Roy John, Malcolm Thomas, Jack Matthews and Cliff Davies.

France and Wales had limited success in the Fifties: they shared the Championship in 1955, Wales won it in 1956 and France in 1959. These victories apart, the rest of the decade belonged to England. In 1953 they won the Championship; in 1954, although they won the Triple Crown, they only shared the Championship in a three-horse race with France and Wales. That year they had a tough pack, which will evoke painful memories in those who played against them: R.V. Stirling (capt.), E. Evans, D.L. Sanders, P.D. Young, P.G. Yarranton, D.S. Wilson, R. Higgins, and J. MacG.K. Kendall-Carpenter. They had a pretty burly back division, too, which included such big men as J.E. Woodward, J.P. Quinn and C.E. Winn, together with the superb skills of J. Butterfield and M. Regan.

Above left The Welsh team which played unchanged throughout the 1950 season to win the Grand Slam. Back row, left to right: Mr I. Jones, J.D. Robins, D. Hayward, E.R. John, R.T. Evans, W.R. Cale, W.B. Cleaver. Standing: K.J. Jones, M.C. Thomas, B. Lewis Jones, J.A. Gwilliam, J. Matthews, C. Davies, G. Williams. Front row: W.R. Willis, D.M. Davies. Left Cliff Morgan.

91

and in the backs. The forwards were C.R. Jacobs, E. Evans, G.W.D. Hastings, J.D. Currie, R.W.D. Marques, P.G.D. Robbins, R. Higgins and A. Ashcroft. The backs were R.E.G. Jeeps, R.M. Bartlett, P.H. Thompson, L.B. Cannell, J. Butterfield, P.B. Jackson and D.F. Allison. Evans also took England to the Championship in 1958 with two wins and two draws, and it is interesting to recall that Ricky Bartlett, sadly deceased, never played in a losing England side during his seven caps over those two years.

The late Forties and the Fifties saw some great teams and players. In ten years from 1948 to 1957, there were four Grand Slams and six Triple Crowns, and the game truly abounded with great players who were perhaps more concerned with the game and its enjoyment, both on and off the field, than the more distracted modern player.

Above *Eric Evans presents the England team to the Duke of Edinburgh during their 1957 Grand Slam season.*

Ken Scotland (right) with Scottish colleague B.C. Henderson.
Far right *Tom Kiernan prepares for another shot at goal.*

Keith Jarrett.
Far right *Ken Jones.*

The Sixties brought only one Grand Slam, by France in 1968, and three Triple Crowns, by Wales in 1965 and 1969 and one by England in 1960. The Championship during this decade was largely dominated by France and by Wales. France won four Championships and shared one, and Wales won three and shared one. When Scotland figured at the top of the table with Wales in 1964, it was for the first time since 1938, while Ireland, after their marvellous post-war start, achieved nothing. There were some terrific players in the Sixties. Full-backs of the calibre of Ken Scotland, Tom Kiernan, Bob Hiller, D. Rutherford, and J.P.R. Williams. Wings like D. Bebb, N. Brophy, A.R. Smith, M.C.R. Richards and Gerald Davies. Centres such as D. Hewitt, D.K. Jones, K.S. Jarrett, M.P. Weston, D. Duckham, J. Spencer, S.J. Dawes, and C.M.H. Gibson. Exceptional half-backs such as D. Watkins, R.A.W. Sharp, B. John, G. Edwards, R.M. Young and R.E.G. Jeeps. There was no shortage of powerful forwards with men such as S. Millar, D.M.D. Rollo, B.V. Meredith, A. Pask, W.J. McBride, W. Mulcahy, D.P. Rogers J. Douglas, J.W. Telfer, N. Murphy, W.D. Thomas B.E. Price, R.J. McLoughlin, D. Williams, K. Kennedy, J.V. Pullin, J. Taylor, K. Goodall, R.J. Arneil, T.M. Davies, G.L. Brown and J. McLauchlan. It is significant that many of these players, who emerged at the end of the Sixties, were to play a major part in the stunning successes of the Lions in 1971 and 1974.

Gareth Edwards.
Left *Dickie Jeeps.*

Ken Kennedy.
Left *Jim Telfer.*
Far left *Bryn Meredith (with the ball).*

Immediately after the war, the various Old Boys teams in London, clubs such as Old Merchant Taylors, Old Millhillians and Old Cranleighans, were still a force in the game, and so were the London Hospitals. Guy's and Mary's were particularly strong and boasted a first-class fixture list. The correspondents of *The Times, Telegraph* and *Guardian* spent a great deal of time and effort reporting the Old Boys' matches. The 1955 Lions had two Old Boys half-backs in Douglas Baker of OMTs and Johnny Williams of Old Millhillians – their selection recalling that of R.S. Spong and W.H. Scobey, two Old Millhillians who were Lions in 1930. Also from the Thirties was the legendary T.F. Huskisson, an OMT who was a fixture in the England side.

Alas, the Fifties and Sixties saw a decline in the fixture-lists of the Old Boys teams and of the Teaching Hospitals. The structure of British

Partisan support at the Hospitals Cup semi-final between Guy's and Middlesex in 1949.

Far right The ritual throwing of bags of flour at the 1958 Hospitals Cup final.

Another hard fought battle between Guy's and Westminster in a 1960 Cup match.

Rugby was moving slowly towards greater centralization and concentration in the major clubs. The only academic institutions to retain their status were the Universities of Oxford and Cambridge. Despite the increasing demand for top 'A' levels by admissions tutors, they managed to keep a first-class fixture list; much of their success is due to the annual Varsity match at Twickenham, which is still a principal and important event in the Rugby calendar. Yet, in 1945, Oxford and Cambridge were at odds with the Rugby Union and threatened to take the match to Wembley. They finally agreed on a fee of £500 for the use of the Twickenham ground, and have continued to play there ever since.

It is interesting to look at the place of Rugby in the history of sport at these ancient Universities. The first Rugby match between the two was played in 1872, when Rugby became the ninth sport to achieve Varsity-match status. Before Rugby there had been Cricket (1827), Boat Race (1829), Rackets (1855), Tennis, (Real, Royal or Court 1859), Billiards (1860), Shooting (1862), Steeplechasing (1863), Athletics (1864). Rugby

was, however, ahead of Soccer, Hockey, Lawn Tennis and Boxing.

Rugby continued at Oxford and Cambridge during the Second World War and there was a war-time series of Varsity matches for which no Blues were awarded. The end of hostilities brought an influx of battle-hardened servicemen, affluent with grants and post-war gratuities. There were naval commanders, squadron leaders, majors and captains galore. One of the outstanding personalities to arrive was B.H. Travers, who captained Oxford in 1947. He was a major in the Australian Army, where he won the Military OBE and was mentioned in despatches. He was a cricket Blue in 1946, an athletics Blue in 1947, and he was also a swimming Blue. He played for England in 1947, 1948 and 1949, and for New South Wales in 1950, and also turned out for the Harlequins and the Barbarians. Nicknamed 'Jika', he was an immense influence on post-war Rugby at Oxford.

Travers and his fellow Colonials were a great reservoir of talent. They were mostly Rhodes scholars and included J.O. Newton-Thompson, S.C. Newman, D.W. Swarbrick,

Photograph before the traditional Stanley's match, 1949. (Oxford team in dark jerseys.) Back row, left to right: G.L. Bullard, J.M. Todd, G.C. Rittson-Thomas, A. Thomas, D.A. Emms, P.W. Kininmonth, W.J. Hefer, M. Terry, P. Duff, W.H. Townsens (touch judge). Middle row: H.D. Small, B. Boobbyer, P.M. Rhodes, H. Thomas, A.B. Curtis, D.W.C. Smith, J. MacG. K. Kendall-Carpenter, J.H. Steeds, P.J. Langley, R.H. Lloyd-Davies, I.J. Botting, C. Holden, T.N. Pearce (referee), R.T.S. MacPherson (touch judge). Front row: D. Jones, L.B. Cannell, T.G.H. Jackson, C.B. van Ryneveld, G.A. Wilson, Major R.V. Stanley, A.N. Vincent, T.W. Price, R. Green, D.H. Keller.

J.V. Smith of Cambridge outpaces the Blackheath defence, 1950.

Photocall for the four internationals in the 1956 Oxford side. Left to right: D.O. Brace (Wales), J.D. Currie (England), M.J.K. Smith (England), P.G.D. Robbins (England).

	OXFORD			CAMBRIDGE	
		Referee: **Mr. L. M. BOUNDY** (London Society)			
1.	**J. S. M. SCOTT** Radley and Corpus Christi	FULL-BACKS	1.	**K. J. F. SCOTLAND** George Heriots School and Trinity	
		THREE-QUARTERS			
2.	**T. BAXTER** Brisbane G.S. and Balliol	LEFT WING RIGHT WING	2.	**P. R. MILLS** Rydal School and Caius	
3.	**M. S. PHILLIPS** Arnold School and Trinity Hall	RIGHT CENTRE RIGHT CENTRE	3.	**G. WINDSOR LEWIS** (CAPTAIN) The Leys and Trinity Hall	
4.	**L. D. WATTS** Bristol G.S. and Wadham	LEFT CENTRE LEFT CENTRE	4.	**H. J. DAVIES** Cowbridge G.S. and Christ's	
5.	**J. R. C. YOUNG** Bishop Veseys G.S. and St. Edmund Hall	RIGHT WING LEFT WING	5.	**M. R. WADE** Wyggeston and Emmanuel	
		HALF-BACKS			
6.	**A. G. R. SHEIL** The Southport School, Australia and Balliol	STAND-OFF	6.	**G. H. WADDELL** Fettes College and Pembroke	
7.	**A. O'CONNOR** Duffryn G.S. and St. Edmund Hall	SCRUM	7.	**S. R. SMITH** Eltham College and Emmanuel	
		FORWARDS			
8.	**L. T. LOMBARD** (CAPTAIN) Kingswood College, S.A. and St. Edmund Hall	PROP LOOSE-HEAD PROP	8.	**D. R. J. BIRD** St. Paul's and St. John's	
9.	**D. M. DAVIES** Cardigan G.S. and St. Edmund Hall	HOOKER HOOKER	9.	**M. T. WETSON** Marling and St. Catharine's	
10.	**D. JESSON** West Hartlepool G.S. and St. Edmund Hall	PROP RIGHT-HEAD PROP	10.	**J. J. RAINFORTH** Oundle and Emmanuel	
11.	**L. I. RIMMER** Birkenhead School and Corpus Christi	BLIND-SIDE SECOND-ROW	11.	**D. G. PERRY** Clifton and Christ's	
12.	**J. R. MONTGOMERY** Michaelhouse, S.A. and Lincoln	SECOND-ROW SECOND-ROW	12.	**V. S. J. HARDING** St. Marylebone Grammar School and Christ's	
13.	**F. H. ten BOS** Fettes College and St. Edmund Hall	SECOND-ROW BLIND-SIDE (2ND-ROW)	13.	**D. A. MacSWEENEY** Rockwell, Tipperary and Christ's	
14.	**S. H. WILCOCK** Kirkham G.S. and St. Peter's Hall	OPEN-SIDE No. 8	14.	**K. R. F. BEARNE** Rydal and Clare	
15.	**W. I. PLANT** R.G.S. Worcester and St. Edmund Hall	LOCK OPEN-SIDE (WING)	15.	**D. C. MILLS** Clifton and Emmanuel	
	Touch Judge: **P. G. D. ROBBINS** (St. Edmund Hall)			Touch Judge: **W. J. DOWNEY** (Emmanuel)	
		KICK-OFF 2.15 P.M.			

An array of current and future internationals in the line up for the 1958 Varsity match.

Above right Oxford and Cambridge join forces to tour Japan, 1959.

M.P. Donnelly, I.J. Botting, A.N. Vincent, C.B. van Ryneveld and M.B. Hofmeyr. The home-grown talent at Oxford in the 1940s was equally impressive, with J. MacG.K. Kendall-Carpenter, L.B. Cannell, G.A. Wilson, B. Boobbyer, G.C. Rittson-Thomas, C.E. Winn and T.J. Brewer. In 1949 there were 11 internationals, actual or future, in residence of Oxford. It was no wonder

that Oxford dominated the post-war Varsity matches until 1952, losing only in 1945 and 1947 when Cambridge had a few personalities of their own such as Eric Bole, the England captain, M.R. Steele-Bodger, the well-known adminstrator, R.H. Lloyd-Davies, J.F. Bance, Logie Bruce Lockhart, and K.A.N. Spray.

The kicking duel in 1947 between the Welshman, Hugh Lloyd-Davies, and Sid Newman was well worth going to see, and so in 1949 was Kendall-Carpenter's covering tackle on the England wing, J.V. Smith, which saved the game for Oxford. After 1952, Cambridge proceeded to dominate matters for the next 12 years, and apart from two wins in 1957 and 1959 Oxford had little to comfort them until they began a recovery in 1964.

Oxford and Cambridge have continued to this day to contribute an enormous number of caps to the various international sides. They have not been alone in this, and in any survey, however brief, of the academic institutions and their legacy to British Rugby it would be remiss not to remember the two Colleges of Physical Education, Loughborough and St Luke's College, Exeter, which have also produced an impressive flow of talented players. Loughborough were a major force in the Middlesex Sevens during the 1960s and '70s. They had world-class players in John Taylor, Gerald Davies, Keith Fielding, Fran Cotton, Steve Smith and Clive Woodward.

OFFICIAL PROGRAMME

ENGLAND (WHITE)				REFEREE: Dr. F. F. Cooper (Middlesex)	THE REST (BLUE)		
1	†D. F. ALLISON	...	Coventry	Full Backs:	1 †J. G. G. HETHERINGTON	Cambridge University & Northampton
2	*J. E. WOODWARD	...	Wasps	Three-Quarters: R. Wing L. Wing	2 †P. H. THOMPSON	Headingley
3	*J. BUTTERFIELD (Capt.)	...	Northampton	R. Centre L. Centre	3 †J. T. HODGSON	Cambridge University
4	*W. P. C. DAVIES	...	Harlequins	L. Centre R. Centre	4 *L. B. CANNELL	St. Mary's Hospital
5	*F. D. SYKES	...	Northampton	L. Wing R. Wing	5 †P. B. JACKSON	Coventry
6	*M. REGAN	...	Liverpool	Half-Backs: Stand-off	6 *M. J. K. SMITH	Oxford University & Hinckley
7	†R. E. G. JEEPS	...	Northampton	Scrum	7 *J. E. WILLIAMS	Old Millhillians
8	*G. W. HASTINGS	...	Gloucester	Forwards:	8 *D. L. SANDERS	Harlequins
9	*N. A. LABUSCHAGNE	...	Harlequins		9 *E. EVANS (Capt.)	Sale
10	*D. ST. G. HAZELL	...	Leicester		10 †C. R. JACOBS	Northampton
11	*R. D. MARQUES	Cambridge University & Harlequins			11 †J. D. CURRIE	Oxford University
12	*P. D. YOUNG	...	Dublin Wanderers		12 *W. HOSKER	Birkenhead Park
13	†P. G. D. ROBBINS	...	Oxford University		13 A. J. HERBERT	Cambridge University & Wasps
14	*I. D. S. BEER	...	Harlequins		14 †A. ASHCROFT	Waterloo
15	†J. W. CLEMENTS	Cambridge University & Old Cranleighans			15 *V. G. ROBERTS	Harlequins
					* International † Previous Total	

Universities, Old Boys and Hospitals were all represented in the final trial of 1956.

To be a Lion, an All Black, a Springbok or a Wallaby is the pinnacle of any Rugby player's achievement. It is the final fulfilment of a playing career. Lions tours usually take place every three or four years, and while tours to Britain tend to be more erratic, all offer the same challenge – the chance to compete against the world's best.

Statistically, over the years, the Springboks are the World Champions, but be careful if you are saying that to a New Zealander! The fact remains that the All Blacks have never won a series in South Africa, although they did draw the series in 1928, whereas the Springboks won a series in New Zealand in 1937.

In the first twenty years after the war, the Lions visited New Zealand in 1950, 1959 and 1966, and South Africa in 1955, 1962 and 1968. Not on any occasion did they win a series. The 1955 Lions came closest: they were the first British Isles team to break the run of defeats in the Southern Hemisphere. They drew their series two-all, and were twice in the lead after winning the First and Third Tests.

The 1950 Lions were the last to go by boat. The whole trip took almost seven months and, for all their deck gymnastics, on the way out, it was not surprising that many of them arrived a stone overweight. This may partly explain why they were soundly beaten by Otago and Southland early in the tour; but then, once they had got fit, they did not lose another provincial game. Because of the war they were an older Lions side than usual, but they enjoyed themselves and were as popular a team as ever visited New Zealand. They played 23 matches, won 17 and lost 5, and in the four Tests they lost 3 and drew 1. In Australia they played 6 games, won 5 and lost 1, winning both Tests. They lost two of the Tests in New Zealand by a mere three points, and their heaviest Test defeat was 8–0 in Christchurch. Their problem was that the forwards were on the light side, and gave away a lot of weight to the big New Zealand pack. The backs had no such problems and delighted the New Zealand crowds with their willingness to run the ball under the guiding hands of the superb Jack Kyle; the New Zealanders rated him as the best player in his position they had ever seen.

Under the captaincy of Karl Mullen, the 1950 tourists had nine of the successful 1948 and 1949 Irish side, including Jack Kyle, Noel Henderson and George Norton behind the scrum, and those exciting flankers Jim McCarthy and Bill McKay, who later was to emigrate as a doctor to Hawkes Bay. There was a huge contingent of 14 Welshmen, and Jack Kyle always speaks extremely highly of Bleddyn Williams, Lewis Jones and Ken Jones as being amongst the best backs he ever played with. The five Scots included Peter Kininmonth, who against Wales in 1951 was to drop an extraordinary goal from the touch-line, and Doug Smith, who was to manage the great

Lions captain Karl Mullen is introduced to New Zealand Governor General Sir Bernard Freyburg during the 1950 tour.

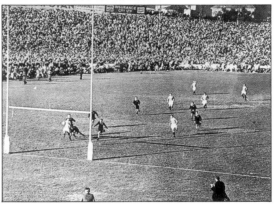

In the same series Ken Jones sprints away from the New Zealand defence to score under the posts after a fifty yard run in the Fourth Test at Auckland.

Lions team of 1971 to New Zealand. England supplied only three players and the manager, Surgeon Captain 'Ginger' Osborne, R.N.

The 1955 Lions were the first to fly. It took 36 hours to Johannesburg in a four-prop Super Constellation. They went out unheralded and unsung, and were accompanied by only two journalists, Vivian Jenkins of the *Sunday Times* and J.B.G. Thomas of the *Western Mail*; they were later joined by Roy McKelvie. They became part of the tour, and were a far cry from the present-day horde of up to thirty media men who go with the Lions.

Bryn Meredith holds off Chris Koch and Bertus van der Merwe (extreme right) as Dickie Jeeps gets the ball away during the Lions' victory in the Third Test at Pretoria, 1955.

Cliff Morgan leads the singing at Port Elizabeth airport at the end of the 1955 tour.

Like the 1950 Lions, they too were hailed as a fun-loving side who embraced the country they toured, which is in contrast to the sometimes dour attitude of recent Lions teams who have spent too much time brooding in their hotels. The manager was Jack Siggins, a tough Belfast Orangeman, who ruled firmly and fairly and demanded only that the players went to bed at a proper hour two nights before a game and trained hard after a night out. The tourists got off to an inauspicious start by losing the first game against Western Transvaal. They then put together six convincing wins against teams that included Orange Free State and Western Province, before a depleted side lost to Eastern Province. Then they had eight high-scoring wins, among them victory in the First Test, and by now the South Africans knew that they faced an extraordinary side and had a fight on their hands.

It was the First Test which finally convinced the host country. A world-record crowd of 95,000, plus an estimated 10,000 gatecrashers, were privileged to watch one of the greatest games of Rugby football ever played. The Afrikaners had come in from the High Veldt and the Karroo to see the Lions thrown to the Christians. Even in those days they were offering £50 a ticket.

The Lions scored first, when Phil Davies cut through the middle and passed to Butterfield who had speed; he took the ball behind him and brilliantly brought it back and put Pedlow in at the corner. Van der Schyff then landed two big penalties, and right-wing Briers scored a lovely try which was converted. At 11–3 to the Springboks it seemed all over, but the Welsh wizard Cliff Morgan brought the Lions back into the game by putting Butterfield over for a try under the posts, converted by Cameron.

At half-time it was 11–8, and a minute later tragedy struck the Lions when the robust Reg Higgins twisted his knee and left the field, to miss the rest of the tour. A man short for the whole of the second half and trailing by three points – it seemed a recipe for disaster; then five Welsh forwards – the two Merediths, W.O.G. Williams, Rhys Williams and Russell Robins – a Scot Jim Greenward and the Irish captain Robin Thompson began to play heroically against the huge Springboks pack. Again it was Cliff Morgan, playing the best game of his life, who struck. Spotting van Wyk late away from the scrum, he rocketed past him and Ulyate for a famous try. Cameron converted and the Lions were leading 13–11. A great run by O'Reilly and a tap over the line by Greenward for a try, converted by Cameron, made it 18–11. Then O'Reilly chased onto a kick-through, made a lovely take and dived over. Cameron converted magnificently from the touch-line, and the score was an almost unbelievable 23–11.

At last the strain of having only seven forwards showed and the Springboks began to pound back. A try by Swart meant that the Springboks needed 10 points with 15 minutes left. The tiring Lions allowed Koch to crash through them for a try, converted by van der Schyff. Five points were needed when in injury-time Briers scored another try, and all that ace goal-kicker van der Schyff had to do was to convert from halfway out. Astonishingly, he hooked it wide, and his dejection was captured

in a famous photograph. The Lions won 23–22. O'Reilly, who had refused to look at the kick, was asked after the match what on earth he had been doing. He replied: 'I was in direct communication with the Vatican.'

The Lions became the toast of Britain and South Africa, and their marvellous back line of Jeeps, Morgan, Pedlow, Davies, Butterfield and O'Reilly became household names. The forwards, however, were perhaps even greater heroes: their resistance, and the way they carried the game to the big South African forwards were critical factors in allowing the backs full rein for their talents. The other factor in the Lions' success was the all-round pace of the whole team. As it turned out, they unexpectedly won their two Tests on the High Veldt, where the grounds were rock-hard and therefore very fast, and then lost the two Tests at sea-level, where the ground was softer.

Danie Craven and many South African critics say that this was the best footballing side to visit South Africa. Not only because they shared the series and broke the existing record by winning 18 matches, or because names like Morgan, Butterfield and O'Reilly became synonymous for thrust and speed, or because they played the finest open Rugby seen in South Africa, but also because there were no unpleasant incidents. Not a player was warned for over-vigorous play, and they won many compliments for being magnificent, fun-loving sportsmen and great ambassadors. Above all, though, they had shown that the Southern Hemisphere could be beaten.

The 1959 Lions, who went to New Zealand and Australia under Ronnie Dawson, were in much the same mould. They did not enjoy such good fortune in the Test series, but in 31 games in New Zealand and Australia they won 25 and lost 6. Their Test record in New Zealand, which is the true yardstick, was: won 1, lost 3. They won both their Tests in Australia.

This team had a residue of six of the 1955 Lions in O'Reilly, Butterfield, Jeeps, Bryn Meredith, Rhys Williams and Hugh McLeod, and they had better full-backs in Ken Scotland and Terry Davies. They too were fun-loving (Andy Mulligan and Tony O'Reilly saw to that) and were also committed to attack. Many of them to this day feel that they fell victim to notorious New Zealand refereeing and were upset at losing the psychologically important First Test in Dunedin by 18 points to 17, when

Mike Campbell-Lamerton struggles to hold Fanie Kuhn during the Second Test at Durban, 1962.

Don Clarke kicked six penalty goals to four British tries. Until 1971 they were regarded as the best British team to visit New Zealand, and they deserved at least to share the series , for their dazzling back play and running were so incisive that no British side, before or since, has scored so many tries. Tony O'Reilly and Peter Jackson, that brilliant elusive wing, scored 36 between them.

Sadly, the expectations produced by the Lions sides of the Fifties were not fulfilled in the Sixties. There was simply not the depth of individual talent available which had existed in the previous decade. The next three Lions teams, of 1962 to South Africa, 1966 to New Zealand and 1968 to South Africa, were uniformly unimpressive and unproductive apart from two wins in Australia in 1966. They achieved not a single win against New Zealand or South Africa. One positive consequence of these tours was to

All Black scrum-half Chris Laidlaw escapes the attentions of Roger Young (on the ground) and Jim Telfer during the First Test at Dunedin, 1966.

Above Brian
Shillinglaw passes to
Arthur Smith during
Scotland's first
international in South
Africa, 1960.
Above right South
Africa v Ireland at
Capetown, 1961.
Right All Black captain
Wilson Whineray
charges away from
Clive Jacobs in the
Second Test against
England at
Christchurch, 1963.
Far right England's
Mike Davis and All
Black Ian Clarke
compete for the ball
during the same match.

precipitate a coaching revolution in Britain.
Organization was improved, and a proper coach
was introduced for the first time in 1971. The
man who got the job, the great Carwyn James,
proved to be an inspired choice.

In 1960 Scotland began a new fashion for
short tours by the four home countries, playing

three matches in South Africa including one Test
which they lost 18 – 10 in Port Elizabeth. This
was followed by a four-match tour to South
Africa by Ireland in 1961, and they too lost the
Test, 24 – 8 in Capetown. In 1963, England
embarked on a six-match tour of New Zealand
and Australia and lost five of their six games;
they lost two Tests in Auckland and
Christchurch, 21 – 11 and 9 – 6, and they also lost
to Australia, 18 – 9 in Sydney. In 1964 it was the
turn of Wales to suffer humiliation in their four-
match tour of South Africa. They won two and

*Syd Millar (with the
ball) leads the Lions in
training before the 1968
tour to South Africa.*
Far right Action from
the Test series which
the Lions lost 0–3, with
one match drawn.

lost two, but sustained a crushing defeat in the Test in Durban by 24 – 3. It was followed by a period of massive soul-searching and led to the reorganization of Welsh Rugby. The annual meeting forced the WRU to make recommendations for the future, and these resulted in the appointment of Ray Williams as the National Coaching Organizer, the introduction of a squad system and the implementation of the *English Coaching Manual,* which had been published in 1951.

The Fifties and Sixties also saw the acceleration of club tours to Europe. Swansea pioneered the way to Rumania in 1954 and to Italy in 1957. They were followed to Rumania two years later by Harlequins, and Llanelli led the way to Czechoslovakia and the Soviet Union.

The first major incoming tour after the war was that of the 1947 Wallabies. The Australians until recently were the Cinderellas of the International Board Countries. Under constant siege from Australia Rules and Rugby League, they are to be admired for their tenacity in fostering Rugby Union in the face of such powerful opposition and for coping so well with the tug-of-war for talent with which they are faced. In 1947 their representatives had a splendid tour. They played 35 games, won 29 and lost 6. In five Tests against the Five Nations they won 3 and lost 2. They beat Scotland 16 – 7, Ireland 16 – 3, lost to Wales 6 – 0, beat England 11 – 0 and lost to France 11– 6. Their strength behind the scrum lay in C.C. Eastes, A.E.J. Tonkin and Trevor Allan. In the pack they had somee pretty hard cases, including that great character Nick Shehadie, who was to become a Knight and Lord Mayor of Sydney, Bob McMaster, a wrestling champion, C.J. Windon, who was to be sent off at Llanelli, and D.H. Keller, who was later to play for Scotland.

The Wallabies came again in 1957 and 1966 with far poorer results. They lost all five Tests in 1957, but won two in 1966, beating Wales 14 – 11 and England 23 – 11. Although both teams had fine captains in Bob Davidson and John Thornett, they were generally short of talent despite the presence in 1966 of one of the greatest scrum-halves of all time, Ken Catchpole, who had grace, genius and a speed of pass that was second to none.

The Aussies were always more laid-back and less dour than the Springboks or the All Blacks, and certainly seemed to enjoy their tour off the field more than most. The All Blacks have

Above left *Wallabies players E. Tweedale (right) and R.E. McMaster discuss tactics during the 1947 tour.*
Above *Lineout action in the Wallabies' game against Hants and Sussex.*
Left *The 1957-58 Wallabies at Eastbourne.*

Scrum-half Connor is put under pressure by Faull in the Australians' final match against the Barbarians at Cardiff in 1958.

Ken Catchpole gets the ball away from the lineout during the Australians' 23–11 win over England on their 1966-67 tour.

often been described by their own historians as the unsmiling giants and the Springboks, their problems exacerbated by language difficulties, have often kept themselves too much to themselves. For all that, the South Africans' love for Rugby is best illustrated by the true story that during the Boer War, Field General S.G.

Maritz of the Transvaal Scouting Corps called a 12-hour truce against the opposing British Forces so that a Rugby match could be arranged between them.

The South Africans came to Europe in all their might in 1951 to play 31 matches; they lost only 1, against London Counties. They crushed Scotland 44 – 0 in a game that, to the chagrin of the Scots, became known as the Murrayfield Massacre. They also crushed Ireland 17 – 5 and France 25 – 3; only against Wales (6 – 3) and England (8 – 3) was it a close-run thing.

Inevitably, the tour was dominated by forwards such as Koch, Bekker, du Rand, Myburgh, van Wyk, Muller, Kenyon and Okey Geffin, who was a siege-gun goal kicker. They also possessed rock-steady backs in Buchler, Ochse and Lategan, and compact and clever half-backs in du Toit and Brewis.

It was the same story in 1961. The Springboks, captained by Avril Malan, played 34 games, won 31, lost 1 and drew 2, and beat all four of the home countries, but less convincingly than in 1951 – 52. They beat Wales 3 – 0, Ireland 8 – 3, England 5 – 0 and Scotland 12 – 5. They drew 0 – 0 with France in Paris in a torrid game. Before the match the French captain, Moncla, demanded that his forwards should stay with the Springboks both physically and psychologically. The clashing of the set scrums in the first quarter of an hour was like a confrontation between two herds of charging wild buffalo. Fortunately Gwynne Walters, the best referee of his time, was in charge and prevented the game from disintegrating into chaos.

The Test pack of P.S du Toit, G.F. Malan, S.P. Kuhn, J.T. Claassen, A.S. Malan, H.J.M. Pelser, D.J. Hopwood and Frik du Preez, who was to become one of the greatest Springbok forwards of all time, was arguably the best pack ever to tour the British Isles. Their backs were never brilliant, but they had a very good runner in the powerful Johnny Gainsford, who was similar in style to the modern-day Danie Gerber. Oxlee was a neat fly-half and they had other powerful backs in Engelbrecht, Kirkpatrick and F. du T. Roux, who was to make a name for himself with his high tackling, which took Richard Sharp out of the 1962 Lions Tour at a very early stage.

The only defeat inflicted on them was by the Barbarians, who therefore won the only Springbok head of the tour. For once in their life, the Baa-Baas departed from the tradition of playing their usual open game and double-

The 1960-61 Springboks arrive at Southampton. Far left *The 1951-52 Springboks. Back row, left to right: G. Dannhauser, S.S. Viviers, B.J. Kenyon (captain), H.S. Muller, P.W. Wessels, H.P.J. Bekker, B. Myburgh, E.E. Dinkelmann, P.G. Johnstone, W.H.M. Barnard, J. Pickard, A.C. Koch, M.J. Saunders, A. Geffin, F.E. van der Ryst, J.A. du Rand, S.P. Fry, C.J. van Wyk. Front row: J. Buchler, D.J. Fry, D.J. Sinclair, A.C. Keevy, J.D. Brewis, J.S. Oelofse, P.A. du Toit, R.A.M. van Schoor, J.K. Ochse, M.T. Lategan, W.H. Delport.*

Left *Hennie Muller leads his team onto the field followed by Okey Geffin before their resounding 44–0 victory over Scotland in 1952.*

Facing page *John Thornett, the Australian captain, is chaired off the field by Phil Hawthorne (left) and Noel Murphy, captain of the Barbarians, after the Wallabies had scored a fine victory in their last match at Cardiff, 1967.*

Tony O'Reilly makes a break for the Barbarians in their 6–0 win over the South Africans in 1961.

crossed the Springboks by taking them on up front. In mitigation, the pitch was like porridge, a characteristic of Cardiff Arms Park of the time. Just as strangely, however, the Springboks decided to enter into the spirit of the occasion by trying to play Barbarian Rugby. The result was that the Baa-Baas won 6 – 0 from two tries by Derek and Haydn Morgan respectively, when they pounced on Springbok mistakes in the first half. One incident which still lives in the memory of those who saw the match was the clattering shoulder-charge tackle by 14½-stone Hadyn Mainwaring on 16-stone Avril Malan. As Malan came charging down the touch-line, Mainwaring dropped him as through he had been shot with an elephant gun; so wounded was Malan that, sadly, he missed the post-match dinner. It was a tackle which entered into Barbarian folklore.

In 1965, the Springboks visited Ireland and Scotland on a short five-match tour and astoundingly they did not win a game. They lost 4 and drew 1; Ireland beat them 9 – 6, and Scotland at last avenged the 'Massacre' by winning 8 – 5. (It is strange that the only one of the four Home Union sides never to beat South Africa is Wales.) In 1968, the Springboks on a short tour of France won 5 and lost 1, but won

both Tests, 12 – 9 in Bordeaux and 16 – 11 in Paris.

This was the end of the good times for South Africa. The rancour of the anti-apartheid demonstrations on their 1969 – 70 tour made it politically impossible for them to continue touring. Although the Lions went to South Africa until 1980, and England went there in 1983, it now seems that only radical political change and the dismantling of apartheid can reopen the door for what is the world's most powerful Rugby nation. Recent events are a little more encouraging, and if President Botha is able to translate his recent promises into reality, then we can hope to enjoy again the challenge of playing the superb Springboks.

The most frequent visitors, and maybe the most popular as well as the most dreaded, are from the furthest point of the globe from the British Isles, from the Land of the Great Long White Cloud, as the Maoris call it. The All Blacks play the most elemental and passionate Rugby with a commitment and a dedication which British teams have been able to match only on rare occasions. Their record against the home countries is as emphatically in their favour as that of the Springboks. They have been to the

Success for the Lions.
Above *Gareth Edwards in action against Northern Transvaal on the undefeated tour of 1974.*
Left *Graham Price puts the pressure on Sid Going during the Lions' 13–9 win over New Zealand in the Second Test at Christchurch in 1977.*

IAN McCALLUM
SOUTH AFRICA

PIERRE VILLEPREUX
FRANCE

JOHN COLE
AUSTRALIA

BRYAN WILLIAMS
NEW ZEALAND

JO MASO
FRANCE

ROLAND BERTRANNE
FRANCE

'JOGGY' JANSEN
SOUTH AFRICA

STEPHEN KNIGHT
AUSTRALIA

GEORGE BARLEY
FIJI

WAYNE COTTRELL
NEW ZEALAND

DAWIE DE VILLIERS
SOUTH AFRICA

ELIE CESTER
FRANCE

HANNES MARAIS
SOUTH AFRICA

PETER JOHNSON
AUSTRALIA

ROY PROSSER
AUSTRALIA

RON URLICH
NEW ZEALAND

JONA QORO
FIJI

COLIN MEADS
NEW ZEALAND

FRIK DU PREEZ
SOUTH AFRICA

IAN KIRKPATRICK
NEW ZEALAND

CHRISTIAN CARRÈRE
FRANCE

GREG DAVIS
AUSTRALIA

BRIAN LOCHORE
NEW ZEALAND

The world-class squad from which the President's Overseas XV was chosen to celebrate the RFU Centenary at Twickenham.

107

Rugby fever.
Above *Bahrain supporters at the Hong Kong Sevens in 1984.*
Above right *The crowd at Ellis Park, Johannesburg during the Fourth Test against the Lions in 1974.*
Right *Welsh supporters enjoy a visit to Murrayfield.*

34 matches, won 32, lost 1 and drew 1. They won four of the five Tests, played a pointless game against Scotland, beat Ireland 6 – 5, Wales 6 – 0 (their first win since 1924), England 14 – 0 and France 12 – 3. These, the fifth All Blacks, were beaten only by Newport, who pipped them by the only score of a drop goal by John Uzzel to nil.

Wilson Whineray's 1963 All Blacks proved too powerful for the University side at Cambridge.
Far left *All Blacks v Southern Counties, 1953.*

British Isles nine times since the war and twice to France. In the period 1945 – 68 they came three times, with the usual devasting results.

After the unoffical tour of the Kiwis in 1945, the next post-war tour was in 1953, under the captaincy of the charming Bob Stuart. (Why is it that the All Black always have a tradition of magnificent captains? In 1962 they had Wilson Whineray and in 1967 Brian Lochore.) Stuart's men played 31 games in the British Isles and France, won 25, lost 4 and drew 2. They played five Tests, won three and lost two. They beat Ireland 14 – 3, England 5 – 0 and Scotland 3 – 0. They lost to Wales 13 – 8 and France 3 – 0, and were the last New Zealand side to concede defeat to Wales.

They were not among the best of the All Black sides to come here, because they were not particularly strong at half-back, but as always they had a strong pack with outstanding forwards in Peter Jones, Tiny White, Ian Clarke, Kevin Skinner and Ron Hemi, who used the tactics of attrition to win their battles. As a team they offered little in the way of running Rugby; their best back, by a mile, was Bob Scott.

The All Blacks did not return until 1963 – 64. When they did at last reappear, they played

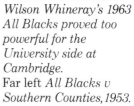

Again, they had a witheringly hard, driving pack, and they were the players who really mattered – men such as Wilson Whineray, Colin Meads, Waka Nathan, Kevin Tremain and Ken Gray. They were also fortunate to have a fantastic goal-kicker in Don Clarke, who seemed able to put them over from anywhere. Whineray became a much respected and popular leader and, when he scored his only try of the tour in the last match against the Barbarians, he was given a standing ovation by the capacity crowd.

Brian Lochore's 1967 side were only the second All Blacks to have an invincible record.

Don Clarke.
Above left *The powerful Colin Meads breaks free in the All Blacks' 33–3 win over the North of England, 1967.*

Fijian hooker Tukana catches Dewi Bebb at Cardiff in 1964.

Above right *The 1952 tourists from Thailand.*

Dartmouth College, New Hampshire on their way to a 5–0 win over the Old Millhillians during their 1958 tour.

They played 15 games, won 14 and drew 1. They won four Tests, beating England 23 – 11, Wales 13 – 6, France 21 – 15 and Scotland 14 – 3. The drawn game was against East Wales at Cardiff. It was a much shorter tour than usual, having been hastily arranged to take the place of a visit to South Africa, which was called off because of problems over apartheid and its application to the Maori players.

The team was managed by Charlie Saxton, so there were glimpses of the old Kiwi style behind the scrum, but it was their ferocious and uncompromising forward play which carried the tour. The sixth All Blacks were relentlessly physical and they destroyed almost every pack they met. Unhappily Colin Meads, one of the greatest forwards of all time, was sent off against Scotland for scything at Chisholm with his boot. Although Chisholm remonstrated on his behalf, feeling that Colin had held the kick at the last second, the Irish referee, Mr Kelleher, stood his ground. The only other instance of a tourist being sent off in an international match in the U.K. was in 1925, when Albert Freethy ordered off another All Black, Cyril Brownlie, at Twickenham in front of the Prince of Wales.

The most interesting and unusual incoming tour was by those exotic South Sea islanders, the Fijians, who in 1964 were invited to the Northern Hemisphere for the first time, by Wales. The tour did not have the approval of the International Board, but it proved to be a highly meaningful and worthwhile exercise; the Fijians were superb value with their free running and handling, and they epitomized the joy of Rugby as a running and handling game. They played five matches, included a memorable Test at Cardiff, for which no Welsh caps were awarded, before 50,000 spectators. A total of 13 tries was scored and the Fijians, who played with 14 men for most of the game, stormed back magnificently in the second half, and in a hurricane finish they came back from a 21-point deficit to score 13 points in the last 12 minutes. They lost by 28 points to 22 and the try count was seven to Wales and six to Fiji. They have been to the U.K. many times since, and are always exuberant and welcome.

PART FOUR

THE POLITICAL YEARS,
1969 – 1984

After the Springboks had comprehensively outplayed the British Lions in South Africa in 1968 by winning three of the four Tests and drawing the other, the spotlight remained on them in 1969 when they made a major tour of the British Isles. This

The Springboks arrive at London airport, October 1969, at the start of their controversial tour of the British Isles.

Five of the tourists take a photocall during a training session at Old Deer Park, Richmond. Left to right: Dow Walton, Dawie de Villiers, Ho de Villiers, Tom Bedford and Frik du Preez.

Police line the front of the stand at Twickenham for South Africa's match against Oxford University.

tour was to prove to be their last to Britain up to the present day, and it was just as notable for the politics which engulfed it as it was for the results of the matches.

In their two previous full tours the Springboks had only lost one match out of 27 in 1951, and one out of 30 in 1960, but in 1969 with intense political pressures undermining their tour they won only 15 of their 24 games which made a nonsense of their clear superiority over the British Isles in the summer of 1968. The groundswell of political agitation had grown during the Sixties and the anti-apartheid demonstrations which erupted throughout the four-month tour were destined to follow and plague South African Rugby from then on. Police escorts became an everyday occurrence, and the abrasive hostility of the groups of anti-apartheid demonstrators must have had a disturbing effect on team morale.

I remember quite clearly the eerie feeling when playing for Scotland against South Africa in their first international on that tour at Murrayfield in early December. There was a huge police presence at the ground, with the terraces behind both sets of goalposts reserved exclusively for the officers of the law with standing spectators restricted to just the East Terrace. The police were there to counter the various threats of destruction which ranged from a plane dropping thousands of tacks and nails onto the pitch to hundreds of spectators invading the field of play to stage a protest sit-in. In the event nothing happened except that Scotland beat South Africa for only the third time in eight internationals.

England inflicted similar treatment at Twickenham a fortnight later, and the only qualified consolation for the Springboks came in January when they drew their last two matches with Ireland and Wales. However, the world of politics gave them their most crushing defeat, and apart from a short tour to France in 1974 they have not been able to tour again in the Northern Hemisphere.

The Springboks had fulfilled all their touring commitments through the Fifties and Sixties but the oppresive, claustrophobic political pressures overwhelmed them during the Seventies. They have not been able to play in Britain, Ireland, France or Australia since 1974, and their only major tour abroad in the last ten years, to New Zealand in 1981, was full of controversy and mass demonstrations. There is no doubt that giant steps have been taken to make Rugby totally integrated in South Africa in recent years, and their supporters feel that no sooner have they fulfilled all the conditions required of them by world opinion than the goalposts are moved.

Their opponents, who are against having any sporting links with a country which practises apartheid, accept that sport generally in South Africa has become increasingly integrated but claims it is impossible to have normal sport in an abnormal society. Both sides feel equally passionately but the current consequences make it most unlikely that South Africa will tour any of the International Board countries in the near future, and to prove that they are still just about the best Rugby nation in the world they have to rely on incoming tours. Their present-day problems have been intensified because even major tours to South Africa are now in decline. The lack of a regular platform for South Africa to display its Rugby prowess has been the most significant change in international Rugby in the Seventies and Eighties.

Putting all political arguments aside, because that is not the purpose of this book, their enforced absence from centre-stage has to be measured, from a purely Rugby point of view, against their world domination of the game in the last hundred years. Their claim to be the top country in the world in the twentieth century is impossible to ignore. Rugby in South Africa is a way of life, and the results fully endorse their status.

They are comfortably ahead in their international matches against England (6 wins, 2 losses, 1 draw), Scotland (5 wins, 3 losses), Ireland (8 wins, 1 loss, 1 draw), Wales (6 wins, 1 draw), France (12 wins, 3 losses, 4 draws), Australia (21 wins, 7 losses), New Zealand (20 wins, 15 losses, 2 draws) and the British Lions (20 wins, 14 losses, 6 draws). Since the turn of the century the Springboks have enjoyed the best international record of any country in the world, and they have been the standard by which other sides are judged. However, with their exclusion from the inaugural World Cup in 1987, added to the fact that they are unlikely to tour abroad or have many incoming official major tours from the International Board countries in the near future, their pre-eminent position will become progressively harder to assess.

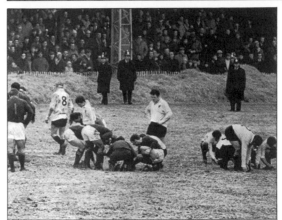

Dawie de Villiers gathers in a loose ball during the match against Cardiff.
Left *The players search for carpet tacks which had been thrown onto the pitch by demonstrators during the match against Western Counties.*
Below *Police were still required when the South African Barbarians toured in 1979.*

The British Isles first went on tour officially in 1910, and since that time there have been only two tours out of 15 in which the British Isles have won the Test series. In 1971 the Lions beat the All Blacks by 2 Tests to 1 with one drawn, and in 1974 the Lions beat the Springboks by 3 Tests to 0 with one drawn. There is no doubt that the early Seventies witnessed British Rugby hit unprecedented new heights, and for a few glorious years they were to remain perched at the summit, the undisputed top dogs of world Rugby.

The success in 1971 was the greatest possible fillip to Rugby in the Northern Hemisphere where it had almost become the norm to be second-best. It was like a child who, after spending a lifetime with his nose pressed up against the window looking at the sweets inside the shop, at last is allowed to taste them. Success tastes better than ever when it is rare and unexpected.

In 1971, after a week of preparation at Eastbourne on the south coast of England, the Lions flew to Australia. Queensland and New South Wales failed to appreciate that the point of the two warm-up matches in Brisbane and Sydney was to give the Lions match practice and a boost to their confidence. Queensland beat the Lions 15-11, and New South Wales only lost 14-12 after missing two kickable penalties late on. These two results guaranteed the Lions did not suffer unduly from complacency or overconfidence when they arrived in Auckland to prepare for the first of the 24 matches in New Zealand.

They beat the Counties and Thames Valley combined side followed by the combined King Country and Wanganui team. Victories followed against Waikato and the New Zealand Maoris before the first major challenge against Wellington who have been for so many years one of the top three New Zealand provinces. The Lions won 47-9, and the whole Rugby-playing world knew that the 1971 British Lions were decidedly a cut above average – a very special vintage. Five more provincial victories confirmed this view, and the first large step on the way to rewriting the history books was taken in Dunedin on 26 June when the Lions beat the All Blacks 9-3 in the First Test.

The British Lions manager, Doug Smith, had predicted at the outset that his team would win the First and Third Tests, lose the Second

and draw the Fourth to take the series. It all seemed a little uncanny when New Zealand squared the series in Christchurch on 10 July by the relatively emphatic margin of 22-12. The Lions continued to win every provincial match up to the Third Test, and assured themselves of a place in history as the first Lions team not to lose a series to New Zealand when they won that match 13–3 in Wellington. Three more provincial successes later and the Lions only had to draw the Fourth and final Test to win the Series. Doug Smith had predicted four months earlier that they would draw the last game and that is precisely what happened in Auckland in the second week of August. The score was 14–14.

No side to tour New Zealand before or since the 1971 Lions has matched their remarkable record. Unbeaten against the cream of New Zealand provincial Rugby, the Lions lost only one of their 24 matches, and in doing so scored 555 points, including 92 tries, whilst conceding only 204 points. The inspiration behind the triumph was unquestionably the brilliant coaching of Carwyn James. A former Welsh international fly-half who had spent most of his career in the shadow of Cliff Morgan, this quiet, unassuming, softly-spoken, highly successful coach of Llanelli masterminded the best four months for British Rugby in living memory. He was the supreme tactician and the most gifted psychologist who brought out the very best from a particularly talented squad of players, and showed great empathy in his handling of individuals.

Rugby has thrown up dozens of great players over the years but only a handful of really outstanding coaches. In the strange world of coaching which is largely peopled by men of Lilliput, Carwyn James ranked alongside those other giants – Fred Allen of New Zealand, Danie Craven of South Africa, Alan Jones of Australia, and Pierre Villepreux of France.

If Carwyn was the guiding light and ultimate catalyst, he had a tremendously capable nucleus of especially talented players around which to build his plan. J. P. R. Williams was one of the best full-backs ever to play Rugby, and whenever people think of a great pair of wing three-quarters the names of Gerald Davies and David Duckham would be very close to the top of the list. Duckham scored 11 tries and Davies 10 to underline their rare skills. John Dawes and Mike Gibson ideally complemented each other in the centre, and there can have been precious few better half-back partnerships than Barry John and Gareth Edwards.

The pack recovered from the loss of both first-choice props, Ray McLoughlin and Sandy Carmichael, through injury in the Canterbury match the week before the First Test. Neither played again on the tour, and Sean Lynch and Ian McLauchlan took over for all four Tests with John Pullin hooking. Willie John McBride, Delme Thomas and Gordon Brown shared the Tests at lock, with Brown the outstanding lineout player and the other two both excelling at the hard graft of forward play. Mervyn Davies was a No. 8 out of the top drawer, being

amazingly versatile as well as a dynamic lineout jumper, and he was flanked by equally gifted footballers in John Taylor (4 Tests), Peter Dixon (3) and Derek Quinnell (1). These were the names that were etched in the memories of everyone who was privileged to see the 1971 British Lions, and their reputation has not diminished one jot in the intervening years.

A handful of these key players joined the 1974 British Lions tour to South Africa, and they were accompanied by another crop of brilliant individuals to form the nucleus of the most successful Lions team ever. They became the only undefeated Lions in history by winning the first 21 matches of the tour and drawing the final Test. The captain was the popular

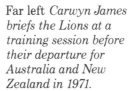

Left *John Dawes, the Lions captain, scores in the 21 - 9 win over Otago.*

Far left *Carwyn James briefs the Lions at a training session before their departure for Australia and New Zealand in 1971.*

Above *Gareth Edwards starts the movement which ended with a try for Peter Dixon.*

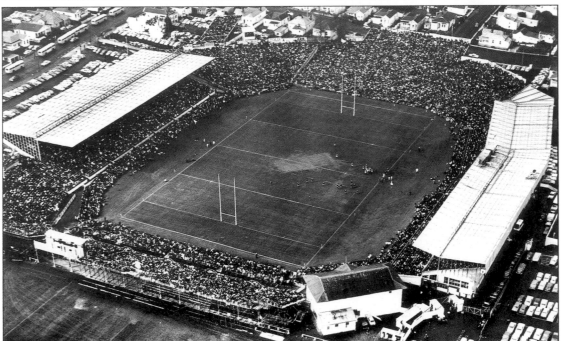

An aerial view of Auckland's Eden Park, packed to capacity for the Fourth Test.

Above *Willie John McBride, captain of the 1974 Lions.*

Irishman Willie John McBride, who was enjoying a record fifth Lions tour. He had been a tremendous servant to Irish and Lions Rugby, and he had earned a fearsome respect and admiration at home and abroad as an uncompromising, ruthlessly determined player. He was a natural leader of men, and he was ably supported by the coach, fellow Irishman Syd Millar. Syd was perhaps not quite as imaginative and creative as Carwyn James but he was utterly dedicated and equally effective. In the next ten years no coach from the four Home Unions was to enjoy anything like the success of either Syd Millar or Carwyn James, and it was to Millar's eternal credit that he kept British Rugby on top of the world in the mid-Seventies.

J. P. R. was still at full-back, but the new three-quarter line read: J. J. Williams, Dick Milliken, Ian McGeechan and Andy Irvine. Phil Bennett partnered Gareth Edwards at half-back. The Springboks were outclassed in the backs, as they had anticipated, but they were shocked to find that their forwards were also second best. Ian McLauchlan, Bobby Windsor and Fran Cotton made a formidable front row. McBride and Gordon Brown were far too good for all the different combinations of locks that

the Springboks tried as they became ever more desperate, and they could not match the Lions loose-forward trio of Roger Uttley, Mervyn Davies and Fergus Slattery.

The Lions won the First Test 12–3 in Cape Town, and they won the Second Test at Pretoria 28–9, scoring 4 tries to 0 in the process. The Lions won the Third Test in Port Elizabeth 26–9 to do what no other major touring side had ever done previously – win a full Test series against the Springboks in South Africa. France and England have beaten South Africa by each winning one international, but Australia and New Zealand and all previous British Lions teams had failed to do what the 1974 side did, and the enormity of their achievement must be measured in those terms. The Fourth and final Test ended in a 13–13 draw. This match finished controversially when Fergus Slattery appeared to score a try in the last minute to clinch victory but it was disallowed by the South African referee. By the time the next Lions tour to South Africa took place in 1980, the Tests were controlled by neutral referees.

Over three-quarters of a million spectators paid $3\frac{1}{2}$ million rand to watch the 22 matches. The Lions set all sorts of records. Their total of 729 points on tour has never been bettered.

Right *Andy Irvine on the burst against Natal with Mike Gibson in support.*
Above *The victorious Lions arrive back at Heathrow.*
Far right *Despite the lack of official recognition there were plenty of enthusiasts to welcome the players.*

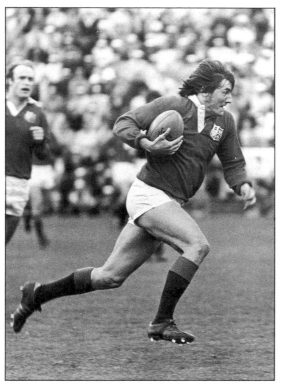

Their 97–0 win over South West Districts was the biggest defeat for a South African provincial team by a touring side. The record 107 tries scored by the Lions in South Africa included 16 against the hapless South West Districts. Andy Irvine's total of 156 points was the most scored by a British Lion in South Africa. The only other side to finish a major tour unbeaten this century were the 1924 All Blacks in Britain. The Lions had scaled the heights in 1971 and had remained there in 1974. The slide back down the other side of the mountain began on the next tour in 1977.

The hallmark of the 1971 British Lions was the wonderful play of the backs. The ran and handled from every conceivable situation and played the most exciting brand of Rugby seen from a Northern Hemisphere side since the 1955 Lions. They counter-attacked from deep defence on countless occasions, and their natural style was breathtaking to watch.

In Britain right through the Seventies those same intuitive skills were present in the Welsh side, and they found plenty of players to co-star along with J. P. R. Williams, Gerald Davies, Barry John, Phil Bennett and Gareth Edwards. The problem which confronted the

Barry John and Gareth Edwards are carried off the field after Wales had beaten Ireland to win the Triple Crown in 1971.

Delme Thomas wins possession in the lineout watched by Jeff Young (2) and Mervyn Davies during the 1971 game against England at Cardiff.

other countries in the Five Nations Championship was that if they deployed their resources to guard two or three players in particular, say Edwards, John and J. J. Williams, then, inevitably, there would be extra space for J. P. R. Williams to explode into the line or for Ray Gravell to punch a hole in midfield or for Gerald Davies to sprint and sidestep down the touch-line.

It was unusual not only to find so many exceptional players at the same time but it was also a pleasant bonus that so many of them lasted for as long as they did. The number of caps the best backs won tells its own story: J. P. R. Williams (55), Gareth Edwards (53), Gerald Davies (46), J. J. Williams (30), Steve Fenwick (30), Phil Bennett (29), Barry John (25), Ray Gravell (23) and John Dawes (22). The best forwards also spanned several years to give marvellous stability to the side: Graham Price (41), Mervyn Davies (38), Allan Martin (34), Geoff Wheel (32), Jeff Squire (29), Bobby Windsor (28), John Taylor (26), Delme Thomas (25) and Derek Quinnell (23).

In the period between 1969 and 1979 Wales won outright or shared the Championship on eight occasions. Admittedly their share of the title in 1973 was not especially glamorous or praiseworthy because that year resulted in a quintuple tie with each of the five countries winning two matches and losing two. On the other hand, it should be pointed out that the Championship was declared null and void in 1972 because some matches were not completed for various reasons. That year Wales had beaten England, Scotland and France, and they would have completed a Grand Slam if their match against Ireland had gone ahead and they had won it. In ten years of fierce competition, only in 1974 and 1977 did Wales fail to finish at the top of the table. Furthermore, six of their seven titles were claimed outright.

The Welsh team arrive in Paris before the win over France that was to give them the Grand Slam.

These glorious years of success were made even more memorable by the spectacular style of their play, and they thoroughly deserved to notch up three Grand Slams in 1971, 1976 and 1978 as well as six Triple Crowns in 1969, 1971, 1976, 1977, 1978 and 1979. If it was hard enough to beat them in their two away internationals each season, it was impossible to beat them at Cardiff Arms Park. Throughout the 11 years from 1969 until 1979 no team in the Five Nations Championship beat Wales in Cardiff. Australia on three occasions and South Africa once also failed to win at Cardiff, leaving only the New Zealand All Blacks in 1972 and 1978 to lower the Welsh colours. Of the 53 matches played in this period Wales won 36, lost 13 and drew 4, and the most fitting tribute to their exciting, expansive style of play can be gauged

Mervyn Davies, captain of the 1976 Grand Slam team.

The Welsh team before their match at Twickenham, 1972. Back row, left to right: Jeff Young, Clive Rowlands (coach), Arthur Lewis, Roy Bergiers, Mervyn Davies, Geoff Evans, Barry Llewelyn, Delme Thomas, Dave Morris. Front row: J.P.R. Williams, John Bevan, John Taylor, John Lloyd (captain), Barry John, Gareth Edwards, Gerald Davies.

by the fact that they scored 904 points including 123 tries.

Gareth Edwards and Gerald Davies, who both first played for Wales in the late Sixties, each scored 20 international tries to share the record before they both retired in 1978. Gareth Edwards also set one record which is most unlikely ever to be beaten – he won his 53 caps consecutively. If you consider that only one international player in a hundred will win over 50 caps, the odds must be one in a hundred thousand that such a player would manage to avoid injury or even the flu for more than ten years, and also not, at any stage, incur the wrath of the selectors. It speaks volumes for the high level of fitness that Gareth attained that he never missed an international during 12 seasons of Rugby at the top.

It was also a reflection on his consummate genius that Wales had such a superb run of success in the Seventies. Stripped of all their famous stars, Wales have failed to earn even a share of the Championship in the first few years of the Eighties.

Derek Quinnell fails to prevent Dave Loveridge's pass during the All Blacks' win at Cardiff, 1978, while (left to right) Frank Oliver, Bryan Williams, Bill Osborne and Brad Johnstone look on.

At a respectable distance behind Wales, France have been the next most successful side in the Five Nations Championship in the last twenty years. They have emulated Wales by achieving the Grand Slam on three occasions in that time, in 1968, 1977 and 1981. They also shared the Championship in 1970, 1983 and 1986, and they have produced not only many of the best and most exciting players at international level throughout this period, they have also played some of the most spectacular and entertaining Rugby. France did not win the title outright until 1959, and by the late Sixties their reputation lay in their ability to unearth

magnificent three-quarters. This assembly line of world-class backs continued in the Seventies and Eighties with centres such as Jean-Pierre Lux, Jo Maso, Didier Codorniou, Philippe Sella and Roland Bertranne, their most capped player with 52 caps, full-backs such as Pierre Villepreux, Jean-Michel Aguirre and Serge Blanco, and wings such as Jean-François Gourdon and Jean-Luc Averous.

The big difference in recent times has been the dramatic improvement in the quality of the French forwards. It began to evolve with men of the stature of Benoit Dauga, Elie Cester, Walter and Claude Spanghero and Jean-Pierre Bastiat who all won plenty of lineout possession

Right (Left to right) Rodriguez, Rives, Lescarboura, Dintrans, Blanco and Estève are serenaded by Dospital and his Basque band at a post-match dinner.
Far right Jacques Fouroux.
Below Another French break-out led by Jean-Pierre Rives.
Below right Didier Codorniou with the ball.

Left *Serge Blanco.*
Far left *Philippe Dintrans.*

Jean-Pierre Bastiat.

and were also natural footballers. They have had top-class hookers such as René Benesis, Alain Paco and Philippe Dintrans flanked by some formidable props, hewn from granite in the indestructible shapes of Jean Iracabal, Armand Vaquerin, Gerard Cholley and Robert Paparemborde. From a succession of brilliant loose forwards, Jean-Pierre Rives, Jean-Claude Skréla and Jean-Luc Joinel with over 120 caps between them would grace any squad of the best players in world Rugby. They now boast tremendous strength in depth, and with their furiously competitive club system they have more good players fulfilling their potential than any of the Home Unions.

Temperamental outbreaks of indiscipline have cost them dear in the 1980s when they might well have collected two more Championship titles, and it can certainly be argued that the rather eccentric coaching of Jacques Fouroux has not always been to their advantage. But they have proved over and over again that in good conditions, with the sun shining, in front of their own fiercely patriotic, partisan, Parisian crowd, they are irresistible and unstoppable. They are justifiably renowned

Robert Paparemborde.

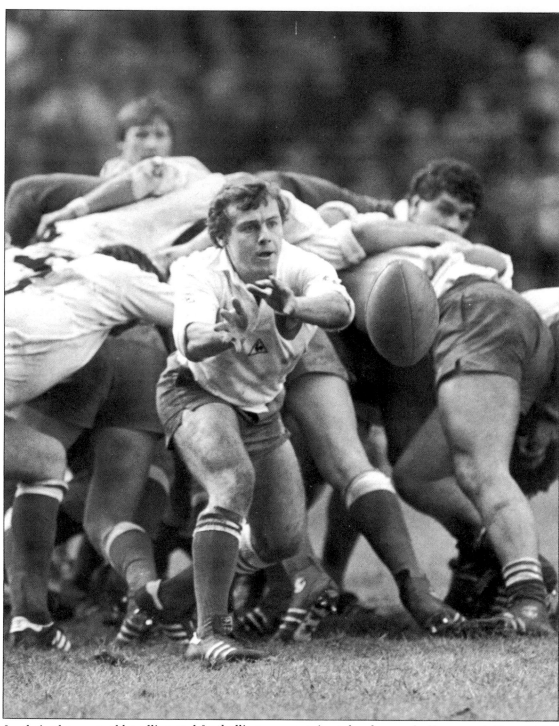

Jérôme Gallion.

for their phenomenal handling and footballing skills, their willingness to run with the ball, their insight into the game, their support play and their ability not only to counter-attack but to create something out of nothing. They have a certain style, class and effervescent *élan* which the Home Unions are struggling to recapture after the heady, halcyon days of the early Seventies.

English Rugby has been haunted by one statistic in the two decades since 1963. Only once in all those years, with all their manpower and resources, have England won the Championship. Between 1883 and 1963, England were outright winners of the title on 17 occasions and they shared the title a further nine times. Twenty-six successes in 80 years is a very respectable strike-rate; once in 23 years is definitely not.

A substantial section of Rugby followers blame poor selection for England's long disastrous run, but though that has been a strong contributory factor on its own, it is too simplistic an explanation. The fact is that the whole structure of Rugby in England is not as strong as it should be, and the system compares unfavourably with other major Rugby-playing countries.

Ranfurly Shield matches in New Zealand and the Currie Cup games in South Africa give the top provincial players the added sharpness, edge and experience which help to distinguish the great players from the merely good players.

Australia are in an equally strong position because their national team is selected almost exclusively from the New South Wales side and the Queensland side. In the New Pacific Championship, New South Wales and Queensland along with Fiji take on the three current outstanding New Zealand provinces – Auckland, Wellington and Canterbury. This is a round-robin tournament which means the Australian selectors can see their best 30 players in action in five matches each.

France and Wales each have an excellent club system which is intensely competitive and encourages the best players to join the best clubs to concentrate the talent in about half a

In New Zealand and South Africa the selectors are able to see their best players in action at provincial level, which means the cream of talent in those countries will be concentrated in six or eight extremely powerful sides, and they will play in a highly competitive series of matches in which only the top players survive and the weaknesses of those just below international level will be exposed. The provincial championship in those two countries goes a very long way to ensuring the selectors can pick the best available Test team. The

dozen sides. Scotland have introduced a league system with 98 clubs participating in seven divisions. The national side is picked almost exclusively from the teams in the First Division and the five districts which take part in a round-robin championship in the first half of the season. From the South, the North and Midlands, Edinburgh, Glasgow, and the Anglo-Scots, the national squad is selected. The Irish have a few top clubs which attract the best players, and the best 60 play in the inter-provincial championship. After Ulster, Leinster, Munster and Connacht have done battle, the teams are chosen for the Final Trial, which gives the selectors a last chance to see their squad in action under pressure before naming their side for the opening international in the

England v Proteas in Cape Town on their undefeated tour of South Africa in 1972 Left Tony Neary scores for England in their 16-10 victory over New Zealand in Auckland, 1973.

The England squad in training, 1974.
Below The Gloucester front row – Blakeway, Mills and Preedy – selected to play in the First Test on the 1984 South African tour.

country but this has been a notable failure in its bid to improve standards. Unlike the leagues north of the border, the teams in the merit tables do not play their matches on fixed Saturdays during the season, which instantly dilutes interest amongst the public and the media; what is more, the clubs in any given merit table do not necessarily all play against each other. This means a team can finish top of their table without playing the sides which finish second and third.

The future must bring improvement. At present the prospect, indeed the Rugby Football Union's promise, of a proper, realistic, meaningful club championship in the 1990s, producing a league system with the best players performing for the best clubs in the First Division is to be welcomed enthusiastically. Further intense club competition would continue to be provided by the John Player Special Cup which has been the only worthwhile barometer for English clubs since its inception as a Knock-Out Cup in 1972.

The County Championship, which began almost a hundred years ago in 1889, has served

Championship. The Irish selectors do not make many mistakes.

However, in England, with the top players spread too thinly across far too many clubs covering the whole country, it is much harder to determine the best 15 players. Instead of leagues like Scotland have, England devised a series of merit tables in every part of the

Dominant figures in the Seventies. Top (left to right) *Hugo Porta (Argentina), Jean-Pierre Rives (France), Gheorge Dumitru (Rumania).*
Centre *Ollie Campbell (Ireland), Fran Cotton and Bill Beaumont (England).*
Bottom *Phil Bennett (Wales), John Rutherford (Scotland).*

Front row power. The imposing French line-up of Cremaschi, Dintrans and Paparemborde.

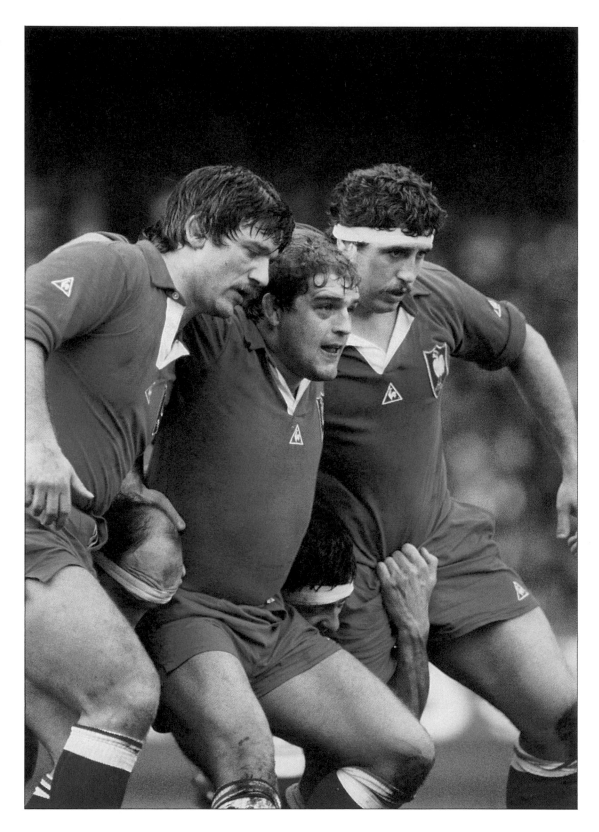

Far left *The Pontypool front row of Graham Price, Bobby Windsor and Charlie Faulkner.* Left *Australia's front three – Ron Graham, Peter Horton and John Meadows – against Scotland at Murrayfield in 1975.* Below *The Lions' combination of Graham Price, Peter Wheeler and Fran Cotton.*

Respected referees.
Top *Jean-Pierre Bonnet (Wales v England, 1979).*
Centre right *Francis Palmade (Wales XV v Rumania, 1978).*
Centre left *Clive Norling (France v England, 1980).*
Bottom *David Burnett (France v Wales, 1979).*

its purpose and is now outdated. Twenty-seven counties are currently involved in the championship which means that over 400 players are on view on a Saturday of county matches which echoes the argument that the available talent is spread too thinly to make a substantial contribution to the national cause. Considerably better than the County Championship has been the Divisional Championship, which was instituted in 1980 and which just happened to be the year that England last won the Five Nations Championship. Surprisingly, this competition was soon dropped but it has now been resurrected, and with the best 60 players in England representing the North, the Midlands, the South and South-West, and London in a round-robin tournament over three successive Saturdays the selectors should be in an excellent position to choose their national squad and international team.

After twenty years languishing in the doldrums, with the only high point coming in 1980, England look at long last as if they are heading towards a better future.

Lancashire, county champions in 1973, provided a succession of internationals through the Seventies. Here scrum-half Ashton receives the ball from, left to right, Neary, Anderson, Seabrook and Leadbetter.

Peter Wheeler with the successful Leicester side after the 1981 John Player Cup final. Their club success led to representative honours for many of the team.

England completed the Grand Slam six times between 1913 and 1928 but there followed a span of 51 years with only one similar success in 1957. After so many barren years the triumph of Bill Beaumont's side in 1980 was particularly popular and welcome. The two guiding lights behind the ultimate triumph of English Rugby over its nebulous system and structure were the coach, Mike Davis, and the captain, Bill Beaumont.

They were admirably supported by a team full of great characters, rich talent and rare

dropped. At last, for one splendid year, these stars came together: Hare; Carleton, Woodward, Dodge, Slemen; Horton, Smith; Cotton, Wheeler, Blakeway, Colclough, Beaumont, Neary, Scott and Uttley. Centres Tony Bond (1) and Nick Preston (2) and lock Nigel Horton (1) also played in the opening two matches.

The quest for the Holy Grail began encouragingly with an impressive win against Ireland at Twickenham by 24–9. Steve Smith, John Scott and Mike Slemen scored the only three tries of the game, and Dusty Hare kicked the other 12 points. England's superiority was

Bill Beaumont manages to get the ball to Steve Smith in the match against Ireland during the Grand Slam season.

Top Mike Davis, an *inspiring coach.*

experience who found a special spirit and dedication as they restored a sense of pride in England's performance. Only 18 players were chosen for the four matches, and this squad contained not only the best team to represent England for a good many years, it was full of famous names. The list of players underlined the solid strength of English Rugby in 1980 and made it all the more remarkable when one tried to comprehend how the selectors had treated so many of the players so badly in the preceding years. First they selected them for the team, and no sooner were they in than they were

total in every respect, and augured well for the rest of the season. Their mighty pack won twice as much lineout possession as Ireland, shaded the set scrums and from that platform secured two-thirds of all the rucks and mauls. They had the best pack in the Championship.

Their powerful juggernaut outclassed France in the second game; the half-backs Smith and Horton were able skilfully to dictate the course of the match, and England won in Paris for the first time in 16 years and for the first time ever at the new French arena, the Parc des Princes. Relishing the command of their forwards, Smith and Horton were again the master tacticians, and it is worth mentioning that these two players had suffered worse than most from the vagaries of English selection in the late Seventies. Horton dropped two goals, Hare landed one penalty, and Preston and Carleton scored one try each.

Wales scored the only two tries of the next game at Twickenham but three penalties from Dusty Hare earned England a one-point victory, and left them on the brink of proving that the impossible was possible, and a Grand Slam was suddenly within their reach. This game was England's only moment of doubt, and it could hardly have been closer and more dramatic.

Welsh flanker, Paul Ringer, who had had a somewhat chequered career prior to 1980, was sent off after a quarter of an hour for a late and dangerous head-high tackle on John Horton. Ringer became only the second player to be sent off in an international at Twickenham; the All-Black, Cyril Brownlie, was the first in 1925. The referee, the admirable David Burnett, did well to control an explosive contest, but indicative of the abrasive nature of the game was the fact that he awarded 34 penalties, and there were also several interruptions to the flow of play while injured players received treatment. Wales, reduced to 14 men, found the odds stacked against them, but the winning points only came in injury time when Hare kicked his third penalty.

Like any good Variety bill, the best was saved till last, and England earned their standing ovation at Murrayfield with a marvellous win over Scotland in the grand climax. The score, 30–12, gave England their highest points total ever in a Calcutta Cup match, and another milestone was reached as Tony Neary, in his 43rd international, became England's most capped player.

It was a classic, highly entertaining match of the highest class, and in scoring five tries to two England earned their Grand Slam triumph in style. The English tries were all scored by backs – one each for Mike Slemen and Steve Smith whilst John Carleton helped himself to three. An English Championship had been a long time coming, but after this thrilling victory the English supporters who had invaded Edinburgh and the estimated 14 million who watched on BBC Television and listened on radio must have thought it had all been worthwhile.

Friendly greetings after England's win in Paris.

Dusty Hare's third penalty goal which defeated Wales at Twickenham.

The line-up for the vital Calcutta Cup match.

Half a dozen clubs have dominated English Rugby during the Seventies and Eighties with each of the four national divisions throwing up at least one side of outstanding calibre.

The geographical complexities of the club system impose certain inevitable limitations on claims that one side is at a given moment the best in the country. Several hundred miles separate some of the top senior sides and it is a regrettable fact that not all the best sides in the North have regular fixtures against the best in the South and South-West.

Happily the introduction of the John Player Cup in the early Seventies has considerably helped to determine the pecking order in the past few years. Before the Cup provided a reliable guide to form, the one side to emerge was London Welsh. In the late Sixties and early Seventies they not only boasted a remarkably successful record, they also played the most delightful brand of Rugby. Their strength was highlighted by the high proportion of their players who represented Wales at that time, culminating in seven being chosen to tour New Zealand with the British Lions in 1971: John Dawes (captain), J.P.R. Williams, Gerald Davies, Mervyn Davies, John Taylor, Mike Roberts and Geoff Evans.

Their wonderful run ended as the Knock-Out Cup started in 1972. Gloucester won the inaugural tournament and triumphed again in 1978 and in 1982, when they shared the trophy with Moseley. The success of Gloucester in this period was built round a formidable mountain of a pack and if their style of play has not always been very aesthetic and rarely excited the purist, it has nonetheless been ruthlessly effective.

Coventry won the Cup in 1973 and 1974 and could justifiably claim to have been the best side in the Midlands in the first half of the Seventies. The North-East took over in 1976 and 1977 when Gosforth deservedly won in successive years with a display of solid, efficient Rugby.

It fell to Leicester to add a new, exciting dimension and raise the whole standard of club Rugby in England with three years of memorable performances between 1979 and 1981. They won the Cup three years in a row and their spectacular style of play was a great credit to their dedicated coach, Chalky White.

They had the most gifted back division in the country with England fly-half Les Cusworth the play-maker, fellow international centres Paul Dodge and Clive Woodward able to provide the power and the dash and, if all else failed, they could always rely on Dusty Hare to kick goals with incredible consistency.

In the last three years Bath have emulated Leicester's achievement, winning the Cup in 1984, 1985 and 1986, and they too have played some great Rugby. They have had a dozen international players in their club during this period of ascendency and apart from their domination in England they have also achieved plenty of success against the best Welsh clubs. In the past twenty years I would suggest London Welsh, Leicester and Bath have produced the three best sides in England.

In Wales four sides can claim to have dominated the game for a reasonable length of time in recent years. The first sustained run of success belonged to Llanelli. They won the Schweppes Welsh Cup four years in succession from 1973 to 1976 and they did it in style with talented players like Phil Bennett, Ray Gravell, J.J. Williams and Derek Quinnell leading the way. In 1974 and 1975 Llanelli also finished top of the Welsh Club Championship. On four other occasions in the last dozen years they have finished in the top four.

In the same period Pontypool have reached the top four on nine occasions, winning the Club Championship on four of them. Pontypool also won the Cup in 1983 and it is worth mentioning to their many critics who have accused them of playing excessively dull, negative nine-man Rugby that their strength was undoubtedly in their formidable pack. Apart from the famous Pontypool front row of Graham Price, Bobby Windsor and Charlie Faulkner, Pontypool have had several other redoubtable Welsh international forwards to stiffen the back five. With players like John Perkins, Jeff Squire, Terry Cobner, Eddie Butler and Mark Brown, it was not a major surprise that they based their tactics round their pack.

Playing much more enterprising and attractive Rugby and enjoying similar success, Cardiff finished in the top four clubs in the League nine times between 1972 and 1985 and they won the Cup in 1981, 1982 and 1984. They have probably been the most consistent side throughout this whole period and in due recognition of their skilful play, several of their gifted players have won international caps.

With not quite such a galaxy of talent to draw on, Bridgend enjoyed a purple patch between 1979 and 1982. In those four years they won the Welsh Cup twice, were runners-up twice and won the League once. Several other clubs, notably Pontypridd, Swansea and Newport have had their moments, but overall they have remained in the shadow of Cardiff, Llanelli, Pontypool and Bridgend.

In Scotland, two clubs have almost exclusively carved up the Scottish Schweppes Club Championship since its inception in 1973. Hawick, in a class of their own, have won the title on nine occasions and Gala, their nearest challengers, three times. Heriot's FP under the captaincy of Andy Irvine became the only other side to win the Scottish First Division title when they finished the 1978–79 season perched on top. Throughout this period Hawick, Gala and Heriot's have provided the bulk of the Scotland international team and no other club could claim to have matched the achievements of these three top sides in the fiercely competitive world of the Scottish league system.

In Ireland, it is easier to select the outstanding club sides in each of the four provinces separately rather then trying to pick the best two or three in the whole of Ireland at any given time. Ulster, Leinster, Munster and Connacht each run a League during the season and have a knock-out Cup competition, and over the years a couple of sides in each area have consistently risen to the top.

In Leinster, Lansdowne and Wanderers

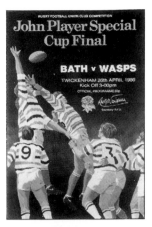

share the best record with three League titles each and four Cup victories. They represent the best of Leinster in the Seventies and Eighties, but not too far behind come St Mary's College and Blackrock College, who each deserve creditable mention.

In Ulster, CIYMS and Ballymena have unquestionably been the most successful two clubs in the Seventies, whilst Bangor have enjoyed the best record in the Eighties. In Munster, Cork Constitution are out on their own with six League titles and four Cup triumphs since 1972. Chasing hard, but at a respectable distance, come University College Cork and Garryowen. Finally, in Connacht, Corinthians and Galwegians are head and shoulders above the other clubs in the area, but it should be added that the general standard in the West of Ireland is not as high as elsewhere and relatively few players from this area have won international caps recently.

John Fidler of Gloucester towers over Leicester scrum-half Stephen Kenny in the John Player Cup final, 1978.

Top *The 1986 final was Bath's third successive win in the competition.*

Top left *Celebrations in the bath at Twickenham after Gosforth had beaten Rosslyn Park in the 1976 John Player Cup final.*

Leicester on their way to another win, this time at the expense of London Scottish.

The Seventies were not a good time for the Irish and the Scots, with the only success coming in 1974 when Willie John McBride led Ireland to the Championship. Nevertheless, from two countries each with a population one-tenth the size of England and, in consequence, limited playing strength, they have left the other Home Unions trailing in their wake in the past few years. Five times in the Eighties the Irish and Scots have either won outright or shared the title. Ireland succeeded in 1982, 1983 and 1985, helping themselves to the Triple Crown en route in 1982 and 1985; Scotland shared the title in 1986 but had their real moment of glory in 1984.

In that year they not only took the title outright, they won the Triple Crown for the first time since 1938 and completed the Grand Slam for the first time since 1925. Kilts had been flying at half-mast for 59 years prior to the 1984 triumph, and the whole of Scotland, not just the Rugby followers, savoured the moment of glory when the crowning victory came at the expense of France in the final game at Murrayfield.

The season had begun promisingly with a 15–9 win at Cardiff against Wales, and the Scots followed up with a home win over England by 18 points to 6 to retain the Calcutta Cup. In Dublin the Scots gained their most emphatic victory when they ran in five tries to beat Ireland 32–9. Some critics said that France, with a display riddled with indiscipline, beat themselves, but if that was the case the Scots went out of their way to give them all the assistance they could muster. The winning margin of 21–12 was convincing enough, and in the final table that season the Scots finished top, having scored 10 tries, France were second with nine tries, Wales were third with five tries, England were fourth with two tries, and Ireland were bottom with one try. For once the Championship accurately reflected the ability of the five countries to score tries.

Captained by Jim Aitken, at 36 years of age not exactly in his first or even second flush of youth, they had a nucleus of some of the best

John Rutherford.

Above right *Alan Tomes gives protection to Roy Laidlaw in Scotland's win over Ireland in 1984.*

Right *The Scottish team leave the field at Lansdowne Road having won the Triple Crown.*

Delight for Scottish captain Jim Aitken, as Jim Calder scores the try against France that gave Scotland their 1984 Grand Slam.

Below Peter Dods who converted that try and added a further penalty before the end.

players in world Rugby. Hooker Colin Deans and tight-head prop Iain Milne were both exceptional players, and so too were all three loose forwards – David Leslie, Iain Paxton and Jim Calder. The half-backs, John Rutherford and Roy Laidlaw, now hold the world record for the most number of appearances together (30), and they were the key figures in masterminding the tactical triumph. Full-back Peter Dods scored 50 points in the season which remains a Scottich record, and his feat emphasizes how important an accurate goal-kicker is under the modern laws. It all added up to a wonderful success story for the Scots' devoted coach, Jim Telfer.

The Irish were also fortunate to have an outstanding coach at this time in Tom Kiernan, the former Ireland and British Lions full-back. He wrought miracles in 1982 and 1983 as he guided Ireland to the top, and there was the same sort of euphoria in Dublin in 1982, when they clinched their first Triple Crown since 1949, as there was at Murrayfield when the

Ollie Campbell.

Above right *Tom Kiernan presents his side to the Prince of Wales before their match with Wales at Cardiff, 1969.*

Above far right *Ciaran Fitzgerald directs his team in 1982.*

Scots celebrated two years later.

Led by their hooker, Ciaran Fitzgerald, the Irish had several experienced forwards to hold the pack together. These included prop Phil Orr, locks Moss Keane and Donal Lenihan, and loose-forwards Fergus Slattery, Willie Duggan and John O'Driscoll. At fly-half Ollie Campbell was a genius of a footballer, and he was also a prodigious goal-kicker. In a highly combative and, at times, exciting three-quarter line, Michael Kiernan and Trevor Ringland confirmed they were both players with glittering futures ahead of them.

They began with a home win over Wales (20–12), they travelled to Twickenham and beat England (16–15) and capped the season at Lansdowne Road with a 22–12 win over Scotland. That year they lost to France but they gained revenge in 1983 and went on to share the title with other wins over Scotland and England.

It was argued by some of the pundits that British Rugby had plumbed new depths in the Eighties, and that Ireland and Scotland were both moderate teams winning Championships of a very modest standard. These sentiments seem quite unnecessarily ungenerous. It was like saying that David was just lucky his missile was not blown off-course on its way to felling Goliath or he would have been obliterated. To put their achievement into a proper perspective, the Irish and the Scots took on the might of England, Wales and France, and they came out on top; furthermore, they both thoroughly deserved their success.

Moss Keane.

Right *Fergus Slattery comes to grips with Jean-Pierre Rives.*

The British Isles' success in the early Seventies was gradually eroded by the steady progress made in New Zealand and South Africa, and the most recent Lions tours have shown a marked decline in the standard of British Rugby. In 1977, the Lions played 25 matches in New Zealand and won all of them except three of the four Tests and the game against New Zealand Universities. Three-quarters of a million people watched the Lions and paid three-quarters of a million pounds for the privilege, but the weather did its best to ruin

the entire venture. Rain plagued the tourists almost every single day for the 14-week tour, and sodden, muddy pitches and a slippery ball became the unacceptable norm.

For the captain, Phil Bennett, the coach, John Dawes, and the 33 players, it was a soul-destroying experience, and yet they came frustratingly close to squaring the Test series with a supreme effort in the Final Test. After losing the First Test 16–12 and the Third Test 19–7, and winning the Second Test 13–9, they led 9–6 in the Fourth Test as full time approached. At that stage, Morgan missed a

Phil Bennett gives some half-time encouragement to his Lions team on the 1977 tour of New Zealand.

137

Stu Wilson scores his 16th try for New Zealand to equal Ian Kirkpatrick's record, in the Third Test at Dunedin, 1983. He was to score three more tries in the Fourth Test.

Beaumont, Wheeler (2), Duggan (8), Price (3) and Bennett (10) watch with delight as Morgan scores in the Fourth Test at Auckland, 1977.

penalty which would almost certainly have given the Lions victory and a share of the Test series. Instead, the Lions tried to cling to their three-point lead for the final few minutes of the match only to be thwarted in injury time when Gary Knight scored a try to win the game for New Zealand.

In 1980 in South Africa the Lions managed to win all 14 provincial matches and the Fourth Test, but unfortunately they had lost the first three Tests and the series. To their credit, the Lions were in contention right up to the last few minutes of each of the Tests they lost. They were crippled by an injury list which necessitated eight players being flown out to replace the eight worst-injured Lions. Other players were injured at critical times to further disrupt the rhythm of the team, and the captain, the redoubtable Bill Beaumont, and the dedicated manager Syd Millar and coach Noel Murphy did a most commendable job to achieve as good a record as they did.

The Lions' Test matches were under the control of neutral referees for the first time with the Frenchmen Jean-Pierre Bonnet and Francis Palmade in charge of two each. The Lions lost the First Test by four points (26–22) and the Third Test by just two points (12–10), and it was only in the Second Test (26–19) that the South Africans won by a margin of more than one score. The Lions' 17–13 victory in the Final Test was a triumph of spirit and determination in the face of adversity at the end of a gruelling tour.

The gradual decline in British Rugby's fortunes had rapidly accelerated by 1983 when Ciaran Fitzgerald's Lions suffered the ignominy of achieving, after Mike Campbell-Lamerton's 1966 Lions, only the second whitewash inflicted on the British Isles this century. Apart from losing all four Tests, two provincial games were also lost to Auckland and Canterbury which meant only 12 of the 18 matches were won.

The First Test was the closest the Lions came when they lost 16–12, but a 9–0 defeat in the Second Test and a 15–8 loss in the Third Test gave the series to New Zealand. The final humiliation came in the Fourth Test in Auckland when the British Lions, rudderless and running around in ever-decreasing circles, went down by the biggest defeat in Lions history – 38–6. Although bad selection and injuries were contributory factors, the main reason for the New Zealand success was that their leading players were better individually and collectively than the Lions. They had a superior mastery of the game's basic skills, and British Rugby was left with much to contemplate as they began the process of rebuilding from the ashes of 1983.

In their complementary role as tourists to Britain, the record of the All Blacks in the Seventies was no less impressive. In 1972–73 they beat Wales, England and Scotland but were held to a draw by Ireland. On their four short tours they only lost one international in total, and that was against England in 1984.

That year they beat Scotland as they did in 1979 when they also defeated England. In 1974 they won their only international against Ireland, and in 1980 they inflicted the same treatment on Wales. In 1978 under the captaincy of Graham Mourie they achieved a notable Grand Slam at the expense of the four Home Unions, and on that tour of 18 matches Munster were the only side to beat them.

Roger Baird seems to have his hands full with Allen Hewson (left) and Stu Wilson in the First Test at Christchurch, 1983.

Far left above *Graham Mourie puts the pressure on England's scrum-half Malcolm Young at Twickenham, 1978. (Below) Andy Dalton (left) and Ciaran Fitzgerald leave the field after the All Blacks' win at Dunedin, 1983.*

Dave Loveridge is protected by John Ashworth (left) and Andy Dalton during the Third Test at Dunedin, 1983.

The laws of Rugby have been changed at periodic intervals to improve the game. It is done primarily for the players but it is also expected to make things better for the spectators. The two most far-reaching changes in the Sixties came in 1964 when, firstly, at a lineout, the three-quarter lines of both sides had to line up at least 10 yards behind the lineout and remain 10 yards deep until the lineout ended; secondly, at scrums, rucks and mauls, the offside line was no longer where the ball was but the hindmost foot of the player's own side.

These two new laws gave backs much more space in which to operate, and most of the recent changes have been designed to encourage players to run and handle by giving them more room and opportunity to indulge themselves. In 1969, the application of the advantage law was extended which meant the referee could let the game flow more often if there was an advantage to the non-transgressing side.

There was also a significant change to the offside law which stated that after the ball had been kicked ahead the team could be put onside not just by the kicker himself as previously, but by any player behind the kicker when he kicked the ball. However, the most interesting change came in the section on foul play which was in many ways a reflection of the changing standards in society at the time. For the first time it was felt necessary by the International Board to put in writing that 'All players must respect the authority of the referee and must not dispute his decisions.' That such sentiments had to be written into the laws of the game would doubtless have had Wavell Wakefield and all the old pioneers of Rugby spinning in their graves.

In 1973 the lineout was becoming an unsightly mess, and the laws were altered to insist on a gap between the two sets of forwards of two feet with players standing one yard apart in their own line. The idea was to eliminate the obvious sources of villainy by having plenty of gaps to allow the referee to see what was going

Jean-Pierre Bonnet signals a try for Scotland to the delight of Jim Calder as Scotland score a resounding 34-18 victory at Cardiff, 1982.

Meirion Joseph keeps a sharp eye on Scottish hooker Duncan Madsen as he moves in on Malcolm Young during the 1972 Calcutta Cup match.

on. Good clean lineout ball, with the back divisions standing 20 yards apart, was expected to favour more open Rugby. Another change was also made to help running Rugby; the knock-on offence was eased. If a player knocked the ball forward but caught it before it hit the ground, play was to be allowed to continue.

In 1975 all the measurements in the laws were changed from yards to metres. Metrification meant the 25-yard line became the 22-metre line, and so on.

In 1977 there was an attempt to reduce the number of matches being won by penalty goals. A start had been made in this direction in 1971 when the value of the try was increased from three points to four. The next step was to reduce the number of offences which allowed a team to kick directly at goal. In 1977, for several minor offences such as a crooked feed or foot-up at the set scrum, a free-kick was awarded instead of a penalty.

In the same year, the 'mark' was changed again. In 1969 a player had to be stationary when calling for a 'mark' or 'free kick' as it was to become known. In 1977, he could only make such a call in his own half of the field, and in 1979 he could only do so inside his own 22-metre area. The dice were being loaded in

favour of the attacking team. There was further evidence of this trend in 1982 when the referee, if in doubt, was instructed to award a set scrum to the attacking team rather than the defending side as hitherto.

In 1979 it was agreed that the referee had an almost impossible task in trying to control every aspect of play, and the laws were changed to empower the touch-judges in international matches to intervene for all acts of foul play which the referee may have missed. This new power of the touch-judge was extended in the 1980s to cover all matches involving touring teams.

The other change worth mentioning was the introduction of replacements. Too often a player with a bad injury stayed on the field ostensibly to help his side, but usually he merely aggravated the injury. In 1968, to combat this, the International Board allowed six replacements to be available at every international match or any game involving a touring team. Two of these six players could replace any players whom the match doctor deemed to be unfit to continue. This sensible law was extended in 1974 to cover other major matches, and it is rare nowadays to witness an injured player remaining on the field.

One of the most interesting developments in the last 20 years has been the increase of short tours to Britain by non-International Board countries. The prolific list tells its own story. Fiji came on tour in 1970 and 1982. Argentina have paid three visits in 1973, 1976 and 1978. Similarly, Japan had short tours in 1973, 1976 and 1983. Canada have also made three tours in 1971, 1979 and 1983 whilst Tonga in 1974, America in 1977, and the Maoris in 1982 have each visited Britain once during this period. Rumania have also spread their wings and visited Britain four times recently to play an international over here. They played in Wales in 1979, in Ireland in 1980, in Scotland in 1981, and in England in 1984. The game is played in more countries now than ever before, and this is reflected in the ever-increasing number of tours.

The expansion of the game has been best demonstrated in the last six years by the success of the Cathay Pacific Hong Kong Bank Sevens, to which teams and press travel from all over the world. This seven-a-side international tournament is without doubt the most spectacular, exotic, best organized Rugby competition of its kind in the world, and it has consistently produced the highest standard of Sevens Rugby seen anywhere.

I was not surprised on my first visit to see quality play from the Australian, New Zealand, Fijian, and British players, but I was staggered at the amazingly high quality produced by countries I never knew even played Rugby. South Korea and Western Samoa were every bit as good as Japan and Tonga. Malaysia, Thailand and Singapore found their lack of sheer size and bulk an insuperable handicap, but against each other they displayed a range of running and handling skills which demanded unqualified praise. Papua New Guinea, Sri Lanka and the Solomon Islands were inevitably outgunned by the teams from the major Rugby-playing countries but they still have a remarkably high level of skill which promises well for the future of the game.

The week of the Hong Kong tournament allows 24 Rugby-playing countries to intermingle for several days, and the huge cross-fertilization of ideas can only be beneficial in the long term to the emerging nations. After the first day of play when the top eight seeded teams meet the smaller fish in a pool system, the second day is divided into three different competitions. The best eight sides to qualify play for the Cathay Pacific Trophy, the next eight have their own knockout competition for the Plate, and the final eight teams for the Bowl.

The strength of this great tournament is that on the opening day the most famous players in the world share a pitch with unknown opponents from countries where Rugby is a minority sport. Hence, I shall always treasure the memory of a thick-set, jet-black Papua New Guinea player called Lucas Senar proudly displaying a photo and press cuttings from the previous year's tournament which showed and described him tackling the legendary Scotland and British Lion full-back, Andy Irvine. For all these players, great and small, Rugby is a way of life, and for one brief weekend each year the aspiring unknown player can rub shoulders with the famous. While tournaments like the Hong Kong Sevens continue to be played, Rugby administrators can be confident that the game will continue to thrive in over 100 countries worldwide.

Below right Tonga (top) at Twickenham, 1974 and the Argentine Pumas (bottom) in France, 1981.
Below Jona Qoro, a key figure on the Fijians' visit in 1970.
Bottom Budge Rogers featured on the poster advertising England's two games in Tokyo, 1971.

The Hong Kong Sevens. Left Korea, winners of the Plate event in 1983. Centre left The Fijian squad, overall winners for the second successive year in 1983. Bottom left Auckland v Singapore, 1981.

The Pan-American Tournament in Hawaii, 1979.

143

Cathay Pacific began their sponsorship of the Hong Kong Sevens in 1976, and it was at about this time that the commercial world as a whole began taking an active interest in putting money into Rugby. In Britain the first major sponsorship came from Imperial Tobacco in 1975–76 when they put up £100,000 over three years to become associated with the English Knock-Out Cup competition. They have supported what is now known as the John Player Special Cup ever since, and their most recent commitment of £315,000 during the three years from 1984 onwards will bring their total financial involvement so far to £872,000.

The other major sponsor in England is Thorn EMI who in 1979 put forward £185,000 to sponsor the County Championship and the Divisional Championship for three years. Their current involvement is £341,000 for the present three-year period. This means that more than £1,500,000 will have been paid over to the Rugby Football Union to disperse in a ten-year period since the start of sponsorship.

The most recent major sponsorship in England has been the generous involvement of Courage, the Brewing Company, in 1985 when they agreed to give their support and their name to the newly devised John Smith

Les Cusworth, in the colours of the Public School Wanderers, holds aloft the Hill Samuel Cup.

Far right Bill Beaumont (Lancashire) with the Thorn EMI County Championship Trophy, 1980.

Above *Sunshine Rugby in Fiji. The crowds enjoy the Lions' visit of 1977.*
Above left *A well-guarded leek.*
Left *The French cockerel at Cardiff in 1970.*

The Hong Kong Sevens. Top *Hong Kong v Bahrain, 1984.* Top right
New Zealand v Western Samoa, 1983. Above *Fiji, winners in 1984.*
Right *American Eagles v Tonga, 1984.*

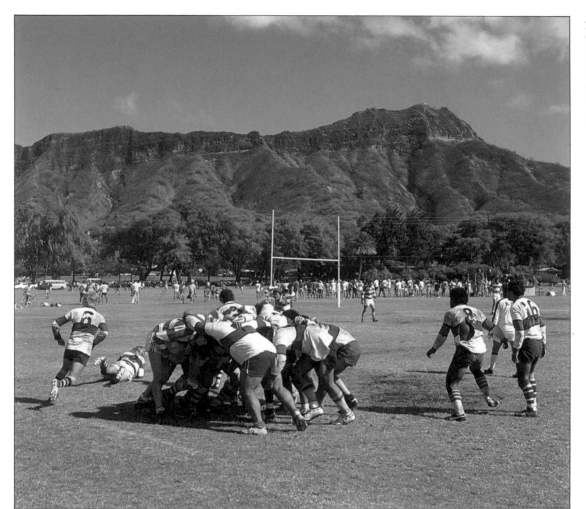

A game for all seasons.
Left *Action during the Pan American Tournament in Hawaii, 1979.*
Below *The 1981 Varsity match at Twickenham.*

Right Keen
competition between
the under-10s of
Stamford and
Stockwood Park in
pursuit of the Mobbs
Memorial Cup.
Below Fun in the mud
in Hong Kong, 1983.

148

National Merit Tables. This could well prove to be inspired sponsorship by John Smith's if their merit tables evolve in the near future into National First and Second Division Leagues. The fervent hope for English Rugby in the Nineties must be just such a league system with the matches played on fixed Saturdays with each club playing every other club in the Division and the winners of the First Division title being regarded as the top side in England each season.

Scotland and Wales soon followed England's example, and both countries received sponsorship from Schweppes in the 1977–78

season. In Scotland Scheweppes have given £250,000 sponsorship to the leagues during a nine-year period. In Wales Schweppes have sponsored the cup to the tune of £250,000 in the same nine-year period. On a considerably lower level, clubs tournaments and competitions have received various amounts of sponsorship, and the link between Rugby and commercial sponsorship is now firmly established in all the major and a great many minor Rugby-playing countries.

The four Home Unions now seek to have all their home internationals sponsored, and they have been very successful after a hesitant start in securing this objective. The lead was given by the Scottish Rugby Union. Breaking from tradition, they took the bold step in 1982 of bringing in the flourishing sports consultancy company, McLaren, Purvis, Palmer (MPP), to run their commercial activities for them. Based in England, MPP opened an office in Edinburgh and soon signed the most lucrative deal of any major Rugby Union in the world when the Royal Bank of Scotland agreed to pay £312,000 to sponsor Scotland's home internationals for a three-year period.

This deal was the major breakthrough, and the other Unions in Britain have been frantically engaged in trying to catch up with Scotland. Initially they were not all wholly successful, but now with the involvement of British Gas, Digital, Save & Prosper, Toshiba and others, virtually every international is now sponsored. In the future, commercial involvement with Rugby must only increase; without it the game would be in dire straits.

Roger Spurrell (Bath) with the John Player Cup, 1984.

Below far left *John Scott, captain of Cardiff, winners of the 1982 Schweppes Welsh Cup final.*

Below and below left *The sponsors get their space on the programmes.*

In glancing back over this 15-year period it is clear that the game was graced by several quite exceptional players. It is hard, if not invidious, to choose just a handful from each of the major countries, but a select few would generally be regarded by their peers, and Rugby supporters everywhere, to be almost indecently talented.

I would hazard a guess that if a world squad was to be picked from the years 1969–1984, there would be an embarrassment of riches from which to choose. The Northern Hemisphere might well provide the full-back with Serge Blanco, J. P. R. Williams and Andy Irvine certain to be in the firing line. Gerald Davies and David Duckham would join Bryan Williams, Grant Batty and Stu Wilson of New Zealand and Brendan Moon and David Campese of Australia amongst the best wings. From so many great centres I would offer Roland Bertranne (France), Mike Gibson (Ireland), Bruce Robertson (New Zealand), and Danie Gerber (South Africa). There is certainly no shortage of half-backs. Fly-half – Barry John and Phil Bennett of Wales, Hugo Porta (Argentina) and Mark Ella (Australia). Scrum-half – Gareth Edwards (Wales), Sid Going (New Zealand) and John Hipwell (Australia).

The great Pontypool triumvirate of Charlie Faulkner, Bobby Windsor and Graham Price would have a strong claim as a unit to make up the front row. But the list of challengers would include Gérard Cholley, Philippe Dintrans and Robert Paparemborde of France, and Gary

Below *Andy Irvine (Scotland).*
Below right *J.P.R. Williams (Wales).*
Below far right *Gerald Davies (Wales).*

Above *David Duckham (England).*
Right *Grant Batty (New Zealand).*
Far right *Stu Wilson (New Zealand).*

Top (left to right)
*Brendan Moon
(Australia), David
Campese (Australia),
Mike Gibson (Ireland).
Centre Hugo Porta
(Argentina), Mark Ella
(Australia), Danie
Gerber (South Africa).*

Below *Frik du Preez
(South Africa).*

Knight, Andy Dalton and John Ashworth of New Zealand. It would not be hard to find a pair of locks from Frik Du Preez (South Africa), Bill Beaumont (England), Willie John McBride (Ireland), Colin Meads (New Zealand), Gordon Brown (Scotland) and Andy Haden (New Zealand). Murray Mexted (New Zealand), Mervyn Davies (Wales) and Jean-Pierre Bastiat (France) would be on the shortlist for No. 8, and the leading flankers would have to include Graham Mourie (New Zealand), Jean-Pierre Rives (France), Jean-Claude Skréla (France), Tony Neary (England), Fergus Slattery (Ireland) and Ian Kirkpatrick (New Zealand).

Few people would challenge the class of all these outstanding players but it is much harder to choose the handful of greatest matches in any given era. At the risk of outraging some people, I would suggest that the following games were well worth crossing the road to see. At Murrayfield in 1971, Scotland led Wales 18–14 in a thrilling match full of movement, skill, character and excitement. Heroic Scottish defence finally broke in the dying seconds and Gerald Davies scored a magnificent try in the corner. 18–17 to Scotland still. From the touchline, John Taylor converted – the greatest conversion since St Paul, Welsh supporters unanimously agreed. 19–18 to Wales.

Perhaps the most memorable classic of all was the marvellous victory of the Barbarians against the All Blacks at Cardiff in 1973. It was a delightful mixture of all that is best in Rugby

with six superb tries and a feast of breathtaking open play. For good measure it produced the try of the decade when early on Phil Bennett sidestepped his way out of deep defence to link with J. P. R. Williams and John Pullin to launch the most sensational counter-attack I have been privileged to see. John Dawes carried on the move, and Gareth Edwards was up in support to sprint the last 40 yards and outstrip the All Black cover to score in the left-hand corner. No other try or match remains quite so indelibly ingrained on the memory but it must be said that the Wallabies' win over the Barbarians in 1984 was also an extravaganza of exciting open play which produced 11 tries and 67 points.

England's victory over Scotland in 1980 to clinch the Grand Slam was very special to England supporters – one swallow in an interminably long summer – and similarly Scotland's storming victory over Ireland in 1984 to capture the Triple Crown after a gap of a mere 46 years was heartwarming for the Scots and appreciated by a wider audience. The manner of those wins by England and Scotland was as important as the results, and the same can be said for the way the All Blacks crushed the British Lions in the Fourth Test in New Zealand in 1983. Top of the list, however, for the great majority of people would be that Barbarians-All Blacks match in January 1973 – a day and a game for the connoisseur to savour.

Top *Murray Mexted (New Zealand).*
Centre, left to right *Ian Kirkpatrick (New Zealand), Graham Mourie (New Zealand), Sid Going (New Zealand).*
Above *Bobby Windsor (Wales).*

The most memorable try. Gareth Edwards scores for the Barbarians against the All Blacks at Cardiff, 1973.

PART FIVE

RUGBY NOW AND THE YEARS AHEAD,
1985 ONWARDS

Right *John Hipwell gets the ball clear before the arrival of Fergus Slattery in Australia's win over Ireland in 1981.*

Below *The Australian squad which won the Hong Kong Sevens in 1983.*

One day you may be a rooster, the next a feather-duster.' Those were the typically pithy, succinct words of Wallabies coach Alan Jones on 24 November 1984, the day Australia slammed Wales at Cardiff Arms Park by 28 points to 9, four tries to one including a pushover try, the ultimate indignity for Wales on their own patch. But the Wallabies need have had no fears about overconfidence for by 8 December they had annihilated Scotland by 37 points to 12 to complete their first-ever Grand Slam tour of victories over the four home countries.

The achievement of that tour certainly gave Australia plenty to crow about, but more than that it finally exposed the level of mediocrity to which British Rugby had slipped since the late Seventies and sent shock-waves of panic and dismay reverberating round these island shores. It also planted Australia firmly back at the top of the international Rugby tree, a position that country had not enjoyed since the last time they had won a series in Britain with Bill McLean's tour of 1947–48. Furthermore, the Wallabies brought with them a thrilling brand of Rugby based on pace, fitness, all-round mobility and skill that must

have been as pleasurable to play as it was to behold. Nor has anything happened since that tour to suggest that the chasm, of Grand Canyon proportions, that clearly separated British Rugby from its Antipodean counterparts has been significantly reduced. For whilst Australia had made a fair advance, international Rugby in the four Home Unions had at best stagnated, possibly even regressed.

The portents, for those who were not aware of what had been happening Down Under in the season that preceded the Wallabies' winter tour, did not seem favourable. Australia had lost 16 of their 20 previous Test matches in

154

the British Isles, whilst in 1983 they had lost the series played in France, and drawn in Argentina. But the controversial appointment of 41-year-old political aspirant Alan Jones as the Wallabies' coach in place of Bob Dwyer, coincided with a rapid transformation in Australia's fortunes. Although Australia lost their three-match series with New Zealand, the outcome was decided by just one point: 24–25 in the Final Test. More significantly, the Wallabies had found in the First Test new lineout skills with Steve Cutler as Steve Williams's new second-row partner and a solid front row of Rodriguez, Lawton and McIntyre.

Australia beat England at Twickenham, 1984.
Left *The Australians outjump England at the lineout.*
Centre *Nigel Melville sets up a rare England attack.*
Bottom *Gould, Lawton and Lynagh put more pressure on the England defence.*

Philip Cox and Mark Ella relax after another victory.

All five were ultimately to complete the Grand Slam series of four Tests in Britain. A short Fijian visit completed Australia's preparations and Andy Slack, the new captain, and Alan Jones, with notable forward assistance from Alec Evans, never looked back.

The eighth Wallabies provided British Rugby watchers with an unparalleled spectacle of thrilling attacking 15-man Rugby that may in retrospect prove to have been a significant watershed in the history of the game. Although they conceded defeat in four of the provincial games, against Cardiff, Ulster, Llanelli and South of Scotland, largely because it was the tour management's policy to ensure that all the fit players had at least one outing each week, the Test record speaks for itself. Four wins out of four, 100 points to 33, 12 tries to 1: that is an impressive success story, whilst the overall tour record shows that they scored 51 tries in 18 matches, against the best that Britain could offer. The hallmark of their game was brilliant back play: the memory of maestros such as

Mark Ella, David Campese, Michael Lynagh, Roger Gould and Nick Farr-Jones is certain to linger long, with their startling array of switches, loops and dummies allied to breathtaking pace and acceleration. But the nuts and bolts of the operation was the performance of the pack: that traditional achilles heel of Australian Rugby, the set-piece scrummage, had been transformed into a *tour de force,* the lineout was no longer a problem and the mobility and ball-handling skills of the back row were of exceptional quality, with Simon Poidevin outstanding.

As a fillip to Australian Rugby, in its continuous battle against competing brands of football – Association, Rugby League and Australian Rules – it was unprecedented, with a television audience of 60 per cent of Australian adults watching proceedings at two o'clock in the morning live from Murrayfield in the Grand Slam decider. For them it was the Grandest Slam of all.

*T*he expansion in popularity of Rugby football has brought with it unheralded developments in unexpected quarters, notably amongst the 'Minis', the Golden Oldies and, most recently, Women's Rugby. Without doubt the most important growth area is that of the smallest members of the Rugby fraternity, those who between the ages of 6 and 13 have taken part in the Mini Rugby explosion.

There is a remarkable buzz of activity and noise at Rugby clubs on Sunday mornings the length and breadth of Britain. These were places which until recently lay silent in the aftermath of Saturday-night festivities. The advent of Mini Rugby has brought about a dramatic change, producing the biggest-ever intake of youngsters into the game of Rugby, and partly compensating for the worrying changes in the educational structure that have so harmed the development of Rugby within the State school system.

It is difficult, as yet, to assess how much the decline of Rugby as a principal game in secondary school education will affect its future well-being, but it is without doubt of considerable significance. It manifests itself in various ways. For example, four secondary schools, each with three or four senior Rugby fifteens, may have been combined to form one sixth-form college with one- and two-year courses and perhaps only one or two Rugby teams, where formerly there may have been at least a dozen or more. Or, a group of schools may have been fully integrated into one large neighbourhood comprehensive with the same overall effect. This is especially catastrophic for Rugby because some of the traditional hot-beds of the sport, the grammar and direct-grant schools, have been swallowed up. Worrying too are the reduced enthusiasm of many modern educational theorists for competitive team pursuits; the reluctance of many present-day schoolmasters to involve themselves in extra-curricular activities; the shortage of that life-blood of Rugby tuition in schools provided by the old St Luke's and Loughborough College trained teachers; the disastrous consequences of the long-drawn-out strike of teachers in State education which, in Wales for example, meant a complete absence of inter-schools Rugby, leading to more emphasis on other leisure-time pursuits or a general apathy towards them. Add these elements together and it is not difficult to

gauge the long-term consequences for Rugby football.

These factors have served to heighten the significance of Mini Rugby for the long-term future of the game. To the eternal credit of many hundreds of clubs, they have taken upon themselves the responsibility of introducing to Rugby thousands upon thousands of youngsters who might not otherwise be given that

Barefoot Mini Rugby for the Under-6s at Hamilton before the Lions' match on the 1977 tour.

Adrian Leather of Ashton-on-Mersey breaks away from the Leigh opposition in an Under-8 match.

Enthusiastic support for the Minis on a Sunday morning.

opportunity. Already the scheme is bearing fruit as the earliest generation of Minis is now filtering through the system to adult playing levels. At the same time the influx to the Colts and youth game at the Under-19 level has also increased and helped to compensate for the reduced supply of recruits at school-leaving age.

This huge voluntary effort by clubs and parents has brightened the previously somewhat depressing prospects for club Rugby without altogether ensuring a secure future. One beneficial by-product has been to increase local involvement in Rugby clubs, swelling memberships as well as bar profits – as much through Sunday orange squash and hot-dog takings as through the traditional beer sales. It has also given to the juniors an early experience of the life-long pleasure and fun that Rugby's social life can provide, albeit in many instances stretching existing club facilities to breaking point!

The real instigator of this simplified version of the 15-a-side game was former Wales Coaching Organizer (now WRU Secretary) Ray Williams, assisted by Don Rutherford, his current RFU equivalent. Mini Rugby, in essence, is a nine-a-side abbreviated form of 'real' Rugby. It stresses handling, running and passing, support play and tackling, whilst kicking is restricted to a minimum. Inter-club matches and occasional festivals are not discouraged but it should always be remembered that Mini Rugby is not an end in itself, nor is winning or losing of importance. It is quite simply an enjoyable way of learning the rudiments and basic skills of the game. First and foremost, Mini Rugby is to be played for fun. A visit to a local club on a Sunday morning will provide ample proof of the success of this remarkable phenomenon.

At the other end of the scale is another and rather more extraordinary development: the rise, on a world-wide front, of Golden Oldies Rugby. In North America and Australasia the burgeoning of the Golden Oldies movement has been quite remarkable, opening a new outlet for physical and social activity for the Over-35s, up to and including those eccentric, foolhardy or fanatical individuals who indulge in Rugby at the age of 70 and beyond! Regular fixtures and local and international tournaments have become a feature of this new realm of Veterans Rugby, culminating in the World Golden Oldies Festival. This was first held in Auckland in 1979 when 200 or so took part. By 1981 there had been a great upsurge in popularity and the *Queen Mary,* anchored as a hotel off Long Beach, hosted almost 1,900 Rugby folk at the California Festival. Two years later it was staged in Sydney with nigh-on 5,000 participants who, for the record, downed 28,000 cans of beer in a couple of days at Randwick, the host club. The oldest participant at that event was 83-year-old Mac Adams, a great-grandfather from Port

The Old Frothonians parade at Twickenham at the opening of the 1985 World Golden Oldies Festival.

Far right POME players enjoy a VIP presentation before their match at the Coogee Oval during the 1983 Golden Oldies festival in Sydney.

Macquarie, Australia.

For the fourth gathering, the event came to London in 1985. Again some 5,000 *aficionados,* representing 22 different countries, indulged in a limited amount of physical effort in some 300 matches at eight different grounds within the London area. The effort expended in the pursuit of fun and revelry was, however, without limit. They represented clubs as disparate as The Tarnished Turtles of the Cayman Islands, The Wagga Wagga Blue Heelers from that self-same Australian outpost, the Takapuna Tuggers of New Zealand, Zrelo Doba of Yugoslavia, Canada's Kawartha Krocks and Calgary Canadian Irish, Japan's Wak Sun and Fuwaku and our own Chelmsford Undertakers, Camberley Gin and Tonics, Guildford and Godalming Gangrenes and Northampton Latter-Day Saints. The event was climaxed by a unique gathering of the entire company at dinner in one hall, the salubrious setting being No. 4 shed at the Royal Victoria Docks in London's East End. It was probably the world's biggest-ever sit-down banquet, and had three 200-foot bars.

All in all, it was an event of 'sweaty scrummaging and serious socializing', as one observer put it. Cliff Morgan called it 'a combination of laughter, delight and fun, an atmosphere of sharing and enjoyment, that gives an important perspective on the game and sport in general.' Prince Philip sent a message of goodwill to the Festival revellers: 'I send my best wishes to all the players and officials and I hope that at least the majority will survive the experience.' They did, and rest assured the greater part and many more recent converts will reassemble in characteristic style in Auckland in May 1987, just prior to a rather more serious and smaller festival of Rugby also taking place there, the first Rugby World Cup.

To Mini Rugby, now 15 years old, and Golden Oldies Rugby, which emanated from Japan in 1947, we must add a new branch of the game – Women's Rugby. For many, Rugby remains the least fitting of all male-dominated sports for females to play, but a growing body of women activists will scoff at such a suggestion. Women's Rugby is widespread and thriving and a serious-minded pursuit for those who take part, especially in the USA where hundreds of clubs compete on a highly-organized basis from coast to coast. It flourishes, too, on the European continent with regular international matches between such countries as France, Netherlands, Italy, Sweden and Spain. In Britain the pioneer clubs have been Magor and Caerleon in Wales, Finchley, Loughborough University and other college and polytechnic sides. At several, such as Caerleon, Wasps and Oxford Old Boys, the women members have established themselves as a section within the men's club; such acceptance is a significant part of Women's Rugby aspirations. The Women's Rugby Football Union was formed in 1984, a National Tournament is now held and in April 1986 Great Britain (the Lionesses?) played a first international against France at the Richmond Club ground, France winning 14 points to 8. The event did much to silence sceptics and announced to a wider audience that Women's Rugby looks to be here to stay.

American Mid-West Ladies on tour in Bermuda.

Play during the final of the French Ladies' Championship, 1973.

Most people would acknowledge that Twickenham represents the home of Rugby Union Football. It is the home not just of English Rugby, but of the Varsity Match, the annual Inter-Services Tournament, and that unique end-of-season festival, the Middlesex Sevens. It is also a home ground for the revered Harlequin Football Club and an occasional recipient of visits from the illustrious Barbarians and other celebrated sides.

But what is this place that ranks alongside Lord's, Wembley and Wimbledon in world-wide sporting renown? To take one view: 'It's a tiresome place to get to, a most uncomfortable, poorly nourished and gloomy place to sit at, and a penance to escape from on a crowded International Day.'

So wrote, in 1944, with a touch of love and hate, one of Rugby's most famous scribes, E. H. D. Sewell, a Harlequin player of 1891. But others, far greater in number, hold Twickenham in awe. For most of them, memories of Twickenham will forever be coloured by fondly recalled days of triumph, like the moment of victory in England's Grand Slam year of 1980 when Dusty Hare kicked the vital penalty goal that beat Wales, or when London was under siege from Arctic weather conditions in 1986, and plastic covers and hot-air blowers contrived to deny the forages of frost and snow, allowing the international against Ireland to proceed in spectacular fashion in an atmosphere of overwhelming bonhomie that epitomized the *joy* of amateur Rugby.

Right The view from the new South Stand.

A rural setting for Twickenham in 1931.

There is more to Twickenham than Rugby alone. It is also 'Twickers' to generations of well-heeled *aficionados* of the game who have thronged the vast car parks and concourses that surround the stadium. They come, as they have always come, with their car-boots laden with fare for *al fresco* meals of champagne and oysters, smoked salmon sandwiches and barbecued chicken legs which fuel the social intercourse in the North and West parking areas before and after the match. Hail fellow, well-met! And all around a herd of sheepskin coats, a legion of British Warms and tweed suits, headscarves and tartan blankets for the ladies, and for the menfolk club ties, Rugby reminiscences and reunions with old team-mates and opposition players. It represents a social scene that to some is as important as the Rugby itself.

Nowadays just as many supporters find their way to this focal point in the London suburbs by taking the train from Waterloo on the scruffy line to Twickenham Station. Arriving in their thousands, they tramp the half-mile across the bridge and down Whitton Road wearing anoraks, jeans and duffel coats, laden with Thermoses of coffee, hip flasks of brandy, or pipkins (plastic, by law) of beer. Or else they pour out from the coach parks in clusters, some on business hospitality packages, with cocktails and a slap-up lunch and tea provided; all are in good heart and voice, with well-oiled throats and well-slaked thirsts, up from Bridgend or Bridgwater, down from Moseley or Manchester. They pour through the Rowland Hill Gates at the main entrance or the turnstiles round the ground, some dallying to barter with touts for tickets they failed to acquire through the restricted club allocation.

By kick-off, 54,000 will be assembled, filling the three grey, cavernous two-tier stands that enclose the East, West and North of the ground, as they have done for fifty years. Now there's a new edifice to the South – a £5 million stand built on futuristic lines that took the place of the old beloved South Terrace. The new stand forms a dominant feature with its private big-business hospitality boxes, Rose Room banqueting suite and Rugby museum and shop symbolic of a new commercial era – the first stage in a grand master plan to modernize the whole stadium.

(For the early history of the stadium, see Part One: 'Twickenham'.)

The home of Ireland's Rugby is the oldest of all the international grounds, and 4 February 1984 was one of Lansdowne Road's red-letter days. Not just because it was a jubilee occasion – the 25th international between Ireland and Wales on the national ground (and the 147th international match to be played there) – it also marked the opening of the new East Stand, the £4 million Triple Crown Stand, by Gerry Reidy, President of the Irish Rugby Football Union.

Lansdowne Road was built on a patch of waste land set between the Lansdowne Road Railway Station and the River Dodder on the outskirts of Dublin. In 1872 a keen sporting enthusiast and graduate of Trinity College, by name Henry William Dunlop, bought the land – seven acres in all – from the Earl of Pembroke. Dunlop then founded on the waste land a sporting organization called the Irish Champion Athletics Club. The club put down a cinder running track, and had a cricket pitch, archery, croquet, tennis, a hurdles course and three plots set aside for football as well as a grandstand to seat 400 people. Significantly, a Rugby club started up – known variously as the Champion Club or Lansdowne Road; eventually it became Lansdowne Football Club, whose home it still remains. They were joined in 1880 by their continuing co-tenants, the Wanderers Club. Ultimately it was to be a Wanderer, H. C. Sheppard, who was to be instrumental in bringing about the harmonious arrangement whereby the Lansdowne Road ground became the property of the IRFU with the two senior clubs remaining as tenants.

Those pioneering days of the early 1870s saw Irish Rugby develop apace, and by 1878, just four years after the formation of the Irish Rugby Football Union, such had been the transformation of the old waste land that it was decided to play Ireland's second international there, against England, transferring from the old venue at the Leinster Cricket Club in Rathmines. The fee for the use of the ground was a princely £5 to Dunlop, and half of any profit over £50 (less expenses, of course).

The full-back and captain, that first day at Lansdowne Road, was R. B. Walkington, the one survivor of Ireland's first-ever international in 1875; he was so short-sighted that he wore a monocle when playing. The result was the now familiar defeat, two goals and a try to nothing, which meant that Ireland had played five international matches without scoring. In fact,

they had to wait until 1880 for a try. Victories then began to flow, Lansdowne Road flourished and only occasional visits were made thereafter to Cork and Belfast for the purpose of staging home internationals.

And what characters the ground has witnessed. In the 1890s – Triple Crown days for Ireland – there was C. V. Rooke, Tommy Crean VC, Louis Magee and that pair of Tipperary

giants, the Ryan brothers. A player relates the occasion the day after Ireland beat Wales in 1896, when C. V. Rooke and the Welsh half-back Llewellyn Lloyd were strolling near Dublin Bay. Said Rooke, the Irish forward, to Lloyd: 'It's by the Grace of God that you're alive today – when I couldn't kick the ball, I kicked you!' Then in the Twenties, there was the robust, indomitable flanker Jamie Clinch, who recounted to me

some years before his death one of his most treasured memories. Running out at Lansdowne Road to play Wales, he heard a Welsh supporter call out: 'Send the bastard off!'

Also in the Twenties Ireland's Rugby home was equipped with massive stands on either side, filled regularly to overflowing, especially in the Golden days immediately after the war. Jack Kyle, Tom Clifford, Noel Henderson, McKay, McCarthy and O'Brien; Karl Mullen too, the captain in Ireland's one and only Grand Slam season of 1948. Then, in 1958, came the first-ever win at Lansdowne Road over a major overseas touring team, Australia, with Kyle still there, the irrepressible Noel Murphy, the swift Tony O'Reilly, David Hewitt – that prince of centres – and a first cap for Ronnie Dawson.

And what legends have graced the Irish stage in later years. The era of Bill Mulcahy led through to the Sixties and a time when it seemed harder to get out of the Irish team than it was to get into it. An age of institutions, rather than transient selections, had dawned, with Tom Kiernan and Ray McLoughlin, young Mike Gibson, destined to become the world's most capped player, Willie John McBride, five times a British Lions tourist, and Fergus Slattery.

Living legends spring to mind when you enter the portals of Lansdowne Road – though the long-absent visitor will blink at how the look and feel of the ground have been transformed by the sudden arrival of the Triple Crown Stand.

Sudden is not as far off the mark as it may sound, since the work from demolition of the old to completion of the new lasted just from March to December of 1983. A fitting edifice it is, too, to celebrate the famous deeds of the Ireland team of 1982, notably their deeds on 20 February that year when Ciaran Fitzgerald's side clinched the crown that had for so long eluded them. That day they beat Scotland 21–12 thanks to Irish fervour on the field, wildly enthusiastic support from the crowd and a slight unassuming fly-half called Ollie Campbell with a magical right boot.

No ground has more tales to tell of international Rugby than the place that welcomes the whole of Ireland, North and South, through its gates to unite in good cheer and steadfastly to keep the cherished ideal of Rugby as a game of, and for, fun. That place is Lansdowne Road.

The home of Irish Rugby.

The Arms Park – rather than the 'National Stadium', as someone suggested it should now be called – is and will forever be the temple of Welsh Rugby. It is a stadium, a theatre, and a stage all in one. In other words it is more than just a Rugby ground, it is a focal point of Welsh pride and passion, and on international days, it is a place of pilgrimage. For in Wales, unlike the other home countries, Rugby has always been the people's game, a blend of sport and religion. Singing and Rugby football are there very much intertwined. Welsh Rugby heroes are national heroes.

It was well over a hundred years ago that the Arms Park's sporting history began. It did so on the ground adjacent to the present main stadium which, since the building of the new stands began in 1968, has become the home of Cardiff Rugby Club. This was land that had been reclaimed as a result of diverting the River Taff away from what is now the city centre. On this same site Cardiff Cricket Club had originally established themselves in 1845, on an area behind the Cardiff Arms Coaching Inn, and it was with the cricketers, many of them also Rugby enthusiasts, that Cardiff Football Club joined forces in 1876 to share facilities at the same training ground with alternate summer and winter use.

As Rugby grew apace, so did Wales's four principal clubs – Cardiff, Swansea, Newport and Llanelli. For the very first home international versus England, in December 1882, the venue was St Helen's, Swansea, and all four principal club grounds hosted the early international matches. Then, as their facilities expanded to allow an ever-increasing size of crowd to view the games, so Cardiff and Swansea became the biennial settings for Wales's home games. This arrangement continued until 1954, when at the end of a very bitter wrangle it was determined that the Arms Park alone would stage Welsh international matches. The principal reasons were that Swansea Corporation owned the St Helen's ground and not the club or the Welsh Rugby Union; the seating capacity there was insufficient; poor traffic access was always leading to congestion on match days, and, perhaps most important, the gate receipts were always £5–10,000 less than at the Arms Park.

More than thirty years on, the new Arms Park is the headquarters of a multi-million pound business employing a staff of 23 in the new Welsh Rugby Union offices that are part of the vast stadium complex that runs Wales's Rugby affairs. Welsh Rugby is justifiably proud

Builders at work to increase the capacity at Cardiff in 1937.

The Golden Oldies Festival, London 1986. Demonstration of the 'short' line-out.

The opening match – Glenfield Grizzlies (New Zealand) v Wak Sun (Japan).

Left *The Chelmsford Undertakers at the opening ceremony.* Right *A Takapuna Tugger.*

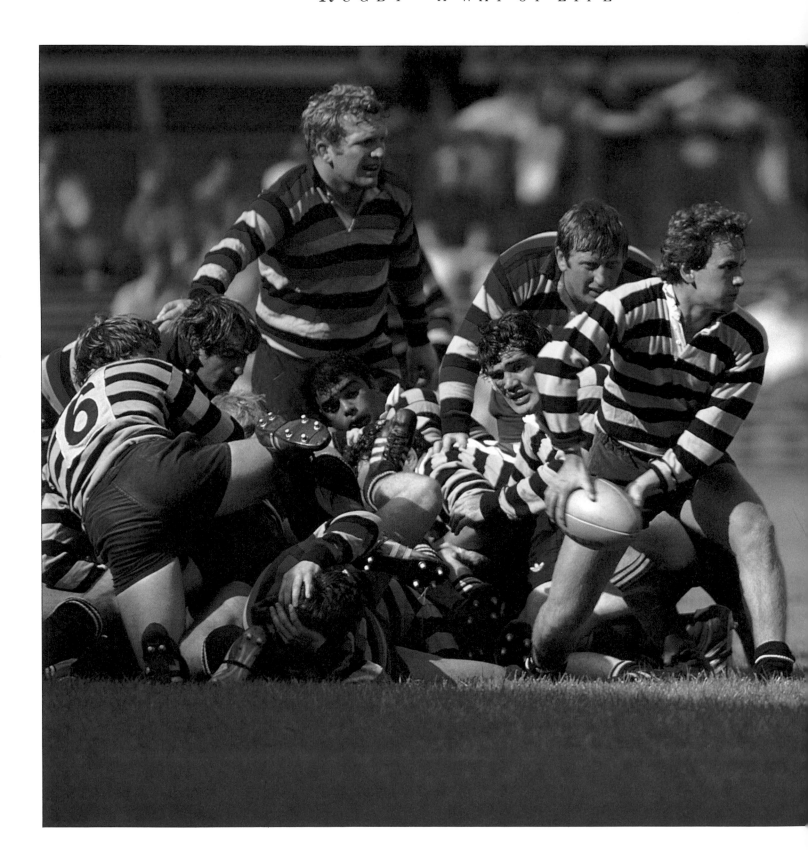

*Club action.
Far left* Wasps v
Lansdowne, 1980.
Left Gloucester v
Bristol, 1977.
Below Harlequins v
Leicester, 1985.
Bottom Liverpool v
Blackrock College,
1979.

Mark Ella sets up a run for Roger Gould during the 1984 Wallabies' final match against the Barbarians at Cardiff.

President's XV combination of Rudi Visagie (South Africa) and Terry Holmes (Wales) in action against England at Twickenham in 1984.

of its achievements in completing, in less than twenty years, an entire redevelopment and reconstruction of the old Arms Park ground. Now the visitor looks upon a huge enveloping horseshoe arena, magnificent in its scale, that gives 33,000 people a superb view from the tiered seating, whilst lower terracing around the pitch and the open Eastern end make the overall capacity nearly 63,000.

It was back in the early Sixties that negotiations began between the WRU and Cardiff City Council, the Cardiff Rugby Club and the Greyhound Racing Company, for the construction of a national ground. Thanks to a bold imaginative bid by the then Cardiff Club chairman, Hubert Johnson, who had addressed himself swiftly to the challenge of other clubs, notably Bridgend, to develop sites for a national Rugby ground, and the sympathetic response to that initial Cardiff plan from the WRU treasurer, Ken Harris, rival schemes were headed off. It was at the culmination of much lobbying and negotiation that Ken Harris unveiled plans for a far-sighted scheme, which entailed re-siting the Cardiff club ground parallel to the main stadium with back-to-back stands and new peripheral developments for the club. The old cricket club and ground would move to nearby Sofia Gardens, new tennis courts would be built and, most importantly, a whole new Rugby playing area would be created, and surrounded by stands costing £9 million.

The new playing pitch was opened amidst the girders and rising frames of the new mushroom-ribbed canopy in 1970. Wales's centenary season of 1981 saw the whole plan well on the way to completion, and when Scotland came to play Wales in January 1984 they ran out into a magnificent and complete sporting arena. Three months later the WRU staged a special match to mark the project's fulfilment – one hundred years to the week since the first international match was staged at the ground.

It was an astonishing achievement for an amateur organization, and a lasting memorial to the vision and business acumen of Ken Harris, especially when you consider that of the total cost of £8,794,500, only £160,000 came from public funds, in the form of a Sport's Council grant. The second century of Welsh Rugby and of Cardiff Arms Park is now well and truly well under way. The ground stands as a magnificent testament to the national game of Wales – bold and imaginative like so many of their players, the realization of a long-cherished dream.

The National Stadium, 1984.

And so to the youngest of the Five Nations Rugby grounds, the old polo ground at Murray's Field, Edinburgh. It is strange that the country which instigated international Rugby, when Scottish club players challenged their English counterparts to a 20-a-side football match, should take the longest to settle in a permanent home. International Rugby began in 1871 on the cricket field of Edinburgh Academicals at Raeburn Place, and it sufficed largely until the turn of the century with occasional visits to Glasgow and Powderhall; then Inverleith became the principal international venue.

It was soon apparent that Inverleith could no longer handle the ever-increasing crowds that flocked to Scotland's matches, and it was decided to move to Murray's Field, the grounds of Edinburgh Polo Club, which had easy access to the city. In 1922 the Scottish Rugby Union announced the purchase, and debentures were later issued to finance this as well as the cost of a main stand, other buildings and the creation of large embankments for standing spectators. There was discussion, too, with the town council over the placing of a new road to run past the ground. Work proceeded well and all was ready by the end of the 1924–25 season.

What an initiation there was for the new Murrayfield, as the Championship season reached an epic finale. Scotland had already beaten France, Wales and Ireland, and the excitement had reached fever pitch by the time England came to Scotland for the inaugural match on 21 March 1925, with the Grand Slam at stake. It was a bright clear spring day and to the astonishment of the SRU a crowd of more than 70,000 came to witness Scotland's proudest day. Phil Macpherson was captain of the Scots, Wavell Wakefield captain of England, and the man who sealed the outcome of the match was the Glasgow Academical fly-half Herbert Waddell, who dropped the winning goal. It was a fairytale end to an historic occasion.

By the mid-Thirties the addition of two end-extensions to the big West Stand more than doubled the seating capacity to over 15,000, whilst a committee box was added with access to improved committee rooms inside. Two former Presidents of the SRU, Sir David Gowan and Aikman Smith, presented one of Murrayfield's most famous landmarks, the clock atop the South Terrace and the original scoreboard, whilst Sheriff Watt presented a flagstaff and flag. But of all the gifts made over the years the most

Preparation for the 1937 Calcutta Cup match.

valuable, without question, has been the undersoil heating system donated by Dr Charles Hepburn in 1959. This continues to function superbly and has ensured that the pitch has remained playable on every possible occasion despite the frequent incidence of frost and snow.

Although triumphs similar to that of the opening day at Murrayfield have been relatively few and far between, there was no doubting the worthiness of the Triple Crown success of Wilson Shaw's side in 1938, the last season before the Second World War. Less happy for Scotland was the game in 1951 against Hennie Muller's South African touring team. It was a match to be known ever after as the 'Murrayfield Massacre' as the Springboks triumphed 44 points to nil (and nine tries to nil), the biggest margin of victory ever in international Rugby. As the Scottish supporter was heard to remark afterwards: 'And we were lucky to get nothing!' One wonders what the Scottish touch-judge that day, Wilson Shaw, made of it all.

Then came a barren period of four seasons without a win for Scotland, and thereafter a further decade of frustration as the Scots suffered at the hands of England fourteen years in a row, and three times were denied the Triple Crown. There were, nevertheless, great players to appreciate on the Murrayfield stage: men such as Ken Scotland, fifth in a line of eight Former Pupils of George Heriot's School to play full-back for Scotland, Arthur Smith the Flying Scotsman, rugged prop David Rollo of Howe of Fife, and Peter Stagg, at 6 feet 10 inches the tallest-ever player in international Rugby.

The Seventies brought a greater share of success, notably against England and even Wales. After the drama of the 19–18 defeat of 1971, not even nine British Lions – J. P. R. Williams, Gareth Edwards, Phil Bennett, Gerald and Mervyn Davies amongst them – could quell the Murrayfield spirit on Wales's next visit, and Scotland ran out victors by 10–9. Then, on 1 March 1975, 104,000 people fought their way into the stadium, leaving several thousand more locked out, and Scotland obliged their faithful throng by beating Wales 12–10.

Nowadays the ground capacity is restricted

and many away supporters off on 'The Murrayfield Weekend' get no nearer to the ground than a colour postcard dutifully sent home to South Wales 'as evidence', whilst the colour television is in reality the supporters' view of the match, watched in some homely bar in the Scottish Borders. But for those who do make it to Edinburgh, it's a long weekend.

A frustrating period of almost-triumph for the Scots came at last to a satisfactory conclusion in 1984, appropriately on the occasion of the hundredth meeting with the Auld Enemie, England; the 18–6 victory gave them their second win in the Triple Crown, after they had already beaten Wales 15–9 in Cardiff. Triple Crown success was consummated at Lansdowne Road, and under veteran prop-forward and captain Jim Aitken, a scarcely endurable wait of 60 seasons at Murrayfield came to the perfect climax as Jim Calder's try sealed the Grand Slam victory against France. There had been only one other day like it at the old polo ground.

Aerial view of Murrayfield on its completion in 1925.

A cacophony of sound, a stark, awe-inspiring oval concrete cauldron, a generous draught of champagne Rugby – these are the principal ingredients that give Parc des Princes its unique character. Since 1973 France have only twice been out of the top two in the Five Nations Championship, and an important factor in their success may be that in that year French Rugby returned to its original home just a short Métro journey from the Arc de Triomphe to Porte de Saint-Cloud on the edge, though not quite out in the suburbs, of the Parisian metropolis.

Parc des Princes is unlike any other international ground. For one thing it is owned and run by the local municipality and is not used exclusively for Rugby. It also stages important soccer matches and on occasion has been on the receiving end of the hooligan influx of so-called Leeds fans or England soccer supporters. Incidentally, I have yet to see one single incident of Rugby crowd violence or trouble at any one of the Five Nations national grounds.

Parc des Princes is entirely a modern construction, built in the early Seventies; when empty, it stands a grey, cast-concrete, almost gaunt arena in a complete oval surrounding the pitch, its lines softened only by the red and blue tiers of plastic seating; at Parc des Princes, everyone can be seated. When full, it resounds

with the noise of a passionate, excitable crowd; whistles, firecrackers and sirens compete against the blaring sound of the bands that make their pilgrimage to Paris from the Rugby-mad domain of the Basque country in the deepest South-West. It produces an atmosphere that tends to intimidate the visitor yet, like Cardiff, seems to inspire the home team. The record of France at Parc des Princes over the last 14 seasons says it all: Ireland and Scotland have never won there, Wales but once, and England twice – a remarkable sequence since that cold day in January 1973 when 37,000 spectators at the new stadium saw Scotland put to flight.

That is the Parc des Princes of the present day, but in an earlier guise it witnessed the very birth of French international Rugby. On New Year's Day 1906, France took the field as a national team for the first time on the original ground of the Parc – and all were agreeably surprised when more than three thousand turned up to watch them. France's first opponents were indeed formidable – the legendary first New Zealand All Blacks of Dave Gallaher. Not surprisingly, with French Rugby in its infancy, New Zealand won 38–8, scoring 10 tries to two by France. At least, from a French point of view, the eight points that they scored were equivalent to one-fifth of the total number of points conceded

Parc des Princes – a multi-purpose stadium which is also home to the national football team.

by that great touring side in the previous 32 matches on tour. And all that before the official union – the Fédération Française de Rugby – had been formed, or even thought of. That was to happen 14 years later.

In the meantime France played 28 internationals, losing 27 of them and winning the other one which, ironically, was played at another ground, Stade Colombes (home of the Racing Club de France), with which the international matches were shared. There in 1911 they beat Scotland 16–15.

There were wonderful goings-on in those days. On the occasion of France's first victory, one of the French players arrived only five minutes before kick-off to find he had lost his place to a local spectator, André Franquenelle. The late replacement played a key role in France's long-awaited day of Rugby success and went on to win two more caps at wing three-quarter!

The impact of that first win was considerable, reflecting a perhaps typical emotional response. In place of a previous lack of loyalty and forbearance in the face of defeat, victory triggered a burst of enthusiastic support verging on fanaticism. Where eight thousand had witnessed France's first success, the next home match was played before 20,000 spectators. It became clear that the original Parc des Princes

stadium would eventually prove inadequate in terms of crowd capacity, and after the First World War the new official governing body of French Rugby decided that all future internationals should be played at Colombes which had a much greater capacity. That was just as well, since by 1924 40,000 people were regularly attending France's matches.

The game continued to flourish until 1931, and then after the England international on 6 April, French international Rugby ground to a halt. For the next nine years France was suspended by the International Board and there were no further matches until after the Second World War. The Board had been provoked into this action by the unsatisfactory nature of the game in France, especially in the club championship where there was brutality on the field, players were poached, cash bonuses paid and top players lived off their earnings from Rugby – allegations that by and large have a familiar ring today.

Parc des Princes languished unvisited by international teams from New Year's Day 1920 until that happy return 53 years and 12 days later when international Rugby was restored to the new Princes' Park and France duly celebrated by beating Scotland 16–13. They won the next five matches off the reel.

Only the ghosts of those early twentieth-century pioneers now mingle with France's present-day heroes at the ground: men such as Henri Amand, France's first captain, Allan Muhr, a giant American in that inaugural team, Marcel Communeau, Jules Cadenat, Adolphe Jauréguy, Rene Crabos and the 'Sultan', Jean Sebedio. They all walked where the great players of today – Blanco, Sella, Codorniou, etc. – now tread, and who follow in a magnificent recent tradition of Rugby flair, that quintessential quality of French Rugby. They follow in the footsteps of others who have brought such Rugby delight with their touch, attacking intent, their magic, their pace and sleight of hand – men such as Lux and Maso, Bertranne and Aguirre, Skréla and Rives who have thrived behind the solid citizens up front who have made it all possible: the likes of Spanghero, Bastiat, Paparemborde and Cester.

It is that prospect of seeing Rugby at its best that whets the appretite for a visit to Parc des Princes which, like French Rugby itself, is altogether a different experience.

I t seems that the current age of Rugby (and by that I mean the last five years) has thrown up more challenges and problems of a more diverse character than have ever confronted the game before. I suppose you could say that it is a natural consequence of expansion and exposure – the larger the animal, the bigger the target. Rugby has changed, through its growth as a world game and as it is played, to the extent that in many aspects it is unrecognizable from the sport of even twenty years ago.

In some ways that has been of benefit, in other ways it has not. The establishment of Rugby as an active leisure pursuit in a hundred countries makes it the world's No. 1 amateur team game. But, as with all sports, it is now taken more seriously than formerly, at all levels. It has suffered (others would argue that is has benefited) from the fact that it is more fiercely competitive than even before, and consequently the demands in preparation and the pressure on players to be successful are greater than ever before. As we have seen, that does not necessarily provide an improvement in the quality of play. The advent of coaches and organized coaching has by no means been a universal blessing. Coaches, like players, may be good, bad or positively harmful, yet their influence is often pervasive, whilst their competence to undertake such responsibilities may be open to question. The highest echelons of the game are nowadays vulnerable to the same dangers of commercial exploitation as have damaged other sports when external forces have taken control. At the same time, the benefits and dependence upon sponsorship have become a vital ingredient of the modern age. Financial considerations, from grass-roots level to the international scene, are now on a much larger scale: Rugby is big business, and requires shrewd financial brains to guide its destiny.

VIOLENCE AND SAFETY

On the field, too, things have changed. Players are fitter, faster, stronger; pressures, as I have mentioned, are greater; the laws are more complex, more difficult to interpret; society is more competitive, more aggressive; frustration is more keenly felt, tolerance is less in evidence. These are some of the factors that contrive to give Rugby a more violent image, especially when the media seem to give greater prominence to the sensational and less

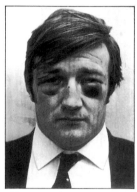

The ugly face of Rugby violence – Sandy Carmichael's battered face following the British Lions' encounter with Canterbury on the 1971 tour.

Top *Chris Ralston shows the injury he sustained in Richmond's match against Llanelli in 1978.*

Far right above *Clive Norling has words with Mark Shaw of New Zealand in 1981 and (below) Roger Uttley receives attention at Twickenham, 1980.*

palatable incidents that the game has always had to endure.

The exposure of violence and its perpetrators (who should be allowed no place on the Rugby field) is no bad thing, but its increased exposure should not allow observers

to conclude that the game is more violent now than at any other period in its history. It may appear to be so partly because the elements of physical contact in the game are harder and more demanding when the players are more powerful and more athletic. So, while the impact of opposing forces is greater, deliberate thuggery and open assault do not appear to be more prevalent. Nevertheless, all brutality is unacceptable, and incidents such as assaults on referees in France by spectators as well as players, all-out warfare on the field in Tonga, a nine-year jail sentence for an Argentinian player who kicked an opponent who subsequently died, the outburst of violence at Bristol that led George Crawford (the referee and a Chief Inspector of Police) to walk off the field, and the fact that, in 1982, 457 New Zealand players were expelled from the field for brutality during a 'clean-up' campaign – all these show that violence remains a world problem. To solve it, the game needs the Unions to agree on a common approach and to impose uniform sanctions. There must be a common wish to banish from the game proven miscreants; to apply legal action for assault so that the guilty are punished in a court of law, and to amend the Laws of the Game to diminish as far as possible causes of frustration occasioned by the rules themselves, or by poor refereeing. All these measures combined would help to alleviate the unsavoury element of the game.

There is also the question of safety. In recent years there has been increasing public concern, supported by the medical profession, over the safety or rather the dangers of playing Rugby, particularly at school level. The foremost area of concern has been over neck and back injuries which by their nature are usually the most severe. The scientific study and analysis of Rugby injuries of this kind has led not just to a growing awareness of specific danger areas in the game but to urgent and positive action to diminish the likelihood of such injuries without abandoning specific aspects of the game in which, very occasionally, appalling accidents have occurred – notably the scrummage. Law changes, at first introduced experimentally, have 'de-powered' the scrummage to a significant extent: referees are required to take strict action at danger-points (notably the scrum collapse), and to stop the game immediately a 'pile-up' forms, and these have been important steps in eradicating potential crisis points. One tragic injury is, of course, one too many, but it would be wishful thinking to suggest that all risk of injury could ever be eliminated from a physical-contact game such as Rugby. Supplementary measures

In French league and cup Rugby violence occasionally spills over to involve not only players but spectators too!

such as the enforcement of new safety studs, checks by referees on the boots of all players at every game, the outlawing of matches between senior and junior players, the demand for the provision of a qualified medical attendant at all games, and also for the teaching of correct and safe techniques – these prove that Rugby is addressing its problems with urgency and concern.

PROFESSIONALISM

Ever since the Great Schism of 1893, following the row on 'broken-time' payments that eventually led to the creation of Rugby League and its paid performers, and later the allegations of monetary transactions (and violence) that resulted in the suspension of international contact with France in 1931, there has always lurked the spectre of professionalism as a threat to the amateur fabric and ethos of Rugby Union football.

Anyone who has been within shouting distance of the game will have heard allegations of illegal 'boot money' payments for players.

Such clandestine transactions have taken many forms ranging from, literally, money in the player's boot and surreptitious 'brown envelope' dealings to less covert and occasionally exposed arrangements between boot manufacturers and the wearers of their products. Most of these payments have involved relatively trivial amounts of money; even so, any payment is beyond the pale in the context of this amateur sport. In recent times, however, there have been so many reports and speculative remarks about money paid to leading players that, if they were verified, these players would properly belong in the ranks of highly-paid professional sportsmen. The main consequence of this would be to make a reality of the Rugby pro circus that some regard as anyway inevitable.

It would not be difficult to compile a thick dossier of allegations of professionalism amongst Rugby amateurs. Given the will to proceed, and perhaps a small army of private investigators, the charges could in many instances be made to stick. The file might include payments made, in cash or kind, to

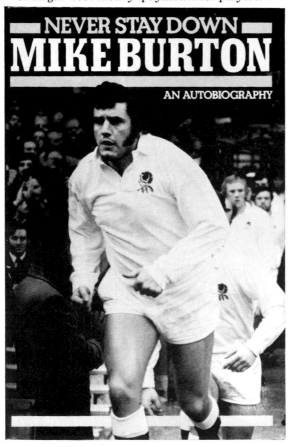

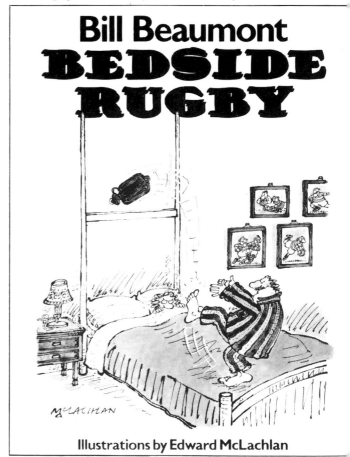

Illustrations by Edward McLachlan

visiting players to Italy and France, to players resident within France, to participants in Rugby coaching schools. It might include excessive 'expense' claims or payments for invitation matches, royalty payments for autobiographies written by, or ghosted for, leading names in the game, and payments received for promotional and commercial activities directly related to the Rugby prowess and renown of individual players. But proving individual breaches of amateur regulations is no straightforward task, and failure to substantiate such claims would very likely prove an expensive fiasco. That has been the crux of the problem for the authorities.

Whilst it has been possible for Rugby to live with the peripheral grey areas of 'shamateurism', the threat to the established pattern of amateur international Rugby is a different matter altogether. The first openly publicised attempts to create a professional Rugby circus involving the world's top players surfaced during the British Lions' tour of New Zealand in the summer of 1983. Behind the

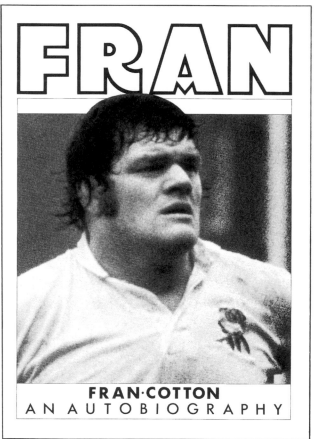

FRAN·COTTON
AN AUTOBIOGRAPHY

attempt was an Australian businessman, David Lord. His scheme, marketed under the name of World Championship Rugby, involved approaches to 208 leading players from eight countries – the Five Nations plus Australia, New Zealand and Fiji. It was claimed at the time that 190 of them had signed binding documents although it later transpired that these may have served to express a declaration of interest more than a positive commitment to participate. However, with payments of the order of £91,000 for the 'star attractions' to play in seven tournaments over a period of two years, such an expression of interest was hardly surprising.

Detailed itineraries were outlined, with venues for the inaugural tournament in the British Isles scheduled to include Stamford Bridge, Wembley, Ninian Park and a host of other non-Rugby venues in Glasgow, Cork, Dublin, Bristol, Leeds, Leicester and more. The plans were eventually abandoned, not, it seems, because players were unwilling or venues unavailable but because the organizers failed to attract sufficient worldwide television coverage, and with it the necessary multi-million pound sponsorship deals. Although the scheme failed, it came a lot closer to fruition than many people realized. Amateur Rugby survived – not through its own efforts, one might add – but the reality of the challenge, once so glibly discounted by Rugby officialdom, was finally understood.

Whether the most recent unauthorized international encounters between South African players (the official Springboks team) and the unofficial New Zealand Test side (playing as the NZ Cavaliers) represent the final advent of professional Rugby is not clear. Despite earlier denials of involvement and subsequent grave warnings to the South African Board issued by the International Rugby Football Board (of which South Africa is a member), and in the face of instructions to their own players from the New Zealand Union to halt proceedings and return home, the four-Test series went ahead in April and May 1986 amidst allegations that the All Blacks players had an outright professional involvement in the tour. The 32-man tour party under the captaincy of Andy Dalton included virtually every one of New Zealand's leading players plus top officials in the coach Colin Meads and the manager Ian Kirkpatrick. Whether or not the participants had flouted the

Warwick Taylor (New Zealand Cavaliers) resists the challenge from South African Jaco Reinack (right) with Danie Gerber and Michael du Plessis in pursuit.

amateur rules is one issue; equally significant is the indisputable fact that this tour cocked a snook at New Zealand's Rugby officialdom. This was a direct consequence of the failure, in the players' opinion, of the NZRFU to resolve the matter of playing contact with South Africa after the official tour there had been cancelled the previous year.

A private court case in New Zealand had ended with the imposition of court injunctions to prevent the tour party from leaving New Zealand. Subsequent attempts to circumvent this ruling by players travelling to South Africa as individuals also fell foul of the law. The consequent frustration for the players over this issue, and not any promise of direct financial reward was, the players claim, the motive behind the breakaway tour. But what is clear is that the whole organization of the tour was undertaken, for the first time in history, by business entrepreneurs outside Rugby's official fold, and, what is more, the South African Board gave the tour their open support once the matches were under way. For the first time Rugby was not its own master: big business, coupled with 'player power', had taken over.

The longer-term consequences of this startling development can, at this stage, only be guessed at. The warning bells had sounded a long time before and the International Board,

Springbok Frans Erasmus on the break against the 'unofficial' New Zealanders.

whilst admittedly never established as or purporting to be a world governing body of the sport, did not respond until the tour was a *fait accompli*. By then the rift was complete, the IRFB exposed as an organization without teeth or executive clout and the whole future of international amateur Rugby thrown into confusion. In the words of Colin Meads: 'The World Cup will blow the IRFB apart ... whether you call it broken-time payments or compensation doesn't matter, the fact is that teams taking part in the World Cup are going to be paid.' If that proves to be the case, it is ironic that the catalyst for that development is a country which has been excluded from the event but which also happens to be as strong as any Rugby nation on earth: South Africa.

From the South Africans' point of view, once they were given the cold shoulder by their fellow members on the International Board, and Rugby within that country began to suffer grievously because of its isolation, did they have any alternative but to go their own way, regardless of the consequences? I think not.

Rugby, then, finds itself at a major crossroads. The nations are set to arrive on a collision course from all directions, and no-one is in control of the traffic lights.

In an age of creeping professionalism, encroaching commercialization and games of Rugby in which winning has become everything, the Barbarian Football Club is something of a refreshing oasis of pure amateurism. Many would say that the Barbarians – the Baa-Baas as they are familiarly known – represent the very last bastion of amateur sport and the Corinthian ideal personified by that outstanding sportsman C.B. Fry who, amongst many other sporting accomplishments, was one of the earliest representatives of the Barbarian FC.

In terms of Rugby the Barbarians have always been more concerned with how the game is played than with the result, and for well-nigh a century the club has remained the most revered touring club in the history of Rugby football. It is a unique club with a unique style. From its unpretentious origins as a 'scratch' team raised by its founder, Percy 'Tottie' Carpmael, to tour the North of England in 1890, the club has grown in the affection and esteem of all Rugby people to its present status as the most famous club in the world, with a resolute commitment to attacking Rugby.

The Barbarians have no ground, no clubhouse, no entry fee, no subscription and virtually no money – match expenses being met by the clubs they visit. Membership is by invitation only and an invitation to play is

The Barbarians at Huddersfield, 1891. Back row, left to right: W. Sugden, A. Rotherham, P.F. Hancock, C.A. Hooper, C.M. Wells, W.H. Manfield, P. Maud, R.T.D. Budworth. Middle row: D.W. Evans, F.H.R. Alderson, W.P. Carpmael, S.M.J. Woods. Front row: A. Allport, F.T.D. Aston, T.A.F. Crow, T. Parker, T.W.P. Storey.
Below right *The Barbarians in France for their match against Racing Club de Paris, 1908.*

Penarth; today the headquarters of the Easter Tour are based in an hotel in the heart of Cardiff city. The traditional warmth of the reception accorded to the Barbarians by the people of South Wales has made Cardiff Arms Park very much a 'home' ground for the big occasions.

The Barbarians play just five regular fixtures a year, including the cornerstone of the club's tradition, the Easter Tour. Originally the tour comprised matches with Penarth, Cardiff, Swansea and Newport between Good Friday and Easter Tuesday. But the increasing demands upon players at club and international level, together with greater work and family commitments amongst younger men have made the Barbarian Committee's task of finding sufficient players of appropriate talents a major problem. Consequently the match with Newport is now played in October whilst the traditional warm-up encounter with Penarth was, with much regret, played for the last time, after 85 years, in 1986. But the other two fixtures remain: against Leicester, the Christmastide festive Rugby highlight, and the Mobbs Memorial Match against East Midlands, played in the spring. This match originated in commemoration of Edgar Mobbs, a great Northampton, East Midlands, England and Barbarian centre three-quarter who was killed during heroic action in the First World War.

In addition, since 1948 the club has been honoured to play every major touring side of the All Blacks, Springboks and Wallabies to visit the British Isles and this sequence of games has produced some of the most memorable ever seen. It began with a famous encounter when Haydn Tanner's Barbarian XV defeated the Australians captained, in the absence of Bill McLean, by Trevor Allan. The standard was set and how well subsequent games have lived up to the inaugural event. One thinks of the outstanding performance of Bob Scott in the

prized as being second only to the honour of representing one's country or the British Lions.

It is in every sense a touring club, and while there are no 'home' matches the Baa-Baas have a spiritual home in South Wales, formerly based on the Esplanade Hotel,

Left and far left *On tour in the Thirties.*

The Barbarians to play Australia in 1948 and (below) the line-up for the match at Cardiff.

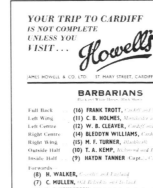

victory for New Zealand in 1954, of Haydn Mainwaring's tackle on Avril Malan during the Baa-Baas' victory over South Africa in 1961, of Wilson Whineray's try that crowned the All Blacks' triumph (by 36 points to 3) in 1964. So many outstanding days to recall in the club's post-war history. But unquestionably the Barbarians' finest hour came on 27 January 1973 versus Ian Kirkpatrick's All Blacks in the 28th and final match of that tour. It was seen by some as a virtual continuation of the epic Test series between the British Lions and New Zealand of 1971, when the Lions had been triumphant for the first time. Although not a 'fifth Test', the two teams contained more than a nucleus of the players from that series; more importantly, the match produced one of, if not the, finest games of Rugby ever seen.

It began with 'that try', when after only two minutes play, a moment of genius from Phil Bennett in defence saw him counter-attack from his own goal-line, side-step three All Blacks and set in motion a bewildering

Dawie de Villiers is chaired off the field by Mike Gibson and Gareth Edwards at the end of the last Springbok tour, 1970.

sequence of inter-passing that ended with Gareth Edwards diving to score at the other end of the field. It was a try that served to inspire everyone present and the match became and will always be remembered as a classic game of Rugby football which the Barbarians won 23 points to 11, four tries to two.

Attacking Rugby is just part of the all-important tradition of the club. Administration of affairs is delightfully informal. The players' Easter Sunday Golf Tournament is seen as being just as important – or so it would seem to the Committee (of eminent former players invited from the four home countries) – as the Rugby played on either side of that day. An invitation to take part in Barbarian Rugby is still made with an eye to choosing the 'deserving' or 'right type' of player, in addition to his needing to be outstanding as a Rugby footballer. And although 'the Esp' hotel is long-gone as the old HQ, the fun and games off the field remain an important part of the Barbarian style.

So one hopes a glorious tradition may continue in spite of changing times and attitudes to sport. The absence of the normal pressures of top representative Rugby, the freedom to attack without fear of recrimination, the natural camaraderie of leading Rugby players from the Five Nations, these are just some of the ingredients that make Barbarian FC so special, and entirely unique to the world of Rugby. From the inspiration of a far-sighted Blackheath player, Percy Carpmael, through

the guiding hands of subsequent club presidents Emile de Lissa, Jack Haigh-Smith, Brigadier Glyn Hughes, down to the caring guardianship of Herbert Waddell, a delightful Rugby experience has evolved. Whilst at the highest level of the game the accent on fun and recreation to be enjoyed in Rugby seems to be of diminishing significance, surely the need for a return to some of the unfashionable ideals of Rugby for pure enjoyment, in a relaxed atmosphere, on and off the field, becomes ever greater. The Baa-Baas provide a restful haven in a tense sporting world. It would be a tragedy, and an indictment of Rugby football if the Barbarian tradition were a casualty of the final submergence of amateur sport.

As so many top international players of almost 100 years of Rugby will avow – in the opening lines of the old Barbarian club song:

'It's a way we have in the Baa-Baas
and a jolly good way too!'

David Duckham at full pace during the memorable game against the All Blacks in 1973.

Below Barbarian team before the match. Back row, left to right: E.M. Lewis (touch judge), G. Windsor Lewis (hon secretary), J.V. Pullin, W.J. McBride, R.M. Wilkinson, D.L. Quinnell, A.B. Carmichael, D.J. Duckham, G. Domercq (referee), D.O. Spyer (touch judge). Middle row: G.O. Edwards, C.M.H. Gibson, Brig H.L. Glyn Hughes (president), S.J. Dawes, H. Waddell (vice-president), J. Bevan, R.J. McLoughlin. Front row: J.F. Slattery, T.O. David, P. Bennett, J.P.R. Williams.

Unlike nearly every other sport, Rugby Union does not have a governing body. At a time when there is a desperate need for leadership and firm control of the game at international level, no organization exists to provide it, and the likelihood of chaos and fragmentation in the international arena looms ever greater.

other countries were suspended until, following independent arbitration in April 1890, the first regulations of a four-nation International Board were agreed upon. With the development of the game in the colonies, representation was achieved by the Southern Rugby Union (New South Wales), Queensland, New Zealand and, later, South Africa, though not until 1948 was full membership accorded to the Australian,

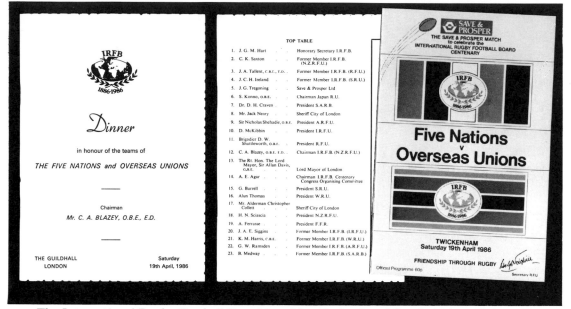

The International Rugby Football Board is not, and has never pretended to be, a world governing body of Rugby – and there has been a notable reluctance, on the part of its members, for it to become so. The IRFB is, rather, a loose and exclusive assembly of eight leading Rugby nations out of the hundred or so which play Rugby on an organized basis. The Board is made up of two representatives from each of England, France, Ireland, Scotland, Wales, Australia, New Zealand and South Africa, with no infrastructure or representation beyond this exclusive band.

Its origins stem from the very start of international Rugby back in 1871 when Scotland first played England. Early disputes made it clear that a common form of laws, and interpretation of them, would soon become necessary. Fifteen years later, in February 1886, Ireland, Scotland and Wales set up the first International Board. England, as the Rugby Football Union, was the dominant force in the game and would have no part of the initial representative body. International matches with

New Zealand and South African Unions. For France the process of acceptance took considerably longer. After sixty years of deliberation, rift and rejection, principally concerning unresolved problems over professionalism, France was finally accepted in 1979 as the eighth member of the IRFB.

The functions of the Board are quite clear and confined to just three areas – determining and safeguarding the principles of amateurism, framing and interpreting the Laws, and controlling all matters concerning international Rugby including matches, tours and anything of international significance. The Board is currently beset by problems on all three fronts. Its responsibilities are clear-cut but its jurisdiction is strictly limited. All internal issues within the individual nations are the sole responsibility of that Union, except insofar as they affect the international scene.

The principal problems we have already outlined. Firstly, concern over the encroachment of professionalism. Although the strict regulations over amateur status have recently been slightly relaxed to allow retired players to accept payment for the writing of books, broadcasting and journalism and other peripheral activities, payment of current players in any form beyond a small daily expense allowance on international tours is not permissible. Secondly, the way the game is played. In particular, the proliferation of penalty goals, the absurd complexity of the Laws, and the varying interpretations placed on them, together with the lack of a common policy for dealing with violence on the field – all these continue to be a source of discontent. Finally, a sphere closely associated with the issue of amateurism, there is the whole matter of international Rugby contact. This embraces the South African question; the rumblings of discontent from countries who remain outside

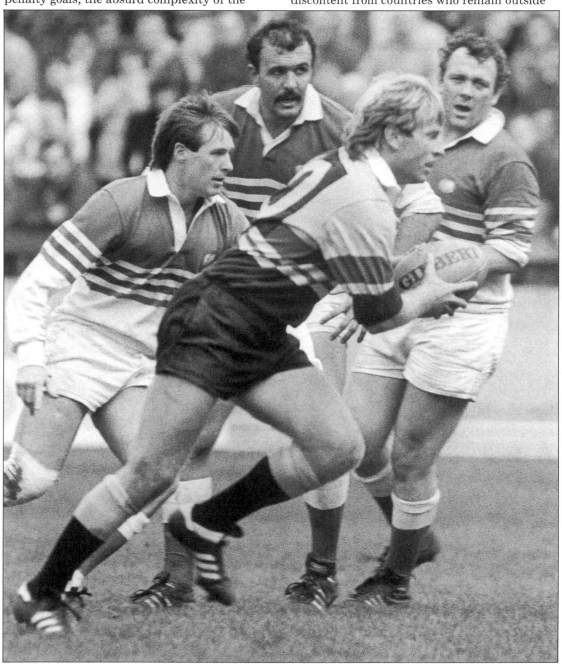

Naas Botha outpaces Dacey, Rodriguez and Whitefoot while representing the Overseas Unions against the Five Nations at Twickenham, 1986.

the membership of the IRFB; the desirability or otherwise of transforming the Board into a world governing body with membership or associate membership for all; and, of course, in the wake of the New Zealand Cavaliers' unauthorized visit to South Africa and their acceptance by the South African Board, not only the issue of future international Rugby, but the viability of the Board itself.

THE INTERNATIONAL BOARD CENTENARY
It was against this backcloth of unprecedented problems at international level that the IRFB Centenary meeting took place in London in April 1986. The celebrations were marked by two centenary matches. First, the British Lions, in the absence of their originally scheduled tour of South Africa, were convened to play the best of the Rest of the IRFB countries in Cardiff (The Rest winning 15 – 7). Three days later the combined talents of Australia, New Zealand and South Africa staged a magnificent display to beat the Five Nations XV 32 – 15 in one of the greatest team performances seen at Twickenham. The occasion also served to emphasize the degree to which Rugby in the Southern Hemisphere has advanced beyond the game played in the home countries. Only

eighteen months previously, British Rugby had been stunned by the superior class of the touring Wallabies. Now the talents of Naas Botha and Danie Gerber from South Africa, of Mark Shaw, Dave Loveridge, John Kirwan and Andy Haden from New Zealand, added to a squad of returning Australians which included men such as Simon Poidevin, Enrico Rodriguez, Steve Tuynman and Roger Gould, provided further evidence, if it were needed, that, as former French fly-half star Pierre Albaladejo commented: 'Their Rugby is on a different planet.' These players from the Southern Hemisphere are the new stars of the game, and as such are also very valuable marketing commodities.

In addition to the celebration matches the Board staged a Centenary Congress which was attended by 54 Rugby nations as far-flung as Chile and China, India and the Ivory Coast, the Soviet Union and the Solomon Islands. The Congress was addressed on the principal issues in the game, discussions were held, and, inevitably in such a fraternal gathering, there was no shortage of cameraderie and fun for the delegates. But no amount of joie de vivre could overshadow the more serious concern expressed by some representatives that greater

Nick Farr-Jones sets up an attack for the Rest of the World against the British Lions at Cardiff, 1986.

186

involvement for them in world Rugby was now required if fragmentation of the game into separate or rival camps was to be avoided.

It seems inevitable that some world representative body must be formed. Already there is the challenge of the only other multinational organization, FIRA (the French-dominated Fédération Internationale de Rugby Amateur) which was born in 1934 following the ban on France, and now encompasses 28 nations from the European continent, East and West, and North Africa. The Fédération has already hinted that a further 12 nations, including North and South America, could be next on the list. Despite the fact that for financial reasons FIRA may not prove to be a viable alternative, nevertheless the IRFB must hope, indeed ensure, that the new offer of associate membership of the Board to all Rugby nations will be taken up. But that is only likely if associate status is guaranteed some meaningful representation.

So, while the 1986 Centenary Meeting of the Board progressed to some degree by amending the Laws to the benefit of the game, by relaxing to an extent the amateur regulations to take some account of the realities of the present day, and by making the offer of a form of Associate membership to the world's Rugby nations, it must remain doubtful whether these advances will be sufficient to keep the lid on a boiling pot. I was more concerned by the fact that, as I looked round the unique gathering of Rugby people on the night of the IB Centenary Banquet, scattered amongst the assembled company were a group of New Zealand players who were flying to South Africa the following day, and in so doing were about to write a new chapter in the history of the game, one that might change the whole character of international Rugby.

THE FIRST WORLD CUP

Finally, I turn to one of the most significant events in Rugby's history. This, barring any dramatic upheavals in the meantime, gives Rugby for the first time a world stage and provides it with an unparalleled opportunity to show the widest possible audience a game. This opportunity is the first-ever Rugby World Cup. The competition for the William Webb Ellis Trophy offers a shop window for Rugby to sell itself and boost its future in the face of so many competing leisure pursuits. Both the watching public and the players welcome the way the best in the world will be pitted against each other to produce a champion team – even though the absence of South Africa will leave the ultimate question unanswered. And while there are reservations over what a serious competition of this nature may do to cultivate professional attitudes, if not indeed professional players, nevertheless it has the support of the players and the guaranteed interest of the world's biggest television audience for Rugby.

The event takes place in Australia and New Zealand. Sixteen nations compete in four pools of four. Thus the emerging Rugby nations have the chance to take their place alongside the long-established leading countries in the kind of worldwide competition for which they have so long clamoured. So Argentina, Rumania, the USA, Canada, Italy, Japan, Fiji, Tonga and Zimbabwe are set amongst Australia, New Zealand and the Five Nations. Hopefully, by the time the 1990 World Cup dawns, access to the competition through regional qualifying tournaments will be open to all.

A SECURE FUTURE

If Rugby at international level appears troubled and tormented and its future direction uncertain, we are referring to a miniscule percentage of those who take part in the game. Rugby at the grass-roots level is Rugby for the overwhelming majority of the game's adherents, and in the final analysis it is their needs and wishes that are of paramount importance, whether he be the junior club man in the 4th XV of a South Wales valley team, the student in the American University campus side or the player who represents the works team in a Japanese steel company.

The bedrock of the game amongst adult players is sound, although the feeding grounds at junior level, whence the senior players emerge, will always need attention and must remain a first priority. The attractions of Rugby as a leisure pursuit are constant and compelling, but to ensure its future vitality and further continuing expansion the game has to sell itself in the local as well as the international market-place. Only then is the future of this greatest of all amateur sports secure, a game that provides for so many millions that unparalleled combination of recreation and fun, both on and off the field. For all of them, Rugby is a hobby for life.

**WORLD CUP
RUGBY**

INDEX

191

The Publishers would like to acknowledge with thanks the help given by J.V. Smith and Len Evans at the RFU Museum, Jenny Macrory of Rugby School and Nick Cain of *Rugby World*.

The Publishers would also like to thank the following sources for their help in providing additional illustrations. (Where there is more than one illustration on a page, the credits start with the picture furthest to the left and nearest the top of the page and work down each column.)

All-Sport 108*a*, 146*a* & *c*, 155*b*, 156, 157*a* & *b*, 162*a*
The Argus 151*f*
Associated Press 83*a*, 98*b*, 99*a*, 109*b*
Associated Sports Photography 134*a*, *b* & *c*, 151*g*
Bermuda News Bureau 159*a*
BBC Hulton Picture Library 10*b*, 15*d*, 21*b* & *c*, 25*b* & *c*, 28*c*, 30*a*, *b* & *c*, 37*b*, 52*a*, 53*a*, 57, 58*a*, & *c*, 63*b*, 72*b*, 78*b*, 80*c*, *d*, *e* & *f*, 90*a* & *b*, 101*a* & *e*, 103*b*, 109*a*
Nato Bernard 178, 179
Mike Brett 136*d*, 150*a*, 151*d*, 152*a*
Alain Cafay 120*a*
Cape Times 51*b*, 100*f*
Colorsport 89*b*, 92*b*, 93*b*, 105*a* & *b*, 106, 107, 108*b*, *c* & *d*, 116*a* & *c*, 118*b*, 119*a*, 120*b*, *c* & *d*, 121*a* & *b*, 122*b*, 124*b*, 125*a*, *b*, *d*, *f*, & *g*, 126, 127*a*, *b* & *c*, 128*a*, *b*, *c* & *d*, 129*a*, 130*a* & *b*, 131*a* & *b*, 133*b*, 135*a* & *b*, 136*a*, 137, 138*a* & *b*, 139*d*, 142*a*, 143*a*, *b*, *c* & *d*, 144*a* & *b*, 145*a* & *c*, 146*b* & *d*, 147*a* & *b*, 148*a* & *b*, 149*a* & *b*, 150*c* &*e*, 151*a* & *c*, 152*c*, *d* & *f*, 154*a* & *b*, 158*b*, 165*a*, *b*, *c* & *d*, 166, 167*a*, *b* & *c*, 168*a* & *b*, 169, 172, 183*a*, 185
Daily Telegraph 174*b*
Eastern Province Herald 98*a*
Mary Evans Picture Library 37*a*
The Evening Post, Wellington 82*c*

Foto-Call 133*a*
Eric Greenfield 92*e*
Higgs & Hill Marketing 160*b*
Tim Hewson 158*a*
The Illustrated London News 15*c*, 20*d*, 22, 25*a* & *d*, 31, 33*b*, 40*b*, 44*a*, 49, 50*a* & *b*, 53*b*, 54, 55*a*, 56*b*, 60*b* & *c*, 61, 63*a*, 171
A.G. Ingram 89*a*
London Transport 45
Ken Kelly 129*b*, 150*b*
Mansell Collection 10*a*, 11
Miroir du Rugby 81
North London Photo Service 93*e*
The New Zealand Herald 30*d*, 73*a*, 79*b* & *c*, 80*b*, 84*b*, 97*a* & *b*, 99*b*, 100*e*, 109*d*
Picture Service 104
The Photo Source 44*c*, 55*b*, 56*a*, 58*b*, 74, 75*a* & *b*, 76*a*, *b*, *c*, *d* & *e*, 79*a*, 82*a*, *b* & *d*, 83*b* & *c*, 91*a* & *c*, 92*c* & *d*, 93*a* & *c*, 100*c*, 101*b* & *c*, 103*a*, 109*c*, 110*b* & *c*, 112*a*, *b*, & *c*, 113*b*, 115*a*, *b*, *c* & *d*, 118*a*, 123*b*, 124*a*, 139*a*, 159*b*, 164, 170, 174*d*
Press Association 93*d*, 119*b*, 150*d*
Sponsored Sport Photography 136*e*
Sport & General 81*a* & *b*, 91*d*, 92*a*, 101*d*, 102, 103*c*, 125*c* & *e*, 142*c*, 145*b*, 160*a*
Sporting Pictures 121*c*
The Star 51*a*, 64*a*, *b* & *c*, 72*d*, 84*a*, 100*a* & *d*
D.R. Stuart 78*a*
Peter Stuart 100*b*
Syndication International 7, 8, 60*a*, 113*a* & *c*, 116*b* & *d*, 117*b*, 141, 152*b*, 155*a* & *c*, 174*a*
Bob Thomas Sports Photography 122*a*, 136*b*, 139*b* & *c*, 140, 142*d*, 150*f*
Topix 110*a*, 117*a*
Western Mail 152*e*

All other illustrations were either photographed for Lennard Books by Adrian Murrell and Bob Martin of All-Sport or were supplied from private collections.

RUGBY · A WAY OF LIFE RUGBY · A WAY OF LIFE RUGBY · A WAY OF LIFE RUGBY · A WAY OF LIFE
RUGBY · A WAY OF LIFE RUGBY · A WAY OF LIFE RUGBY · A WAY OF LIFE RUGBY · A WAY O
RUGBY · A WAY OF LIFE RUGBY · A WAY OF LIFE RUGBY · A WAY OF LIFE RUGBY · A W
LIFE RUGBY · A WAY OF LIFE RUGBY · A WAY OF LIFE RUGBY · A WAY OF LIFE RUGBY · A W
OF LIFE RUGBY · A WAY OF LIFE RUGBY · A WAY OF LIFE RUGBY · A WAY OF LIFE RUGB
WAY OF LIFE RUGBY · A WAY OF LIFE RUGBY · A WAY OF LIFE RUGBY · A WAY OF LIFE RU
WAY OF LIFE RUGBY · A WAY OF LIFE RUGBY · A WAY OF LIFE RUGBY · A WAY OF LIFE
A WAY OF LIFE RUGBY · A WAY OF LIFE RUGBY · A WAY OF LIFE RUGBY · A WAY OF LIFE
GBY · A WAY OF LIFE RUGBY · A WAY OF LIFE RUGBY · A WAY OF LIFE RUGBY · A WAY OF LIF
UGBY · A WAY OF LIFE RUGBY · A WAY OF LIFE RUGBY · A WAY OF LIFE RUGBY · A WAY O
RUGBY · A WAY OF LIFE RUGBY · A WAY OF LIFE RUGBY · A WAY OF LIFE RUGBY · A WA
E RUGBY · A WAY OF LIFE RUGBY · A WAY OF LIFE RUGBY · A WAY OF LIFE RUGBY · A WA
LIFE RUGBY · A WAY OF LIFE RUGBY · A WAY OF LIFE RUGBY · A WAY OF LIFE RUGBY · A
OF LIFE RUGBY · A WAY OF LIFE RUGBY · A WAY OF LIFE RUGBY · A WAY OF LIFE RUGBY
AY OF LIFE RUGBY · A WAY OF LIFE RUGBY · A WAY OF LIFE RUGBY · A WAY OF LIFE RUG
WAY OF LIFE RUGBY · A WAY OF LIFE RUGBY · A WAY OF LIFE RUGBY · A WAY OF LIFE RU
· A WAY OF LIFE RUGBY · A WAY OF LIFE RUGBY · A WAY OF LIFE RUGBY · A WAY OF LIFE
BY · A WAY OF LIFE RUGBY · A WAY OF LIFE RUGBY · A WAY OF LIFE RUGBY · A WAY OF LIFI
UGBY · A WAY OF LIFE RUGBY · A WAY OF LIFE RUGBY · A WAY OF LIFE RUGBY · A WAY OF L
RUGBY · A WAY OF LIFE RUGBY · A WAY OF LIFE RUGBY · A WAY OF LIFE RUGBY · A WAY O
E RUGBY · A WAY OF LIFE RUGBY · A WAY OF LIFE RUGBY · A WAY OF LIFE RUGBY · A WAY
IFE RUGBY · A WAY OF LIFE RUGBY · A WAY OF LIFE RUGBY · A WAY OF LIFE RUGBY · A W
F LIFE RUGBY · A WAY OF LIFE RUGBY · A WAY OF LIFE RUGBY · A WAY OF LIFE RUGBY ·
OF LIFE RUGBY · A WAY OF LIFE RUGBY · A WAY OF LIFE RUGBY · A WAY OF LIFE RUGB
AY OF LIFE RUGBY · A WAY OF LIFE RUGBY · A WAY OF LIFE RUGBY · A WAY OF LIFE RUC
A WAY OF LIFE RUGBY · A WAY OF LIFE RUGBY · A WAY OF LIFE RUGBY · A WAY OF LIFE
Y · A WAY OF LIFE RUGBY · A WAY OF LIFE RUGBY · A WAY OF LIFE RUGBY · A WAY OF LIFE
GBY · A WAY OF LIFE RUGBY · A WAY OF LIFE RUGBY · A WAY OF LIFE RUGBY · A WAY OF LII
RUGBY · A WAY OF LIFE RUGBY · A WAY OF LIFE RUGBY · A WAY OF LIFE RUGBY · A WAY OF
RUGBY · A WAY OF LIFE RUGBY · A WAY OF LIFE RUGBY · A WAY OF LIFE RUGBY · A WAY O
FE RUGBY · A WAY OF LIFE RUGBY · A WAY OF LIFE RUGBY · A WAY OF LIFE RUGBY · A WA
LIFE RUGBY · A WAY OF LIFE RUGBY · A WAY OF LIFE RUGBY · A WAY OF LIFE RUGBY · A
OF LIFE RUGBY · A WAY OF LIFE RUGBY · A WAY OF LIFE RUGBY · A WAY OF LIFE RUGBY
AY OF LIFE RUGBY · A WAY OF LIFE RUGBY · A WAY OF LIFE RUGBY · A WAY OF LIFE RUG
WAY OF LIFE RUGBY · A WAY OF LIFE RUGBY · A WAY OF LIFE RUGBY · A WAY OF LIFE RU
· A WAY OF LIFE RUGBY · A WAY OF LIFE RUGBY · A WAY OF LIFE RUGBY · A WAY OF LIFE
BY · A WAY OF LIFE RUGBY · A WAY OF LIFE RUGBY · A WAY OF LIFE RUGBY · A WAY OF LIFE
JGBY · A WAY OF LIFE RUGBY · A WAY OF LIFE RUGBY · A WAY OF LIFE RUGBY · A WAY OF L
RUGBY · A WAY OF LIFE RUGBY · A WAY OF LIFE RUGBY · A WAY OF LIFE RUGBY · A WAY
RUGBY · A WAY OF LIFE RUGBY · A WAY OF LIFE RUGBY · A WAY OF LIFE RUGBY · A WA
IFE RUGBY · A WAY OF LIFE RUGBY · A WAY OF LIFE RUGBY · A WAY OF LIFE RUGBY · A
LIFE RUGBY · A WAY OF LIFE RUGBY · A WAY OF LIFE RUGBY · A WAY OF LIFE RUGBY · A
OF LIFE RUGBY · A WAY OF LIFE RUGBY · A WAY OF LIFE RUGBY · A WAY OF LIFE RUGE
AY OF LIFE RUGBY · A WAY OF LIFE RUGBY · A WAY OF LIFE RUGBY · A WAY OF LIFE RUC
WAY OF LIFE RUGBY · A WAY OF LIFE RUGBY · A WAY OF LIFE RUGBY · A WAY OF LIFE RU
· A WAY OF LIFE RUGBY · A WAY OF LIFE RUGBY · A WAY OF LIFE RUGBY · A WAY OF LIFE
BY · A WAY OF LIFE RUGBY · A WAY OF LIFE RUGBY · A WAY OF LIFE RUGBY · A WAY OF LIFE
JGBY · A WAY OF LIFE RUGBY · A WAY OF LIFE RUGBY · A WAY OF LIFE RUGBY · A WAY OF L
RUGBY · A WAY OF LIFE RUGBY · A WAY OF LIFE RUGBY · A WAY OF LIFE RUGBY · A WAY
RUGBY · A WAY OF LIFE RUGBY · A WAY OF LIFE RUGBY · A WAY OF LIFE RUGBY · A WA
FE RUGBY · A WAY OF LIFE RUGBY · A WAY OF LIFE RUGBY · A WAY OF LIFE RUGBY · A W